3⁰⁰

To Eldon + Laurie
    A little something to help you remember your
visit to Chambersburg. This is Chambersburg's historical
claim to fame. Enjoy.
                    With fondness,
                    Tom + Dell

Table of contents

Acknowledgements

The Greater Chambersburg Chamber of Commerce appreciates the efforts of numerous individuals who have helped create *Southern Revenge*. Through their time and effort, the story of the Burning of Chambersburg — a devastating incident of the Civil War history of the nation — has been told.

"For what better way to learn of peace than to know about war."

Special thanks and acknowledgements are extended to Cinda LeFurjah and Harold Collier for carrying the idea of the book until it became a reality. To the authors Ted Alexander, Jim Neitzel, Virginia Stake and William P. Conrad for bringing the work to fruition by contributing their historical knowledge, research, writing skills, time and talents. To Jim Neitzel and Cinda LeFurjah for the graphic design, typesetting and layout of the book.

The following people and organizations are also commended for their invaluable help in completing Southern Revenge: Bob Gottschalk, Murray Kauffman, John Benchoff, Mike Winey, Matt Penrod, Randy Hackenburg, Dr. Richard Sommers, Dennis Frye, Rica Alexander, Jane Alexander, Helen Giltinan, Lillian Coletta, Beth Baer, Dale Gallon, Victoria Linetsky, the Kittochtinny Historical Society, the Coyle Free Library, Franklin County Heritage, Inc., and Lillian S. Besore Memorial Library.

Preface

One hundred and twenty-five years ago the townspeople of Chambersburg, Pennsylvania experienced the most traumatic and devastating time of their lives.

After two previous invasions from Confederate forces during the Civil War, the residents were threatened again, but this time with more dire consequences. Rebel cavalry galloped into Chambersburg in late July, 1864, and demanded money. The Rebels seemed bent not on conquering the town, but bringing it down in flames. If the townspeople would not, and could not, meet ransom demands, then Chambersburg would be burned. The Rebel threats were challenged, and Chambersburg, specifically the downtown area, was put to the torch.

The burning of Chambersburg was immediate and devastating. Families ran from their burning homes, fleeing for their lives as the life they had known went up in a great black pillar of smoke.

The rebuilding of Chambersburg began as quickly as it was destroyed. Brick by brick the town and townsfolk rose from the ashen rubble as a phoenix of sorts — stronger, more beautiful and more spirited than before.

It is the uncommon spirit of Chambersburg Past that is commemorated . . . it is the unique spirit of Chambersburg Today alive and well that is being celebrated during this 125th Anniversary of the Burning of Chambersburg.

***

We draw your attention not so much to Davison Greenawalt and his farming family and German heritage for their uniqueness, but rather because they represent a typical picture of life and living in Chambersburg as the Civil War was about to begin. The Germans, along with the Scotch-Irish, represented the backbone of this community.

***

By 1755, approximately 60,000 to 70,000 Germans were living in Pennsylvania.

Family patriarch Johann entered the United States somewhere during the great influx of Germans between 1720 and 1730. Ships were arriving almost daily from the fatherland at New York City and Philadelphia, each teeming with 600 to 700 immigrants.

By 1755, approximately 60,000 to 70,000 Germans were living in Pennsylvania. After disembarking at Philadelphia or moving from New York state, most Germans settled in York County. It was from Hanover in York County that Johann moved to Chambersburg around 1775 as America was about to win its freedom from England.

After two girls, Eliza and Susan, the eldest son, Henry, was birthed in Chambersburg in 1811. As Godfrey established a farm in Hamilton Township, the children continued to come. One child, Charlotte, died in infancy, and finally, the tenth child, Samuel F., was born in 1829. You will hear about him later.

***

The northwest corner of the diamond in the mid 1800s.

Word of the Southern attack quickly whipped through Chambersburg that early day in April. News of the rebellion would quickly reach farms and outlying areas. The Greenawalt farm was about three miles outside of town, right where Route 30 and the Warm Spring Road intersect. Since Chambersburg was near the Maryland border, an impending Civil War and the volatile politics which surrounded it were always discussed by townsfolk in the courthouse or in the many hotels which characterized the town.

John Brown, the abolitionist, had already spent time in the town to plot his takeover of Harpers Ferry, and Frederick Douglass, the famous Negro orator, had spoken here. Men like Alexander McClure, well-known town lawyer and politician, had even attracted one of the founding fathers of American newspapers, Horace Greeley, to speak at an annual agricultural meeting in 1854.

Within a day, President Lincoln would call for volunteers throughout the Free States. Chambersburg was typical of towns and cities throughout Pennsylvania and patriotism ran high. Flags were quickly unfurled and flown at the Chambersburg National Bank on the square, as well as many businesses and hotels, and private residences. Within a week, young men had signed up for a three-month tour of duty (the Rebellion, everyone was sure, would be crushed by then), kissed their loved ones good-bye, and were loaded on trains streaming out of Chambersburg bound for Harrisburg.

***

But we are getting a little ahead of ourselves. More about life in Chambersburg and nine-year-old Davison Greenwalt and his family.

Chambersburg, in the first year of Abraham Lincoln's presidency, was a town of about 5,000 people surrounded by a growing agricultural community. The town had a square, called a diamond in 1861. The fountain did not exist. It was erected in the mid-1870s to commemorate the county men who fought in the Civil War. The diamond in 1861 was dominated by the Franklin Hotel, the Chambersburg Bank and such businesses as the Jacob Hoke and Company dry goods store.

The 1860 census indicates there were 2,496 farms in Franklin County, with pigs being the main farm animal. There were more than 33,000 accounted for, with 15,000 sheep and 11,000 horses and 11,000 cows tallied. There were 55 asses and mules. Farmers cranked out 784,639 pounds of butter, 714,857 bushels of wheat and slaughtered 268,402 animals.

There were 5,256 people living in Chambersburg and the most populous township was Antrim Township, which also had the highest valued properties. Greene and Montgomery townships followed in population. Hamilton Township had 1,529 people and was one of the few townships without a post office. There were 42,122 people living in the county.

Chambersburg had 19 public schools and required students to attend for nine months. There were five males and 14 females teaching, with the males being paid on the average of $50 a month while the women earned $26. Townships, except Antrim with 20, had fewer schools than Chambersburg and paid much less. In Davison's township, Hamilton, there were eight schools; children went for five months, 8 men taught, and they made $23.75

The bridge on North Main Street over the Falling Spring.

a month. Besides public schools, there were a number of renowned private academies.

In the 1830s, large sheds were in the diamond where farmers, mostly the German families like the Greenawalts, brought their produce to sell. By 1861, the sheds were long gone and a market house was constructed on the corner of Queen and Second streets for the buying and selling of produce and meats. That Market House was later converted to the borough hall. The courthouse was torn down and rebuilt in 1842 for $45,545.

The roads were hard-packed dirt which carried a steady stream of people and cargo north and south, east and west. A loaded wagon could make it to Pittsburgh and back in three weeks. A tavern and a hotel, called a hostelry, were usually about a mile apart on the turnpike from Philadelphia to Pittsburgh. In larger communities such as Chambersburg, there was a greater concentration, and Chambersburg had many of them, from the Golden Lamb Hotel

At right, a typical news item in a local newspaper describing a game law of the time.

The Game Law - The game law fixes a penalty of $5 upon any person who kills or destroys certain birds out of season, as follows: - Partridges from the first of February to the first of September; Quails and Rabbits from the first of February to the first of October; Woodcocks from the first of February to the fourth of July. It is during the time named that the species are propogated, and to destory them at that time tends to their total extinction, hence the law for their protection.

and the Montgomery House to the Franklin Hotel.

At night, wagons and buggies were often gathered in front of these taverns and hotels and following a fine meal, someone broke out a violin and, before long, people were dancing the Virginia Reel. "Captain Corn," one name for liquor in those days, was imbibed freely.

Three fire companies were dedicated to keeping the town safe. The county jail was 63 years old. Industry was growing. T.B. Woods was four years old, the Cumberland Valley Railroad was 24 years old. There were paper mills, tool makers, tanneries, furniture factories, and stagecoach makers. A "poor house" had been built by the town. And someone living in Chambersburg in 1861 could expect to probably be buried in Cedar Grove Cemetery.

County commissioners in 1861 were J.A. Eyster, Jacob C. Good and James D. Scott. Sheriff was Jacob S. Brown. The District Attorney was George Eyster. There were two George Ludwigs in town. One was a jeweler and one was a brewer. David M. Leisher was a blacksmith. William H. Micheals was a 20-year-old night watchman with the Cumberland Valley Railroad. N. Pearse Grove, son of a wagonmaker, was a house painter. Thomas Kennedy, later the president of the Cumberland Valley Railroad, was a lawyer. Two 22-year-old lawyers were just beginning to make their marks: Hastings Gehr and George Oberkirsh Seilhamer.

Mary Ann Grove, a well-to-do spinster, lived on South Main Street. Daniel Gehr, Hasting's father, was a Whig and a Republican and was the area's most successful stagecoach manager as well as a stockholder in the railroad. The esteemed lawyer and later politician John McDowell Sharpe was 31 years old. Jacob Suesserott was a 32-year-old physician. Peter

Pre-burning drawing of Franklin County Court House. Notice side entrance located on right.

Nicklas had just recently taken over the Nicklas carpet business on South Main Street, when his Uncle George died. George L. Miles ran a bakery and restaurant.

Colonel Alexander K. McClure, newspaper editor, state legislator and vehement opposer of the slavery, lived on an estate north of town called Norland (where Wilson College is located). William H. Lippy was working with his father, David, as a building contractor. They had built several major buildings in town, including the Presbyterian Church. William Heyser, the Sunday School Superintendent at the Reformed Church, who would die within two years, was the bank president. A. H. McCullough, son of the Hon. Thomas Grubb McCullough, who studied medicine and law, and organized the first Know-Nothing Society on May 11, 1854, was the general ticket agent for the Cumberland Valley railroad on the day the telegram announced the attack on Fort Sumter.

***

Davison could watch from almost anywhere on his farm all the hundreds of wagons which trekked to and from Pittsburgh, and through Chambersburg to important economic points east, like Philadelphia, Baltimore and Washington. The wagons had two cargos: people and belongings heading west for a new life, and goods and services manufactured back East. Some of the goods were made in Chambersburg. There were other means of transportation. Stagecoaches were an essential form of travel. Many travelers simply rode horses.

If Davison and his family would want to go to Chambersburg, they had to ford the Conochocheague stream at Loudon Street. There were no heavy bridges in Chambersburg. Foot bridges existed on Lincoln Way (known at that time as Market Street) and King Street, also known as Cow Street. Sometimes the Greenawalts had to wait, since so much traffic had to ford the stream there.

Farming families like the Greenawalts did not depend heavily on local merchants

There were several reasons for trips to town. For goods and services, Chambersburg had most of what someone in 1861 might come to expect. There were merchants of all kinds, from Jacob Hoke's store on the square, probably the largest dry-goods merchant in town, and Huber's Hardware, to Miss Hetrick's Hat Shop on South Main Street. Most stores remained open until 9 or 9:30 p.m. It was easier for the stores to remain open later. Gas lights on the square which illuminated the area so well had been installed. Two men, A.C. McGarth and Abraham Myers, came in 1856 to put in the gas system and now McGrath was the superintendent of the Gas Works.

Farming families like the Greenawalts did not depend heavily on local merchants for they were self-sufficient. But if the family ever stopped in Eyster Bros. store just off the square on South Main St., Davison no doubt wandered over to see clerk Edward Grove who delighted everyone with his trick. Grove could imitate the sound of a chick and when he sold a dozen eggs, he would "peep." Children like Davison loved his trick, but they still had to hear the jolly clerk assure them that the eggs were good.

***

On the days when Davison would accompany his family to Chambersburg for an extended time, he might have stopped by to see his uncle. Samuel F. Greenawalt, the youngest son of Godfrey and Anna, was the 32-year-old owner of a thriving livery and stables business. (It was in the rear of the Mansion House. You got to the business by the back alley.) The goods he manufactured had a reputation of superior quality and he handled only the best horses. He lived on the southwest corner of Main and Queen Streets with his second wife, Anna Mary Brough, with two children from his first wife and two children with Anna.

> ## Davison Greenawalt lost a brother not yet a year old and a five-year-old sister within one month in 1851 to childhood diseases.

Davison no doubt enjoyed the spirited nature of his uncle who became a community leader with an eye for improvement in several areas. Described as willful and possessing an iron will, he spearheaded the drive to have an election to build the city's water works. He was a sheriff at one time. He was a member of the town council and had extreme interest in the maintaining and upgrading of the town's roads.

He was a valued member of the Friendship Fire Company and he would go on to dabble in various businesses as well as farming and politics. He died at 48 in 1877.

***

The Greenawalts always came for church. The Greenawalts were a prominent family of the Reform Church, now known as the Zion Reformed Church on South Main Street. Davison's grandfather, Godfrey, was a Trustee Under Charter and Petitioner for Charter who helped incorporate the church in the borough in 1819. Davison's father, Henry, was a deacon and served as a trustee twice, one being in 1861. Reverend Fisher was delivering sermons from the pulpit in 1861.

There were eight churches in Chambersburg in 1861 and they played a vital role in the community, since religion was the backbone of family life then. During the war years, pastors like Reverend Dr. Conrad of the First Lutheran Church would denounce the war, Northern Copperheads, and anyone who had something good to say about the South. Some churches, such as the Methodist and United Brethern, would have winter revivals for four or five weeks which played before packed houses every night. People would become so involved they would pace the aisles and chant hymns.

If the Greenawalts ever needed "doctoring," they would come to town. There were a dozen physicians in town in 1861, and they were held in high esteem. One doctor, John Montgomery, would practice for decades, and his name is still well-known. One of the best-loved doctors of the area was Dr. William Boyle, who had his office on Market Street. He had a large practice, and made house calls. Disdaining a horse and buggy, Dr. Boyle made his rounds in town on foot. Dr. Boyle was a self-made doctor, something impossible now, and he also dabbled in other things, such as being the editor of the *Valley Spirit*.

Medicine, at that time, was moving away from the dark ages of lancing and bleeding. Physicians, however, still had to contend with diseases now long gone. A dysentery epidemic struck Chambersburg in 1850. Cholera ripped through the area in 1832 and again in 1852, claiming many lives. Children at that time were susceptible to many diseases, and few families escaped childhood mortality. Davison's family, had tragic consequences, with two

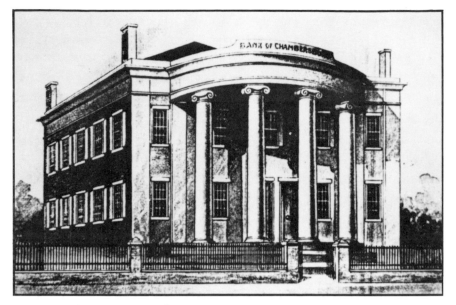

The Bank of Chambersburg, 1860s.

children dying exactly one month apart in 1851 from childhood diseases. Samuel, not yet one year old, died on May 23 and five-year-old Charlotte died June 23. Davison would be born approximately ten months later.

There were some activities in Chambersburg which would draw the Greenawalts to and near town, one being the agricultural fairs held on the grounds of the Agricultural Society of Franklin County, about a mile west of Chambersburg close to the Greenawalt farm. They were held in October. The town was alive with people. Old style hacks and stagecoaches would haul people to and from the fair for 20 cents. The hotels were filled.

Most everything raised from the ground was displayed by proud farmers, from apples (Rambo, Queen, Green and Yellow Pippens were the only ones then) to cabbage. The best in cattle, hogs, sheep and horses were shown, and trotting and running races were popular. The most popular fowl of the day was the Creole chicken, considered one of the best laying birds in the 1860s.

Balloon ascensions were extremely popular in 1861, and crowds would pack the square from the middle of July through the first of August to see aeronauts gas up their balloons from a gas main on the square.

> **During annual agricultural fairs in October, the town was alive with people, and old style hacks and stagecoaches would haul people to and from the fair for 20 cents.**

Circuses would attract several thousand people to Chambersburg and they often came from Pittsburgh like the Dan Rice Circus, a frequent visitor and real favorite. When the circus came to town, it would pass by Davison's farm and he would join many young boys, most who came from Chambersburg, to escort the entourage to town. Circuses had few varieties of animals in those days, outside of elephants, camels and caged monkeys. There were plenty of horses and ponies, of course, as well as a child's favorite, the clown.

If the Greenawalts had been wealthy enough, they could have sent Davison and his brothers and sisters to the Chambersburg Academy, a well-thought-of institution which required tuition. It still benefited from the reputation of one of the most accomplished private teachers in Pennsylvania in the 1830s, William Van Lear Davis, Esq. There were nine public schools in Chambersburg. Philip M. Shoemaker was the county superintendent. Davison, like so many country boys, walked to a rural school. The main books were the primer, spelling book, first, second, third, fourth and fifth readers; the two Arithmetics, Grammar, Geography, History and Copy book. The rod and the ruler, of course, were not spared.

***

Although the Greenawalt family would never benefit from fire protection, the town itself felt quite safe with three fire companies: Friendship, Hope, and Hook and Ladder. The Friendship Fire Company was located at the Courthouse in a two-story brick building. The Hook and Ladder Company was in the east end of the old Market House. The Hope Company was on Third Street opposite of the railroad depot.

Each company had a hose reel, suction and gallery engine. They had up-to-date equipment, although bucket brigades were often used. The companies were dedicated, but Friendship and Hook and Ladder companies carried bitter rivalries. At fires, they often fought with one another and even directed water streams at each other. Davison's uncle, Sam, was often a mediator in the rivalries.

***

Although German farming families such as the Greenawalts were dedicated to their land and cared little for news, Davison could stop by John M. Cooper's building on South Main Street just off the diamond and pick up a copy of the *Valley Spirit*. Cooper was the editor of the paper which was owned by George H. Mengel & Company. It was a Democrat paper, espousing the virtues of the Breckenridge wing of the party and had impact on state politics. There were one semi weekly and three weeklies in Chambersburg. The semi-weekly, begun in 1861, was called the *Dispatch*. It would last for two years. The three weeklies were the *Repository and Transcript, Reformed Messenger* and the *Valley Spirit*. The *Repository*, owned and edited by Andrew Rankin, was on the diamond. Reverend Fisher edited the *Reformed Messenger* in the Mansion House. The *Messenger* was a house organ of the Reformed Church.

The Methodist Church in Chambersburg, 1861.

WHITE SWAN HOTEL

Having purchased this well-known hotel, *long known as Miller's and recently as Weist and Grove's*, the proprietor pledges himself that no pains shall be spared to minister to the wants of his guests.

The character heretofore sustained by the *House* as a comfortable *Home* for the *Sojourner*, shall not suffer in my hands if a constant effort to please and accommodate will sustain it. The proprietor therefore solicits a continuance of the liberal patronage heretofore extended to the White Swan.

In addition to large Stablings, he has TWO LOTS and a pair of HAY AND STOCK SCALES for the accommodation of *Drovers* and *Butchers*.

MICHAEL GROVE,
Proprietor
Chambersburg, Pa.

It was with the *Messenger* that Moses A. Foltz was associated in the spring of 1861. Foltz, the most well-known newspaperman in Franklin County journalism history, would be associated with several papers and his family played a role in the development of today's *Public Opinion*, which began in 1869. Foltz developed the *Public Opinion* out of the *Country Merchant* which he started in 1866. Foltz, a deacon in the Greenawalt family's church for 27 years, married Charlotte Sophia Etter, Davison's cousin.

***

Basically, Chambersburg was a prosperous community on the eve of the Civil War. The economy was growing, the borough was expanding, and the rapid influx of immigrants was making the area divergent and vibrant. In April 1861, when war broke out, Chambersburg would begin to be reshaped as no one could imagine. It would be a staging area for several campaigns and would be visited three times by enemy forces.

***

Davison Greenawalt began farming with his father in 1872 and remained there for five years before leaving for California. While in California, he studied horticulture. In 1878 he returned to his birthplace and devoted the remainder of his life to fruit-raising and established the Siberia Fruit Farm on part of the Greenawalt farm. He became an acknowledged expert in fruit-growing and followed his uncle into politics, aligning himself with the Republican party as a township delegate to the county convention as well as being a member of the convention.

Davison was married twice, and had seven children with his second wife, Mary Ida Miller, whom he married in 1880. The family became members of the First Lutheran Church. Davison cared for his mother at his home in the early 1900s.

On June 6, 1929, Davison died of natural causes, five weeks after celebrating his 77th birthday. He is buried in Norland Cemetery north of Chambersburg.

CHAPTER 2

John Brown's summer of discontent

It was in early June 1859, almost six months to the day before abolitionist John Brown would be hanged for his failed raid upon the Federal arsenal in Harpers Ferry, Virginia, that a soft-spoken, bearded man arrived in Chambersburg at a boarding house on East King Street.

He was with two men he identified as his sons, and when he asked Mary Ritner to rent a room or two in her boarding house, he identified himself as Isaac Smith.

Mrs. Ritner would remember him as a serious man, one who would come and go over the next few months with his sons and other men, whom he said were his employees. Isaac Smith said he was in the business of developing mines.

The reason Mrs. Ritner, a recently widowed woman in her late 50s, would remember is because soon after the tragically-flawed raid on Harpers Ferry on October 16 she would discover she had housed Brown and his followers throughout the summer and early fall of 1859.

Brown and his men were in and out of Chambersburg during that period although one man, John Henrie Kagi, who was Brown's "Secretary of War" in Brown's elaborate scheme to create his own government and free the slaves, stayed throughout the summer and fall. Kagi was known to Mrs. Ritner as J. Henrie.

John Brown planned part of his ill-fated Harpers Ferry Raid in Chambersburg during the late summer of 1859.

In retrospect, there would be no reason for anyone to find this Isaac Smith and his men suspicious. Chambersburg, like so many towns and villages along the Pittsburg Turnpike, was used to travelers, speculators and strangers.

***

John Brown was not much of a success in life. He failed in almost everything he did. The son of a Calvinistic father, he had been a postmaster, a tanner, a surveyor, a speculator in real estate, a horse breeder and he ended his working career as a farmer, horse breeder and selling agent. He also fathered 20 children with two wives. By the time he failed as a selling agent, his views on slavery were beginning to consume his life.

He was 59 years old in 1859 when he finally settled on working out of Chambersburg to bring to fruition his dream of emancipating the millions of slaves in the United States. By then he was a hunted man, wanted for ordering the execution-style murders of pro-slavery men along the Pottawatomie Creek in Kansas.

The violence in Kansas no doubt pushed him to the point that he not only could participate in violence but also that violence, not negotiations and meetings, was the solution to ending slavery. Every time he spoke to his followers, often described by him as his "flock of sheep," he reminded them that violence was the only way.

The year preceding his stay in Chambersburg was spent developing his Provisional Constitution, a new government which would establish him as "commander in chief," and create "president" and "vice president" positions, as well as a "Supreme Court" and a one-house "Congress." The naming of Kagi as "Secretary of War," in light of his plans to take up arms, provide them to shackled slaves everywhere and lead a revolution, was an important and vital act.

Once he explained his new government to his "army" — never numbering more than 20 or 30 — he spent that year moving throughout New England, Pennsylvania, Ohio and

John Henri Kagi, Brown's Secretary of War, spent more time in Chambersburg than any other of Brown's men. Kagi boarded at Ritner's from July to October 1859.

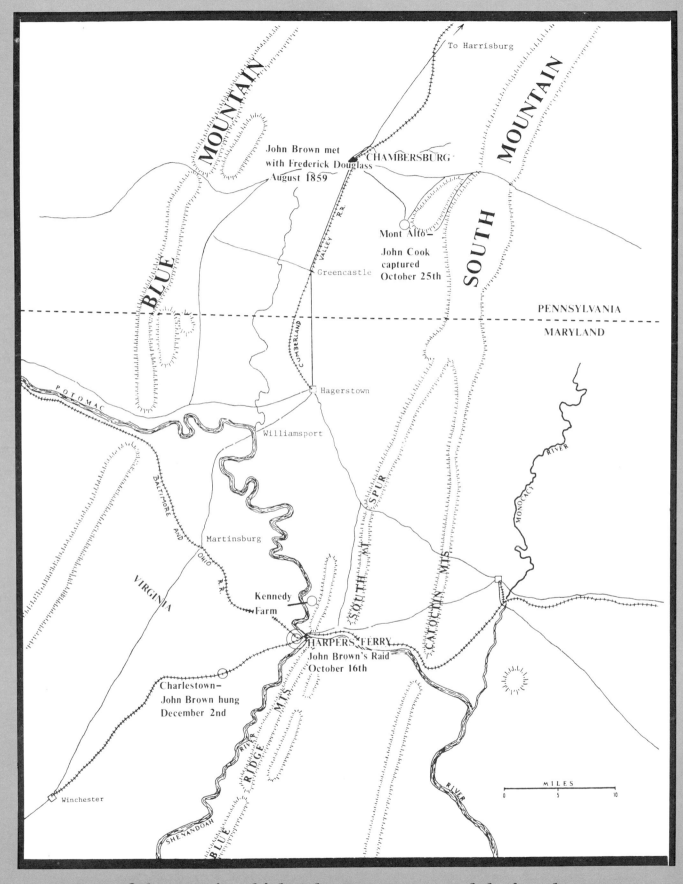

A map of the area in which John Brown operated during the summer and fall of 1859.

Here are early 20th century views of the warehouse on North Main Street which Brown used to store weapons.

Canada to enlist support for his insurrection. He was challenged from time to time as he secretly met with his loyal followers about the use of violence. But for Brown, by this time, there was no turning back. There was only one way to free the slaves. There was only John Brown's way. And he often referred to himself as the "avenging agent of the Lord."

***

Brown might have chosen Mary Ritner's boarding house for a specific reason. There is no doubt that from Mrs. Ritner's second floor back window he could look across the open spaces of the northern part of the borough and see the rear of the Oakes and Caufman's warehouse. The warehouse, located on North Main Street, was next to the Falling Spring, approximately where the entrance to United Towers is today.

It was there that on August 11 that 15 boxes were stored after being unloaded from the Cumberland Valley Railroad. Brown told those who were asked, such as the employees of the warehouse, that the boxes contained hardware which he would use to develop his mines. The boxes, however, contained Sharpes rifles and Maynard revolvers.

Brown might have chosen the Ritner boarding house because he had known about the Ritner family background. The Ritners were sympathetic to the plight of slaves and were part of the Underground Railroad system. Mrs. Ritner and her husband Abram had been active in helping blacks; they even had some political clout since Abram Ritner was related to a Joseph Ritner, former governor of Pennsylvania.

Other boxes which arrived on September 17 were stored in the Oakes and Caufman warehouse. Those boxes carried pikes to arm liberated slaves until firearms had been distributed and the slaves had been trained to use them.

Brown decided to use Chambersburg as a base camp because it was the hub of the Cumberland Valley Railroad. The railroad, established in 1837, was well-run and rather dependable. It was linked to Harrisburg to the north which meant Brown could travel east and west more easily.

To the south, it linked with the Franklin Railroad which went to Hagerstown, Maryland. The Franklin Railroad was not nearly as developed as the Cumberland Valley Railroad. On some stretches, horses were used to pull the railroad cars. Nonetheless, Brown decided that, when the time was right, the guns and ammunition could be transported well enough and from Hagerstown his army could take them to Harpers Ferry.

> **Brown often moved between Chambersburg and Harpers Ferry to develop his plans to raid the Federal arsenal.**

To carry out his revolution, Brown had long ago decided that a raid on a Federal arsenal was important not only to draw attention to his revolution, but also to secure the guns needed to arm the slaves. Harpers Ferry suited his plan for several reasons. By seizing this Federal arsenal, Brown thought he could carry on a guerrilla war throughout the nearby Blue Ridge Mountains. Finally, if he failed, he was near enough to a northern state to escape to safety.

He often moved from Chambersburg to Harpers Ferry to develop his plans, and he rented a house on the Kennedy farm about seven miles from Harpers Ferry. He used the name of Isaac Smith again, but said he was a cattle buyer from New York. It was in the farmhouse that he reminded his followers that this was the right arsenal to attack. He said that this area was teeming with slaves crying out to be freed. In some respects, he was right. There were 84,000 free Blacks in Maryland and 87,000 slaves. In Virginia, there were 58,000 free blacks and 491,000 slaves, more than in any other state.

But in this farmhouse, his followers would once again challenge him on his ideas. They would point out that perhaps these slaves were reasonably content and well-treated (which was often the case), and that they would not respond to his calling. Again, Brown would become enraged, and become more resolved that his way, the way of violence, was the only way.

***

Some Chambersburg residents other than Mary Ritner would remember John Brown. Emma Jane Ritner, who was just a young girl, wrote a letter in which she recorded what she could remember of Brown's stay in her mother's boardinghouse. Emma said that Brown was "an old gentleman who came in a white canvas covered wagon ... He stayed only a few days but all through the summer he came at intervals. He was strong and vigorous. I think it was only his white hair and beard that caused us to think of him as an older man. We children loved him. He was carrying guns and ammunition to Harpers Ferry instead of farming tools. My sister and I often rode with him for a mile or two and walked back."

Although Franklin Keagy, a Chambersburg resident, and Emma Jane Ritner were in the best position to have seen John Brown, two more Chambersburg residents observed him. Colonel A. K. McClure, prominent Chambersburg politician and abolitionist, recalled: "I saw

Brown's major followers

Owen Brown . . . son of Brown, he escaped the disaster of Harpers Ferry and headed north, passing through Chambersburg.

Albert Hazlett . . . following the raid, he escaped but was captured near Carlisle. He was taken to Charles Town and hung.

At left, Francis Jackson Merriam . . . he had Alexander McClure prepare a will; he successfully escaped from Harpers Ferry.

At right, John E. Cook . . . some evidence suggests he may have spent some time in Chambersburg. Following the raid, he was captured near Mont Alto, placed in the Franklin County Jail and eventually executed.

Above, Osborne Perry Anderson . . . one of seven who escaped Harpers Ferry. He was nearly captured in Chambersburg where he was given food.

This is the fire engine house inside the U.S. Armory Compound at Harpers Ferry where John Brown and his men made their final stand.

Kennedy farm. Once in this town, they boarded the train and went to Harrisburg. They were headed for North Elba in New York state, the place where Brown's wife had resided for many years.

After the raid, several of Brown's men escaped and filtered back through Pennsylvania and most especially back into Chambersburg. There were seven of Brown's men who managed to get into this area at that time. They were Owen Brown, Barclay Coppoc, Francis J. Merriam, Charles P. Tidd, John Edwin Cook, Osborne P. Anderson, and Albert Hazlett.

Five of the seven men traveled together; they were Brown, Coppoc, Merriam, Tidd, and Cook. At Mont Alto, Cook separated from the other men in order to attempt to secure provisions for the group of fugitives. Cook was captured and eventually spent time in the Chambersburg jail. He had hoped to see his wife and child who were in Chambersburg, but after

Emmanuel Chapel, Mont Alto . . . Episcopal place of worship, built for workers of nearby iron furnace. Tradition has it that John Brown (AKA Isaac Smith) taught a Sunday School class for Blacks here in 1859.

Artist's depiction of Brown being led to the gallows, appropriately entitled, "Last Moments of John Brown."

the Raid occurred Cook's wife and child were helped by some local residents to leave the area and seek refuge in New York state with the lady's uncle. Cook, himself, was sent from Chambersburg to Charles Town, where he perished upon the gallows.

Owen Brown, Tidd, Coppoc, and Merriam were fortunate to escape from the area. Merriam was placed upon a train near Scotland while Brown, Tidd, and Coppoc traveled in a northwestern direction up through Pennsylvania toward Ohio. Hazlett and Osborne P. Anderson also came into the vicinity of Chambersburg. Anderson was given food by someone in Chambersburg while Hazlett was given a ride in a buggy some miles outside of Chambersburg by a gentlemen who lived in Quincy. Authorities almost captured Anderson while he was in Chambersburg, getting food from a friend. Hazlett was captured near Carlisle and eventually hanged. Of the seven men who made their way back into Pennsylvania, five of John Brown's men outwitted their would-be captors, for Anderson, Owen Brown, Tidd, Merriam, and Coppoc eluded the authorities. Cook and Hazlett did not escape detection and lost their lives in Charles Town.

* * *

In addition to the Ritners, Alexander McClure and his wife were sympathetic toward the abolitionist movement. His wife was probably the lady who wrote to John Brown while he was in prison in Virginia after the Harpers Ferry Raid. At least Mrs. McClure's initials match the ones that appeared on a letter that was sent from Chambersburg on November 26, 1859. The letter said: "... I had hoped that your life would be spared, until the recent public declaration of Gov. Wise, when he visited you in prison to tell you that he cannot temper Virginia justice with mercy - that darling attribute of Him who shall judge us all. A million hearts will be saddened by your execution, and a million more will feel keenly on the issues it will thrust upon the world that never felt before. Its fruits must be left to time; God only knows them. As a wife and mother, I have regretted that an act springing from deep-seated convictions of duty - however, mistaken, morally or politically - should desolate a home by the gibbet. But fear not for those who shall mourn your untimely and cruel end. He who tempers the wind to the shorn lamb will not forget them; and the voices of mothers of the North,

Brown's grave at North Elba, New York.

with the true-hearted men, will provide them with all temporal comforts."

McClure, who was a lawyer, also had dealings with Francis Merriam prior to the raid, for this particular follower of John Brown had a considerable amount of money and felt the need to make a will before traveling to Harpers Ferry. Merriam contacted Colonel McClure and solicited his help in drawing up a will. Not only that, but McClure also had contact with John Cook when Cook was in the Chambersburg jail. McClure felt he could help Cook gain his freedom through legal means, but just to be sure he had even devised an escape plan. However, Cook was spirited out of Chambersburg and returned to Virginia for trial and hanging before McClure could help.

John Brown was hanged on December 2, 1859. Later in that month, four of Brown's disciples, were hanged. A Chambersburg resident by the name of B.L. Maurer viewed the happenings in Charles Town. Maurer learned that Copeland and Shields Green were to die at eleven o'clock. He watched as the prisoners were loaded onto a furniture wagon. The wagon took the prisoners to the field about a quarter of a mile away. Soon the prisoners were on the fall; and after a prayer was offered, the sheriff cut a rope and Copeland and Green were, in Maurer's words, "swinging between heaven and earth." Copeland's neck was not broken, and he struggled. Green died easily. This was ironic, for it was Green who trembled violently as he climbed into the wagon. Copeland had remained calm.

Around 11:30 the same procedure began again, but this time it was Cook and Edwin Coppoc who were to die. As these two men climbed to the gallows, they seemed to gain control of themselves although at times earlier they had given in to despair. As the ropes were adjusted, Cook said, "Be quick, or quick as possible." Coppoc repeated the sentiment. Soon the men were dead.

After viewing the hangings, Maurer returned to the hotel where he was staying, ate dinner, and then proceeded to make his way back to Chambersburg. A chapter of history had been written on that fateful day in December, and it would not be long before the country would be divided into two armed camps. Within a few short months the Civil War had begun. John Brown was dead by then, but perhaps he was correct when he said to Frederick Douglass that he was worth more dead than alive.

CHAPTER 3

Chambersburg braces for war

n April 12, 1861, Confederate forces began shelling Fort Sumter, and the following day it surrendered. On April 15, President Abraham Lincoln issued a call for 75,000 volunteers to suppress the rebellion.

The same day Lincoln issued his call for troops, Colonel A.K. McClure of Chambersburg, a prominent Republican leader, met with the President, General Winfield Scott, and Pennsylvania Senator Simon Cameron. As a result of this meeting, McClure wired Harrisburg that the state was to furnish 14,000 men and two regiments were needed immediately.

Chambersburg was soon filled with volunteers from all over the county. On the evening of April 17, a public meeting was held in the Franklin County Courthouse. Community leaders spoke out against the rebellion. Men, both young and old, vowed to fight to their death to save "Old Glory." At this time several committees were formed to support the war effort.

The Committee on Contributions received pledges of several thou-

Major General Robert Patterson was the 69-year-old Union commander who was given the duty of staging an army in and around Chambersburg in 1861. He was instructed to contain the Confederate forces in the Shenandoah Valley. His failure to do so led to the first Confederate victory at Manassas and his dismissal.

Andrew Curtin, wartime Governor of Pennsylvania, visited Chambersburg a number of times throughout the Civil War. The first was in May 1861, to review the troops under Patterson.

impending Rebel raids into Pennsylvania. In late April, Chambersburg braced itself for an attack from Maryland. Area residents were urged to collect arms for the defense of the county seat. In May, a party of wood cutters was fired on by a group of alleged "Pennsylvania Secessionists" near Shade Gap, and one Chambersburg newspaper editor urged that all such "Northern traitors should be shot down like dogs." Another rumor placed a thousand Cherokee Indians at Harpers Ferry with "tomahawks, scalping knives and rifles" prepared to invade the Cumberland Valley.

By early May, 1861, more than 3,000 soldiers were camped at the fairgrounds west of town as well as on a farm east of town.

In response to the Confederate threat, real or imagined, Union troops started to concentrate at Chambersburg. By May, the 7th, 8th and 10th Pennsylvania regiments (3,000 men) were camped at the Fairgrounds just west of town and on the Eberly farm east of Chambersburg. The courthouse and several private dwellings were also used to quarter troops.

On May 3 a freak storm blanketed the area with four to five inches of snow. This contributed to an epidemic of "spotted fever." Many of the soldiers slept on the ground without tents and were exposed to the snow and rain during the same period. A hospital was established in the Mansion House on the corner of the diamond and East Market Street, and

The scenes above are special sketches by an artist which appeared in the July 6, 1861 issue of Harper's Weekly. They depict camp life between Chambersburg and Greencastle.

the ladies from the town's churches got together to bring food to the sick. As sickness spread among the troops, a general hospital was established in Franklin Hall, the town's commercial and entertainment center, located on the northeastern corner of the diamond.

During this same period, a grand review was held in the town diamond. The ladies of Chambersburg presented a "handsome" flag to the 7th Pennsylvania. Later in the day Governor Andrew Curtin arrived on a special train and reviewed the troops.

While Confederate forces, under General Joseph E. Johnston, gathered at Harpers Ferry, another army, led by General P.G.T. Beauregard, was concentrating some 20 miles southwest of Washington at Manassas, Virginia. With these threats right on the Union border, a nervous President Abraham Lincoln pressed his military commanders to take action.

Even though most of the Union army was composed of raw recruits, Lincoln reminded General Irvin McDowell, newly appointed commander of the Department of Northeastern Virginia, that the enemy was just as inexperienced. While McDowell hastily prepared his army to

An epidemic of "Spotted Fever" whipped through the soldiers' ranks and they were cared for in makeshift hospitals.

Patterson's Army seen in the square of Chambersburg as it departs the area.

strike the Confederates at Manassas, another Union force was ordered to contain Johnston in the Shenandoah Valley. This action would prevent him from joining forces with Beauregard at Manassas.

The command of this effort would fall to 69-year-old Major General Robert Patterson. A veteran of both the War of 1812 and Mexican War, Patterson was to rendezvous his troops at Chambersburg, train them as much as time allowed, then move south across the Potomac and pin down Johnston. The old general wasted little time getting more troops to Chambersburg. By June 1 more than 8,000 soldiers were camped in and around Chambersburg. On Sunday, June 2, General Patterson arrived on a special train from Philadelphia. The general, with his entourage, was met at the railroad station by his staff and a large body of soldiers. There followed a grand parade over the town's streets to the "delight of many" but to the dismay of the more religious citizens, who felt this was a violation of the Sabbath. Following this martial demonstration, Patterson set up headquarters in a large stone building opposite the Montgomery Hotel, which had formerly been used as a Female Seminary.

General Patterson's headquarters were in a large building across from the Montgomery House.

Within days, army camps in and around Chambersburg swelled to nearly 20,000 strong. This army was not only Pennsylvanians but men from other parts of the Union, such as Rhode Island, Connecticut and Wisconsin.

With this many troops, difficulties arose which attracted the concern of town authorities.

Abner Doubleday, famous Union commander, was a captain in the artillery stationed in Chambersburg in 1861.

Newspaper artist's depiction of Colonel George H. Thomas' Brigade of Patterson's Army crossing the Potomac at Williamsport, Md.

The rate of crime rose sharply with greater incidents of robbing, assaults, and public drunkenness. Prostitution became a problem as ladies of the night plied their trade in the camps and on Chambersburg streets. A robbery of a man and his lady at a Chambersburg hotel was committed by four soldiers. The men were never arrested, and a chorus of protest came from the newspapers. One editor commented, "Such conduct should call down the indignation of every true soldier. It will lead to serious results if carried on much further. Soldiers, as well as civilians must learn to respect the laws, if not, must abide the consequences of their violation." Another editor commented on the rise in crime by saying, "The Criminal Docket was larger than it has been for several years.

> **With so many Federal troops, Chambersburg residents saw major increases of incidents involving robbing, assaults and public drunkenness.**

Almost every grade of crime was before the court." Soldiers who misbehaved were placed in the guard house which, in this case, was the cellar of the courthouse. More obstreperous men were bound by ropes and placed in a separate part of the cellar. Others, such as three Rhode Islanders, were drummed out of the service.

The most heinous crime committed by soldiers while in Chambersburg occurred on June 1. A black man was slain in cold blood. According to a written account by Jacob Hoke: "In the afternoon of Saturday, June 1st, the horrible tragedy of the killing of the colored man, Frank Jones, occurred.--Jones, it was said, kept a disorderly house in that part of town known as "Wolfstown." His place was the frequent resort of soldiers, and for some cause on that afternoon they attacked his place, forcing open the windows, upsetting the stove and beating

Signs of the times

With thousands of soldiers in its midst, Chambersburg was transformed from a tranquil, rural community to an active military base.

During the Civil War, the residents of Chambersburg would experience the influx of tens of thousands of soldiers both blue and gray living in their community.

The soldiers who came would shape the daily life of the community for the residents of Chambersburg were in the minority in their own town.

The following articles from the semi-weekly *Dispatch* in Chambersburg during the summer of 1861 reflect the turbulence of the times.

The Hospital.

An apartment for the reception of sick soldiers has been fitted up in one of the rooms known as the "Mansion House." Beds, and everything necessary for the comfort of the sick, have been prepared under the directions of Surgeon THROOP and his Assistants; and those who may take sick at the encampments will at once be removed to these snug quarters where they will be under the care of skillful physicians and attentive nurses. Our ladies too have been patriotically and industriously at work preparing bandages, scraping lint, collecting old linen, and other articles necessary for hospital use. While among us the sick soldiers will be sure to receive every attention that the kind hearts and willing hands of our ladies can bestow upon them.

CHAMBERSBURG HOSPITALITY -- OPINIONS OF THE SOLDIERS -- The soldiers from Philadelphia and Camp Scott, who have been for the last few days quartered amongst us, are unanimous in our praises of the kindness and hospitality of the Chambersburg people. One of them, from Camp Scott, said to us a day or two ago, that "The Chambersburg people were the *best people he had ever seen.*" Of course the expression was a little extravagant, but he was just about leaving, and said it in the fullness of his heart. Another publishes a Card in our present issue, which is also very flattering, and certainly will be duly appreciated by those for whom it was designed.

Such testimonials show not only the due appreciation of the soldiers' service by our people, but that the hearts of our brave defenders are also in the right place, and reflect mutual credit upon both.

—— Signs of the times ——

HOME AFFAIRS

BALLOONS FOR THE BATTLE-GROUNDS -- A number of large balloons have been prepared for the use by our Government during the war. The Rhode Island Regiment which passed through this place on the Tuesday morning last, was supplied with one. The balloon will be used to obtain views of the position and movements of the enemy.

STABBED WITH A BAYONET -- In noticing the case of the stabbed soldier in our last issue, it appears that our informants did injustice to the Lieutenant. The officer and many of the privates of his company agree that the Fifer was served just right.

The wound was not as severe as was first supposed.

ANOTHER SOLDIER GONE -- Yesterday the regular troops performed the melancoly duty of burying one of their comrades. The ceremonies were conducted, the corpse preceded by a company or two and followed by his horse bearing his weapon and uniform, his company with arms reversed, bringing up the rear.

The flag, under which he served his country, covered his coffin in its passage to the grave.

SHOT HIMSELF -- Mr. John Fisher, proprietor of the Southern Hotel, while amusing himself with a loaded revolver, Sharp's Patent, accidentally discharged the weapon, wounding himself severely. The ball entered the abdomen below the stomach and at first it was thought to be fatal. He seems to be doing well.

BURIED AT LAST -- A day or two ago, one of the companies quartered here received two days rations, but the men concluded that, as the beef was entirely dead, it ought not to be treated disrespectfully. Accordingly, about twenty-five men, headed by the 1st sergeant, proceeded with it on a wheelbarrow to a field near by, and buried it with becoming honors.

THE FOURTH IN CHAMBERSBURG -- Hot and sultry, the Fourth passed by in Chambersburg without any demonstration whatever except a few small Pic-nic parties. The churches were all closed as well as the stores and other places of business, and the little boys appeared to monopolize all the "goings on" by shooting fire crackers at the street corners. After dark a few Rockets were sent up, and numerous Roman candles made their light to shine. None of them could head off the comet, and pretty early in the evening Sky Rockets and Roman Candles ceased their blazing, and the comet was left to shine undisturbed among the permanent residents of the Heavens.

Jones and his wife. In the confusion Jones discharged his gun, the contents of which wounded two soldiers in the legs. The cry then raised, 'kill the nigger, kill the nigger'."

Several soldiers took pursuit and tracked Jones to a home where he was hiding in a chimney. Jones was then dragged out and brutally beaten and shot, at least five times by a lieutenant.

General George Cadwalader, Philadelphia native, lawyer and Mexican War veteran, commanded the 1st Division of Patterson's Army.

His body was transported to the jailhouse lawn, and an inquest and arrest warrants were issued, but nothing was followed up.

On June 7 Patterson's army headed south. Advance elements led by Colonel George H. Thomas camped at Greencastle that night. Meanwhile Stonewall Jackson's cavalry chief, Turner Ashby, disguised as a horse doctor, had penetrated Patterson's lines and rode into several of the Chambersburg camps, returning to Virginia with "an immense amount of information."

In the face of Patterson's advance into Maryland, Johnston withdrew from Harpers Ferry, moving his force to Winchester. On July 2, Major General George Cadwalader's division of Patterson's army forded the Potomac at Williamsport. A few miles into Virginia, the Yankee invaders met elements of Johnston's army at the "Battle of Falling Waters." Then Confederates, under Thomas J. Jackson (later to be known as Stonewall) defeated Patterson's men in the only sizable engagement of this little mentioned campaign. Even at that, it was a small affair. The Federals suffered 4 killed, 16 wounded, and 49 captured. The Southern forces reported twenty wounded. The next day Patterson occupied Martinsburg. The main resistance there came from a young damsel named Belle Boyd, who shot and killed a drunken soldier who had entered her home and threatened her mother.

Once in the Shenandoah Valley, Patterson became very cautious. At Bunker Hill the advance stopped. The commanding general now feared he would be hampered by lack of supplies. The army, now down to 13,000 due to sickness, desertion and the reassignment of some regiments, was moved to Charles Town. Patterson's indecisiveness and withdrawal to Charles Town gave Johnston the chance he wanted. On July 17, his men were marching toward Piedmont where they boarded trains for Manassas. This movement saved the day for the Confederates at 1st Manassas and sealed the fate of General Patterson's military career.

Two days after the Federal debacle at Manassas or Bull Run, Patterson read in a newspaper of his relief from command. As he returned to Philadelphia, he passed through

Soon after Patterson led his men south, his indecisiveness quickly led to the end of his military career.

Chambersburg on a regular passenger coach with few people recognizing him.

Chambersburg had played a key role in one of the first campaigns of the Civil War. It was a campaign that failed. Nonetheless, the tone had been set. Chambersburg would remain an important military staging and supply center for the rest of the war.

Franklin County supplied about 5,000 men to 27 different regiments and batteries and 62 companies throughout the Civil War. Their experiences were wide ranging and at times overlapping. Length of service varied from unit to unit. Usually it was for three years.

The 2nd Regiment of 3 months men was raised with great haste to meet President Lincoln's April 15, 1861 call for 75,000 men to put down the rebellion. "As fast as companies and squads were accepted, they reported at Camp Curtin, Harrisburg." Elections for officers were held, and Frederick S. Stumbaugh of Chambersburg was made colonel.

Three of the ten companies were raised in Franklin County, those being Companies A, B and C. This represented the county's first manpower contribution to the war effort, and though this regiment served only three months, most of the men, including Colonel Stumbaugh, would join other regiments and fight in many battles throughout the war.

Though shots were fired, the 2nd Pennsylvania would not see any serious fighting in its short term. Assigned to General Robert Patterson, the 2nd did much marching in those frantic days after the war began. It was Patterson's task to control the Confederates in the Shenandoah Valley. His 20,000 strong army, then at Chambersburg, was ordered to Williamsport, Maryland. The 2nd broke camp in Chambersburg and proceeded by rail to Hagerstown, Maryland. Patterson's forces crossed the Potomac on the 2nd of July and advanced on Martinsburg, Virginia. The enemy fell back to Winchester, Virginia, to make its stand. Patterson's men did much demonstrating and driving in the enemy's pickets in response to news on July 16th that Confederate General Beauregard's Army was to be attacked by Union troops at Manassas. The purpose of this demonstrating was to prevent the Confederates at Winchester from going to aid Beauregard. On the 17th, Patterson, rapidly but inexplicably, transferred his force to Charles Town, Virginia, allowing Johnston to join Beauregard. By this time, the 2nd Regiment's term of service had expired, and it was sent to Harrisburg to be mustered out July 26.

6th Reserves (Company D Washington Rifles, Capt., later Lt. Col., William D. Dixon commanding, from Franklin County)

The regiment was organized at Camp Curtin, Harrisburg, in late June, 1861, and drilled for several days at Camp Biddle, Greencastle, before being ordered to Washington via Baltimore. In Baltimore, the regiment ran into some excitement when a soldier accidentally discharged his rifle and almost caused a repeat of the bloodbath of April 19, when a Massachusetts regiment opened fire on a riotous civilian crowd. "With great difficulty (they were) kept from discharging their pieces at their supposed assailants." The regiment reported to Washington strong and healthy but within a short time the material environment of D.C. in the summer turned it into an "invalid organization with a sick roll numbering hundreds."

First action was under General McCall at Dranesville, Virginia, December 20, 1861. Some volleys were exchanged with the rebels, a charge was made, and a

Captain Joseph A. Davison served with the 6th

Lt. Col. William D. Dixon . . . 6th Pa. Reserves

caisson and some prisoners were taken. Their first fight was a victory. Wm. VanDyke of Co. D was killed. Nothing then until March, 1862.

The 6th fought on the Peninsula with General McClellan through the Seven Days, then returned to participate in the 2nd Manassas battle and the Maryland campaign. At South Mountain, September 14, 1862, Co. D with four other companies was ordered to attack the rebel 8th Alabama. They "dashed like a steed . . . against the very muzzles of their guns." It helped break the Confederate line. Thomas Campbell, John Fry, and J. McLaughlin of Co. D were killed in this action.

The regiment served with the Army of the Potomac until June 11, 1864. At Bethesda Church, its final action, the 6th, then only about 150 strong, captured 102 prisoners and buried 72 rebels whom it had fought against.

Ten men of Co. D died or were killed in its service.

12th Reserves (Company K McClure Rifles of Franklin County). The regiment was originally raised in July 1861 for three months service but was not accepted. Instead the men were mustered into the reserves for three years. None of this regiment had previous military experience except for the McClure Rifles which had been attached to volunteer militia. Company K was dissolved July 20, and the men were transferred to other companies in the regiment.

After the end of July 1861, the 12th was ordered to Harrisburg by Governor Curtin to protect the state arsenal from disbanded three months men who were threatening an attack. This delicate assignment was handled well, and no incident occurred.

The regiment, along with the other reserves, was then sent to McClellan's army on the Peninsula before Richmond and first became involved in serious combat at the Battle of Mechanicsville, where it earned the praise of Confederate General Roger Pryor. The reserves became involved in covering the Army of the Potomac's retreat during the Seven Days and witnessed the great convulsing "of the Earth itself" as the cannonading and carnage were described.

The regiment returned to Northern Virginia to fight with Pope at 2nd Manassas and again with McClellan at Antietam. At Gettysburg the 12th again was a spectator to, as well as a participant in, the great panorama of the battle from its position on Little Round Top. Grant's overland campaign in 1864 marked the climax of the 12th's service; Bethesda Church was its final action. Its term expired, and the 12th returned to Harrisburg and was mustered out June 11, 1864.

43rd Regiment 1st Light Artillery (Battery A from Franklin County) three years service on the 13th of April, 1861, James Brady, a citizen of Philadelphia, issued a call for volunteers for a Light Artillery Regiment.

"In three days 1,300 men were enrolled . . ." but General Patterson, at the time in command of Pennsylvania troops, rejected it because it was not a militia organization. Eight hundred of the men, eager to be in the service, enlisted in other regiments from New Jersey and New York. One Company joined Colonel Baker's California Regiment. The place of these 800 was filled in part by a company of Franklin County men, subsequently known as Battery A.

Battery A was commanded by Captain Hezekiah Easton and was the first of the regiment to see action. This was at the Battle of Dranesville, December 20, 1861, but it suffered no loss or injury.

Battery A was attached to the Pennsylvania Reserves and participated in McClellan's Peninsula Campaign. At Gaines Mill, June 17, 1862, the battery's infantry support was ordered away, leaving the guns exposed. Seeing this, the enemy immediately charged the battery, killed Captain Easton, and captured all the guns. The battery was given new guns, John G. Simpson was made captain, and the battery fought with the Reserves at 2nd Bull Run, South Mountain, and Antietam. Fredericksburg was another battle in which it served. Battery A was then sent to Norfolk and fought out the war with the Army of the James, also known at various times as the 7th and 5th Corps.

The end of the war saw Battery A demolishing rebel fortifications and arsenals in Richmond and removing guns and ordnance. In July, the battery returned to Harrisburg and was mustered out on the 25th, 1865. Twenty-one men from Franklin County died in its service.

3rd Cavalry (Company H partially recruited in Franklin County).

The Third Cavalry was recruited in the spring and summer of 1861 for three years and for a time was called Young's Light Kentucky Cavalry. Colonel William Averell, a West Point graduate, was named in Washington to command the regiment and immediately began drilling them and instilling them with an esprit de corps that never failed. The Third was involved in all major campaigns of the Army of the Potomac from McClellan's Peninsula battles on through the final pursuit of Lee to Appomattox Court House. The list of battles and skirmishes is a long and distinguished one. While many veterans left the Third at the end of their terms in July 1864, enough others stayed to maintain a three-company batallion.

They served with the 77th Regiment

Assistant Surgeon Jacob S. Maurer | *John Purvins, Co. A* | *Capt. William Skinner, Co. A*

77th Regiment (Companies A and partially D, G, H from Franklin County) was authorized by the War Department to include eight companies of infantry and one of artillery (which was Muehler's Independent Battery B).

Frederick S. Stumbaugh, a prominent citizen of Chambersburg and former colonel of the 2nd Pennsylvania three months militia, raised the regiment in August 1861, and served as its colonel. Peter Housum, of Franklin County, was Lt. Colonel. At Camp Wilkins near Pittsburgh, the men were drilled, and on October 18 they were sent west to Louisville, Kentucky. At first their march south to join Buell's Army was slow. "Proceeding leisurely forward . . ." the regiment wouldn't reach Buell at Nashville until March 2, 1862. The fall of Forts Henry and Donelson two weeks earlier had opened the Cumberland and Tennessee rivers. General U. S. Grant meant to take advantage of it. He moved his force to Pittsburgh Landing on the Tennessee. Buell's Army got busy repairing the Nashville and Decatur Railroad, which was meant to be an important line for Grant's movements. On April 6, Confederates under General Albert Sidney Johnston unexpectedly attacked Grant, and the battle of Shiloh raged. Buell's Column was ordered up. The 77th saw some limited fighting on April 7th with three killed and seven wounded. The 77th was the only Pennsylvania regiment at Shiloh.

The regiment then became involved in the Perryville Campaign but missed the battle as it was engaged in maneuvers against Confederate Kirby Smith's force.

In November, Stumbaugh was promoted to brigadier general. His appointment somehow fell through, however, and he resigned his command. Lt. Colonel Housum took over and led the regiment until January 1, 1863, when he died of wounds suffered at Stone's River.

The 77th fought many battles with the Army of the Cumberland including Chickamauga, Siege of Chattanooga, Sherman's Atlanta Campaign, Franklin, and Nashville. General Rosecrans called the 77th the "banner regiment at Stone River . . . They never broke their ranks." Its service throughout the war was excellent.

Following the surrender of the Confederates east of the Mississippi, hostility in Texas still prevailed. The 77th was sent to keep things quiet, and there it finished its term. It was mustered out, finally, on January 16, 1866, in Philadelphia. Company A of Chambersburg suffered 41 deaths throughout its encounters.

Company H, consisting partly of Franklin County men, enlisted, marched and fought; but because it was not fully recruited, it was never formally organized. The men were never paid for their service and were disbanded in November, 1862.

Independent Battery B (Muehler's) originally recruited for service with the 77th Pennsylvania Regiment, Battery B would serve only a short time with the regiment before it became independent.

Battery B was recruited in part from Franklin and Erie Counties and was mustered in November 6, 1861, at Pittsburgh under the command of Captain Charles F. Muehler. After this, the battery was sent to the Army of the Cumberland at Louisville, Kentucky, and participated in movements against Confederate General John Hunt Morgan. The battery missed the battle of Shiloh, arriving late with Buell's Column but campaigned actively with the army through northern Mississippi and Alabama. The battery then missed the Battle of Perryville, October 8, 1862, (arrived late) but fought hard at Stone's River and won the praise of General Rosecrans. It was engaged in Chickamauga the following fall, where Alanson Stevens, who had succeeded Captain Muehler, was killed. Chattanooga, Missionary Ridge, Sherman's Atlanta Campaign, Franklin, and Nashville were other severe contests that Battery B took active parts in. The Battery was mustered out of service October 12, 1865. Twenty eight officers and 26 enlisted men died or were killed in its service.

87th Regiment ("New" Company K from Franklin County).

The designation "New" Company K meant that the company was raised late into the war to fill the ranks of those whose term of service had expired. On the 13th of October, 1864, the original 87th lost nearly half its men when their terms ended. Veterans and recruits were consolidated into a batallion of five companies. In March 1865, five new companies (one was "New" Company K) were assigned to the battalion, bringing it up to full strength. On April 2, it took part in a charge on the Confederate lines at Petersburg. On April 6, it participated in the fighting at Saylor's Creek, losing only one wounded. The 87th was mustered out at Alexandria, Virginia, June 29, 1865. One man from Franklin County, Samuel A. Myers, died in its service.

103rd Regiment ("New" Company A recruited in Franklin County).

The designation "New" Company A meant that the company was raised late in the war to fill the ranks in place of those whose three year term had expired or in place of those who were captured. "New Company A" was assigned to the 103rd because of the latter. On the 20th of April, 1865, at Plymouth, North Carolina, after being under siege for three days, the original 103rd surrendered to the enemy. "New" Company A, along with seven other new companies, was attached to the 103rd and served in and around New Bern, North Carolina, until the close of the war. It was mustered out June 25, 1865. Captain Elias K. Lehman commanded "New" Company A.

107th Regiment (Companies B McClure Light Guards, H and K raised in Franklin County).

Recruited in part by Robert W. McAllen of Franklin County, the 107th was organized for three years service at Harrisburg, March 5, 1862. Thomas A. Zeigle was made Colonel, Robert McAllen, Lt. Colonel.

In late April, the 107th was assigned to McDowell's Corps. McDowell, at that time, was near Manassas facing towards Richmond, hoping to support McClellan's army, which was then on the peninsula and advancing on the rebel capital. Stonewall Jackson diverted his attention with his lightning quick movements in the Shenandoah Valley, and McDowell was forced to deal with him, never making it to Richmond.

On July 16, at Warrenton, Virginia, Colonel Zeigle died in camp. Command should have been given to Lt. Colonel McAllen, but McAllen was himself too ill and needed to be discharged. Mexican War veteran Thomas McCoy took over command.

The 107th was involved in the confusion surrounding Pope's and Bank's armies following McClellan's repulse at the Seven Days battles. Robert E. Lee sent Stonewall Jackson north, and McDowell tried to cut him off at Culpepper, Virginia, but Banks beat him. McDowell's Corps would sit out the battle of Cedar Mountain only two miles from the fighting. They watched it but were not called up until it was too late. Jackson, victorious, kept on, while McDowell circled to join Pope. The 107th was sent to Thoroughfare Gap to delay Confederate General Longstreet's approach and almost missed 2nd Manassas. It fought also at Antietam, Fredericksburg, Chancellorsville, and Gettysburg. At Gettysburg, Lt. Colonel Jas. MacThompson and Captain Jacob V. Gish of Franklin County were wounded and captured. The regiment missed the Wilderness but joined Grant's overland campaign in midstride, fighting from Spottsylvania to Petersburg. Five Forks on April 1, 1865, was its final engagement. It took part in the great review of the armies in Washington and was mustered out July 13. Sixty men from Franklin County died in its service.

11th Cavalry (Company D partially raised in Franklin County).

The 11th was organized at Philadelphia in the fall of 1861 by Colonel Josiah Harlas as an independent regiment known as Harlan's Light Cavalry. Special authorization had to he obtained from the Secretary of War since the regiment was raised from different states — Iowa, New York, New Jersey and Pennsylvania. Its independent status was revoked because of its irregularity, and the regiment was designated Pennsylvania Cavalry.

In the spring of 1862, the 11th was split apart; a detachment was sent to Portsmouth, Virginia, and the remainder joined the Army of the Potomac at White House, Virginia. The regiment was reunited after a short time. During the war, detachments of the 11th were frequently given duty away from the regiment.

The 11th served principally on the peninsulas of Virginia and at Suffolk, White House, Portsmouth, and Bermuda Hundred toward the end of the war. The 11th did make some movements into North Carolina, but because it spent much of the war dispersed, with its companies on various duties, its effectiveness as a regiment was minimal. Nonetheless, together or in pieces, it fought many skirmishes and battles; it captured much arms and equipment (110 pieces of field artillery, 41 mortars, 6 heavy guns and 120 carriages and caissons). The 11th was mustered out at Richmond, August 13, 1865.

Pvt. John F. Pfoutz, Co. A, 126th   *1st Lt. William H. Mackey, Co. H, 126th*   *George Colby, Co. K, 126th*

The 126th Regiment was a nine months unit raised in response to a call for men from President Lincoln and, more directly, Governor Curtin in August 1862.

The idea of the nine months men was to encourage older, family men and businessmen, who might not want to enlist for three years, to participate in the war. Draft was employed only when necessary to fill the quota. In the case of the August call, the draft was not used widely as it wasn't needed. Response was excellent, and fourteen regiments were raised. Most of these spent their terms in garrison duty and saw no fighting. In fact, only three suffered any battle casualties. One of those that fought was the 126th.

Soon after Chancellorsville in 1863, where it took a bloody loss, the 126th was returned to Harrisburg and mustered out on May 26, 1863

Made up mostly of men from Franklin County, the 126th represented the county's largest single contribution of manpower during the war — eight companies of infantry, approximately 800 men. These men were young (average age 23), many had served previously in the 2nd Pennsylvania, and many were professional men — lawyers, dentists, medical doctors, though most were laborers and farmers. They were "the very pick and pride of Franklin County..." They served with distinction, first in a supporting role during the 2nd Bull Run and Maryland campaigns, then actively at the battles of Fredericksburg and Chancellorsville, where they fought heroically and suffered greatly.

Corp. Benjamin
Dawney, Co. H, 126th

Lt. Col. D. Watson
Rowe, 126th

Pvt. Seth Dickey, Co.
C, 126th

1st Sgt. George F.
Platt, Co. D, 126th

Major Robert S.
Brownson, 126th

1st Lt. Stephen O.
McCurdy, Co. G, 126th

J. F. Smith, Co. C,
126th

*The 126th Regiment
was the county's
largest contributor
of manpower during
the war.*

1st Lt. James McCull-
ough, Co. C, 126th

Thomas A. Creigh,
Co. C, 126th

2nd Lt. Clay Mac-
Cauley, Co. D, 126th

S. J. Patterson, Co. C,
126th

Capt. William McDowell, Co. I, 158th

Pvt. William Stumbaugh, 158th

Pvt. Nicholas Greenawalt, Co. D, 158th

Lt. Michael Miller, Co. B, 158th

Col. David B. McKibben, 158th

Lt. Col. Elias Troxell, 158th

At Fredericksburg, the regiment took part in the fourth and final Union charge up Marye's Heights. The 126th took part in Burnside's Mud March in January 1863, but otherwise it was a quiet winter. Spring brought a new campaign and the battle of Chancellorsville. The second day found the regiment, along with its brigade, in a vulnerable spot near the Ely's Ford Road. It survived, but it took a bloody loss with 9 killed, 49 wounded, and 11 taken prisoner. A week after the battle, the regiment returned to Harrisburg to be mustered out May 26, 1863. The return home was special as townspeople, family, and friends turned out for parades and ceremonies honoring their returning loved ones.

158th Regiment (Company B Letterkenny Guards, Company D Wiestling Guards, Company E Border Guards, Company G Franklin Guards, and partially Company I Mountain Rangers and Company F Oakville Guards from Franklin County).

The 158th was organized at Chambersburg in early November, 1862, for nine months service. David B. McKibben of the regular army was made colonel, Elias S. Troxell, Lt. Colonel and Reverend Daniel Hartman became regimental chaplain. All three of these men were from Franklin County. At the close of the month, the 158th was sent to Suffolk, Virginia, where it was instructed and drilled thoroughly in preparation for war. One month later, the regiment went into winter quarters at New Bern, North Carolina.

In the spring of 1863, Confederate General D. H. Hill was sent into North Carolina to operate against Federals at Washington on the Tar River. Hill invested the Union garrison there, and the 158th under Lt. Colonel Troxell was sent, with other troops, to relieve Washington by water. "While on the way, the vessel on which it was embarked ran aground, in the midst of a terrible storm, and lay for two days and nights at the mercy of the waves. It was finally rescued, with the loss of stores, and proceeded on its way up the Pamlico River." A short distance below Washington, the expedition was stopped by obstructions in the channel, and heavy batteries were placed to dispute any passage. The men boarded gunboats in order to run this blockade, but pilots could not be found, and the idea was given up. The expedition returned to New Bern to begin a trek across country to relieve Washington. At Swift Creek, enemy skirmishers were driven in, but no more fighting took place. "The enemy, seeing that he was about to be met in a fair field, abruptly raised the seige, and retired to Goldsboro."

> **The 158th, organized in late 1862, helped harrass Lee's retreating troops following Gettysburg and was mustered out on Aug. 12, 1863.**

The 158th then participated in General Dix's movement toward Richmond from Fortress Monroe. This advance was meant as a feint to prevent the reinforcement of Lee's army and was somewhat successful. The 158th was then ordered to Harpers Ferry and helped harass Lee's army during its retreat from Gettysburg. Once Lee had made good his escape, the 158th's term of service was winding down. On August 12, 1863, at Chambersburg, the regiment was mustered out. Fourteen men from Franklin County died or were killed.

16th Cavalry (Companies E and H from Franklin County).

Organized in November 1862, at Camp McClellan for three years service, it was mounted and equipped by the 23rd and sent to Camp Casey, Bladensburg, Maryland, for instruction. On January 3, it was sent to the army near Falmouth, Virginia, and was assigned to Averell's Brigade. Colonel John Irvin Gregg, Mexican War veteran and regular army man, was regimental commander. Lorenzo D. Rodgers of Franklin County was named Lt. Colonel. He resigned May, 1863.

Its first battle was at Kelly's Ford, March 17, where the 16th dismounted, charged, and scattered a squadron of rebel cavalry, suffering only a slight loss. On June 9, 1863, the largest cavalry battle of the Civil War was fought at Brandy Station, Virginia; the 16th missed the action as they had just turned in their saddles for exchange and were not issued new ones in time. The regiment would not fight much at Gettysburg but was active in the pursuit of Lee's Army, engaging his cavalry in a sharp clash near Martinsburg, Virginia, July 18. Six were killed in that encounter. William M. Goodman and Samual A. Rorebaugh of Company H were killed two days prior at Shepherdstown, Virginia; Lewes Hoffmaster of Company H was captured at Shepherdstown and died at Andersonville Prison, Georgia. The regiment campaigned through the fall and winter, many being killed and wounded. In February, a detachment from the 16th under Captain Adam J. Sayder of Company H, joined Kilpatrick's legendary raid on Richmond that failed and in which Colonel Ulrich Dahlgren was killed. The regiment served around Richmond and Petersburg through the remainder of its term, harassing Confederate supply lines as well as engaging in many battles. These battles included the fight at Yellow Tavern, where General Jeb Stuart was slain. It helped chase Lee to Appomattox, and, on August 7, 1865, was mustered out at Richmond, Virginia.

Twenty-five men from Franklin County died.

17th Cavalry (Company G from Franklin County).

The 17th was raised in response to a call by President Lincoln for the state to provide three regiments of cavalry; it organized at Camp Simmons near Harrisburg, October 18, 1862. Josiah Kellogg, formerly of the First U.S. Cavalry, was made colonel.

Its first fight was at the town of Occoquan, Virginia, on December 22, where it encountered and chased Hampton's Legion from South Carolina. Christmas was spent skirmishing with Confederates. With Joe Hooker in command of the army the following spring and a new campaign brewing, the 17th prepared itself. It was one of only three regiments of cavalry to accompany Hooker's columns in their movement toward Chancellorsville, May 1863. At that battle, the 17th was used as support for batteries of artillery squarely in the way of Stonewall Jackson's flank attack. "Formed in single line, with sabres drawn, with order to charge in case the enemy came to the guns ... thus was the mad onset of Stonewall Jackson's army checked by artillery, supported by a single line of raw cavalry."

Under Buford, the 17th fought against Heth's Division on the first day at Gettysburg near the Lutheran Seminary. "For four hours, and until the arrival of the First Corps, Buford held at bay a third of the entire rebel army." Early the following year, a detachment from the regiment, about 200 men, were involved in Kilpatrick's catastrophic raid on Richmond. Then

Pvt. Conrad Stumbaugh, 21st Cav.

2nd Lt. John H. Harmony, Co. L, 21st Cav.

Pvt. Joseph Pfoutz, 21st Cav.

Pvt. Joseph Boughey, Co. K, 21st Cav.

Pvt. Theodore Colby, Co. B, 21st Cav.

Pvt. Samuel Mowers, Co. D, 21st Cav.

the spring campaign began. The 17th, attached to Sheridan's cavalry corps, rode and fought courageously from Catharine Furnace in the Wilderness through Todd's Tavern and in all the subsequent movements of the corps. At Cedar Creek, in October, a detachment from the regiment served as an escort for Sheridan on his famous "ride" from Winchester to the battlefield to rally his men.

In 1865 it saw more hard fighting. Brigade commander General Devin wrote in his farewell order to the 17th: "In five successive campaigns, and in over three score engagements, you have nobly sustained your part. Of the many gallant regiments from your state none has a brighter record, none has more freely shed its blood on every battlefield from Gettysburg to Appomattox. Your gallant deeds will be ever fresh in the memory of your comrades . . . ."

165th Regiment (Company A from Franklin County).

The 165th was organized in November 1862, near Gettysburg as a nine months service drafted militia unit. Charles H. Buehler, formerly of the 2nd and 87th Pennsylvania Regiments, became colonel. The 165th was sent immediately to Suffolk, Virginia, where it spent most of its service guarding the approaches to the mouth of the James River. In April 1863, Confederate General James Longstreet took 40,000 men into that area to drive out or destroy the Federals. Longstreet laid siege to the Union post for a month but abandoned his effort and withdrew towards Petersburg. In June 1863, the 165th was involved in General Dix's brief diversionary campaign against Richmond. This concluded the regiment's term of service. It returned to Gettysburg to be mustered out July 28, 1863. Three men from Franklin County died.

21st Cavalry.

Two 21sts were raised. The first was a six-month regiment recruited in July and August 1863. Companies D, H, I, K, L, and M were made up of Franklin County men responding to the urgent call of President Lincoln and Governor Curtin. At an instructional camp near Chambersburg, officers were selected, and William H. Boyd made colonel, Richard F. Mason, Lt. Colonel. Colonel Boyd was not from Franklin County but was widely respected for having been active with the Lincoln Cavalry in skirmishing against the advance of Lee's army in the Cumberland Valley during the Gettysburg campaign. All the field officers were experienced cavalrymen. Companies H, K, L, M and two others were then detailed to Pottsville and Scranton. Five others, including D and I went to Harpers Ferry and spent the fall and winter engaged in arduous work in the Department of the Shenandoah.

In January 1864, authority was given to reorganize the regiment for three years service. All units returned to Chambersburg, and those who wished to quit did so while the others were mustered in for the long term. New recruits filled the ranks, and all the field officers stayed with the exception of a Major Jones. In May, the regiment was ordered to Washington where, to their dismay, their horses were taken away. They were armed and equipped as infantrymen and sent to Virginia to join the Army of the Potomac.

As infantryman, the regiment was first involved in heavy fighting at Cold Harbor, losing 11 killed and 46 wounded. Among the wounded was Colonel Boyd, who was discharged. Then at Petersburg, on the 18th of June, the 21st came under even more destructive fire. A member of the regiment identified as J D H wrote in his pamphlet, "Travels and Doings," that the 21st was ordered on the evening of the 18th to charge a rebel fort. "We fixed bayonets, and went up the hill on a yell, while the rebels opened upon us a perfect hailstorm of iron and lead from their muskets, and from sixteen pieces of artillery.

If Cold Harbor was hard, the fight of the 18th of June was harder. We charged the brow of the second hill, and the rebel fort lay directly in front of us ... about 150 yards. Here we found we could go no further. He, who went beyond this, went to his grave." Eleven were killed, 79 wounded including Lt. Colonel Mason, 1 was missing in the charge.

On October 5, 1864, the regiment was pulled out of line and sent to City Point, Virginia, where it was remounted, re-equipped, and assigned to General David Gregg's cavalry division. As cavalrymen, the 21st was engaged in a very sharp clash at Boydton Plank Road. It burned Confederate stores at Stony Creek Station and rode on the Bellefield raid. Heavier fighting followed in the spring during the final campaign. On April 5, at Paine's Cross Roads, Virginia, Gregg's division struck a rebel wagon train, destroying 200 wagons and capturing some 900 mules. The 21st lost 98 killed, wounded, and missing in less than half an hour. Contact with the enemy was kept up. In the days that followed Appomattox Court House, the 21st made an unsuccessful charge against Rosser's cavalry. They were ignorant of Lee's surrender.

Following the surrender, the 21st headed for North Carolina with Sheridan's cavalry corps in hope of fighting Joe Johnston's army, but Johnston too surrendered, and the war was over for these men from Franklin County. On July 8, 1865, they were mustered out and went home. The regiment death toll was 151, and 267 were wounded.

184th Regiment (company F from Franklin County).

The 184th was organized at Camp Curtin, May 1864, for three years service. On May 14, the 184th, under Major Charles Kleckner, was ordered to join the Second Corps, Army of the Potomac, then campaigning in Virginia. The 184th caught up to the Army as it was crossing the Pamunky River on May 28th. On May 29 it was led into battle at Totopotomoy Creek. General Grant's insistence on pressuring the enemy kept the regiment very active and kept it skirmishing on the way to Cold Harbor. On the second day of that battle, its brigade was led "in two desperate assaults upon the enemy's works, forcing it to lose 67 killed with 113 wounded. It was also forced to leave some of its dead in the enemy's intrenchments ... For its unflinching bravery it was warmly commended by its brigade commander." Lt. W. D. Williams of Company F was mortally wounded in this engagement, and Captain. Henry K. Ritter was wounded. For the next ten days the regiment remained on the front line, skirmishing heavily. It then moved with the corps, crossed the James, and on June 16, attacked, without success, the enemy fortifications south of Petersburg. Two days later the attack was repeated. In each assault the loss was heavy. Much more so, though, on the 22nd. During yet another assault, 52 men were killed and wounded and 115 taken prisoner. "Out of 500 men who stood in the ranks on the banks of Totopotomoy, on the 29th of May, 350, including 12 officers, had been either killed, wounded, or taken prisoners, in a period of 25 days - a loss unprecedented. Of the number taken prisoner on the 22nd, 67 died at Andersonville, and a number died at Salisbury and Florence."

Yet the fighting was not over. Bolstered by three new companies of recruits, the 184th remained along the Petersburg line until the city fell and then aided in the pursuit of Lee's Army. It fought at Saylors Creek, High Bridge, and Farmville and was at Appomattox Court House for the surrender. The 184th then marched all the way back to Washington and participated in the grand review of the armies. Company F was mustered out July 14, 1865, after losing 27 men to battle and disease. Eight of those died at Andersonville prison, Georgia, and another man died while held captive at Danville, Virginia.

22nd Cavalry (Company L under Capt. Thomas French from Franklin

County).

The 22nd was formed by the consolidation of the Ringgold Cavalry with a battalion of six months men including Co. L raised in response to the rebel invasion of June-July, 1863. The six months battalion served prior to the consolidation, guarding the fords of the Susquehanna above and below Harrisburg as well as picketing roads leading into the Cumberland Valley. It joined in pursuit of Lee's army after Gettysburg. In February, the battalion was sent to Chambersburg and was recruited as a three year regiment. There it was joined with the Ringgold Cavalry. It then proceeded to Cumberland, Maryland for instruction. In April, about 700 men of the regiment who were not yet mounted, were sent to a general camp of rendezvous for cavalry in Pleasant Valley, Maryland. There they were given horses and trained how to use them.

In its first battle, the 22nd fought as infantry against Jubal Early at Leetown, West Virginia, in June 1864, while covering General Sigel's withdrawal from Martinsburg, West Virginia. It was then remounted and helped cover General Sheridan's retreat from Cedar Creek. Captain French was among the wounded in this action. In the meantime, the detachment that had been left in Cumberland the previous April had been active in movements with Generals Sigel, Hunter and Crook and fought at the battles of New Market and Kernstown that summer. The detachment then joined General Averell's command in chasing the rebel McCausland after the burning of Chambersburg. The two detachments were rejoined in Hagerstown, Maryland, in August and served in Averell's advance on Martinsburg. The advance was a failure, and many casualties were suffered. Darkesville, Bunker Hill, Stephenson's Depot and Bucklestown were sharp fights. The 22nd then joined Sheridan's force and helped smash the rebels at Winchester, Fisher's Hill, Mount Vernon Forge and Cedar Creek.

The 22nd spent the winter operating against guerillas in Hardy, Hampshire, and Pendleton Counties, West Virginia. The duty, over "mountain roads covered with ice and snow and swept by wintry blasts," was arduous but successful. In April 1865, nearly half of the regiment was mustered out. The remainder was consolidated with the 18th Pennsylvania Cavalry, forming the 3rd Provisional Cavalry, which served chiefly in West Virginia. Co. L mustered out October 31.

200th Regiment (Company G partially raised in Franklin County).

The 200th was organized September 3, 1864, at Camp Curtin to serve for one year. On the 9th of September, the regiment was ordered to join the Army of the James and was posted near Dutch Gap, Virginia, where it repulsed a Confederate attack on November 19. The 200th was then sent to the Army of the Potomac at Petersburg, where it became involved in the siege operations. Perhaps the most desperate fighting the 200th experienced was the following March 25, when three Confederate divisions attacked and captured the Union Fort Stedman, breaking the Union line. General Hartranft's division of Pennsylvanians, of which the 200th was a part, rushed up. The 200th made two separate advances which cost the regiment dearly but succeeded in stalling the Confederate attack. For this, the 200th earned the praise of General Grant. Its loss was 14 killed and 109 wounded. It fought hard again at Fort Sedgwick along the Jerusalem Plank Road, April 2, and was one of the first Union regiments to enter Petersburg the following day. The 200th was involved in the chasing of Lee to Appomattox following the South Side Railroad. It went into camp at Nottoway Court House, April 9, and stayed there until Johnston's surrender in North Carolina. It was mustered out May 30, 1865, while new recruits were transferred to the 51st Pennsylvania.

201st Regiment (Companies I and K partially raised in Franklin County).

The 201st was organized at Harrisburg in August 1864, as a response to President Lincoln's July 18th call for 500,000 more men. It proceeded to Chambersburg and went into camp five miles out of town where the pike crosses Back Creek. There it was properly schooled and drilled. The 201st spent most of its term split up and attached to various guard and provost duties. Much of the regiment, including Companies I and K, served along the Manassas Gap Railroad. Their duty there ended in November 1864, after the tracks were destroyed, and the regiment proceeded to Alexandria, Virginia, Camp Slough. There it was engaged in guard duty on trains and fortifications. It escorted recruits and stragglers on their way to the front, and many of the officers were used on a general court martial. The regiment reassembled in Harrisburg, June 1865, to be mustered out.

202nd (Company G partially raised in Franklin County).

The 202nd was organized September 3, 1864, at Camp Curtin and sent to Camp Couch, Chambersburg, for drill. September 29, the regiment was sent to the Manassas Gap Railroad to protect the line from enemy guerillas, chiefly John Mosby. General Sheridan had begun his Shenandoah campaign, and the railroad was a vital supply line for his army. The duty was very trying for the 202nd. Frequent harassment by rebels kept them anxious. "If a soldier went outside the lines, he was immediately set upon, and either murdered or sent away into captivity." One incident where rebels derailed a train and fired into the survivors of the wreck particularly upset them. For revenge Charles Albright, Colonel of the 202nd, ordered every building burned within a one mile radius of the wreck, and a system of rounding up prominent rebels and forcing some of them to ride the trains was instituted, which virtually ended all harassment of the trains.

Once Sheridan's success was assured, the Manassas Gap Railroad was torn up and the 202nd assigned to a portion of the Orange and Alexandria Railroad from Bull Run to Alexandria. After Lee and Johnston's surrender the 202nd was ordered to the Anthracite Coal regions of the state. August 3, 1865, it was mustered out in Harrisburg.

205th (Company G partially from Franklin County).
207th (Company F partially from Franklin County).
208th (Company B partially from Franklin County).
209th (Company D and partially G from Franklin County).

These regiments are lumped together because they were all raised at approximately the same time, under similar circumstances, and all were assigned, along with the 200th, to General Hartranft's Pennsylvania Division and attached to the IX Corps at Petersburg, Virginia. Under Hartranft these regiments fought together and shared experiences.

The 205th and 207th were brigaded together, as were the 200th, 208th and 209th. All were involved in the terrible fight at Fort Stedman, where the division sealed a hole in the Union line, and all were involved in the attack that finally broke the Confederate stronghold. As a division, they entered Petersburg on April 3, and briefly helped to keep order in the burning city. They then moved out along the South Side Railroad, repairing track and attending to Confederate prisoners. They missed the surrender at Appomattox. In May and June 1865, the regiments were individually mustered out in Alexandria, Virginia.

210th Regiment (Companies D and I from Franklin County).

The 210th was organized in September 1864, at Camp Curtin and sent to Petersburg to join the 5th Corps on duty there. Hatcher's Run, October 27 and 28, was its first action, but the fighting was minimal. In December, it was involved in the Bellefield raid, doing much

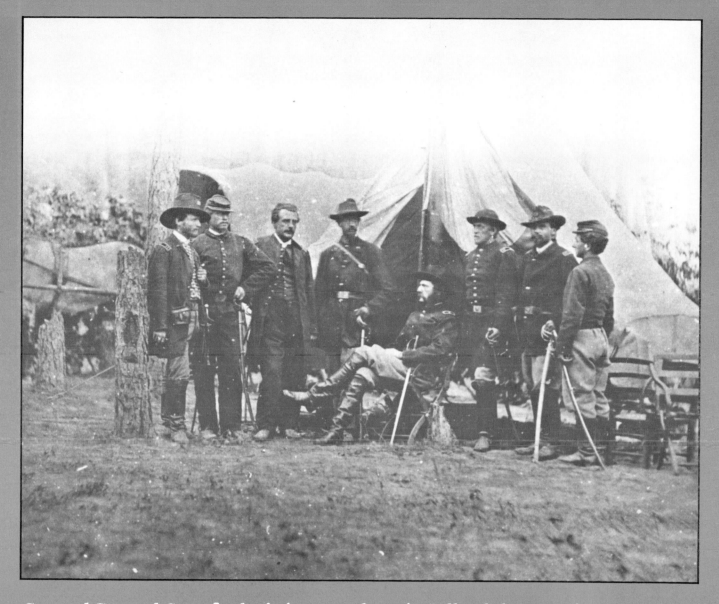

General Samuel Crawford, sitting, was born in "Allendale" mansion near Fayetteville six miles east of Chambersburg in 1829. Crawford was the highest ranking Chambersburg area native to serve in the war. He graduated from the University of Pennsylvania Medical School in 1850 and served as an assistant surgeon in the U. S. Army at a number of posts in the West until 1860. He was then transferred to Charleston Harbor where he commanded a battery at the bombardment of Fort Sumter. Crawford was promoted to Brigadier General in 1862. He won praise from Nathanial Banks for his performance during the Shenandoah Valley Campaign of 1862 and saw heavy fighting at Cedar Mountain where his brigade suffered 50% casualties. He was severely wounded at Antietam but recovered to lead the Pennsylvania Reserves at Gettysburg. Crawford fought in the major battles of the Eastern Theatre through Appomattox. Following the war he served with the regular army at various posts in the South until his retirement in 1873 when he moved to Philadelphia. He died there in 1892 and is buried in Laurel Hill Cemetery.

destruction to the Weldon Railroad and Confederate stores located along it. Many took ill following the raid due to fatigue and exposure suffered during the raid. The chaplain, Reverend Taylor Swartz, was among those who died. Sergeant David Summers and Private David Fulton of Company I and Private Emanual Boon of Company D died, too.

On March 27, movement upon Gravelly Run began. The 210th took the advance. In the three days that followed, the regiment experienced its most bitter fighting. When it was finished, 35 were killed including Colonel William Sergeant, 115 were wounded, and 150 were missing. Its next fight was April 1 at Five Forks. "In a charge made upon the enemies works, it displayed its wonted courage . . . with the corps, it followed closely the retreating (enemy) and at Appomattox Court House, was upon the front line to the last, the flag of truce proclaiming the surrender, passing through the lines of the brigade in which (the regiment) stood." The 210th participated in "the grand review of the National Troops" in Washington. It was mustered out May 30, 1865. Recruits were transferred to the 51st Pennsylvania. Thirteen men from Franklin County died.

Besides these regiments, approximately 500 black men from Chambersburg and Franklin County served in Union black regiments during the war.

CHAPTER 4

"Jeb" Stuart launches the first raid

Friday, October 10, 1862, was a bitter and cold rainy autumn day. At Jacob Hoke's dry goods store on the Diamond, business was slow, so he began restocking the shelves with some of the goods that had been hidden away when invasion had seemed imminent the month before.

About 4:30 in the afternoon, Hoke had one of his few customers. "He looked the very ideal of a soldier," remembered Hoke, "...Tall - about six feet, well shaped, and muscular." The stranger wore a regulation Federal blue greatcoat, but the rest of his clothes had a decidedly "butternut" hue. He wore a sabre and at least two pistols at his sides and seemed to be taking an inventory of the store. After asking Hoke for a pair of socks, the stranger took his time making a selection, all the while continuing to survey the goods surrounding him.

When the soldier finally found the pair of socks he was looking for, Hoke asked him directly, "Are you from the Army of the Potomac?"

"No, Sir. I'm from Virginia: Just from the sod."

"When he handed me a piece of silver in payment for his purchase, my suspicions were confirmed," wrote Hoke. "That he was a rebel, and a scout from the approaching foe, there can be no question."

Before the day was over, Jacob Hoke would see a good many more rebels.

After their mauling in Maryland, the Confederate Army of Northern Virginia lay stretched along the Opequan Creek between Winchester and Martinsburg, Virginia. Every day, it grew stronger, as stragglers, new recruits, and recovered wounded came back into the ranks. By early October, the army had more than doubled since the Battle of Antietam.

General Robert E. Lee knew, however, that this army had had a long, severe summer of campaigning. Everything from shoes and clothes to rifles were badly needed. These veteran troops needed more time to rest and refit before they could take to the field again.

General George B. McClellan's Union Army of the Potomac still lethargically hugged the north bank of its namesake river and daily received more of the vital materials that could soon have it on the offensive again. The army's two primary lines of supply were the Baltimore and Ohio Railroad and the Cumberland Valley Railroad, which fed into Hagerstown, Maryland from central Pennsylvania.

Studying maps at his headquarters near Winchester, Lee saw that five miles north of Chambersburg the Cumberland Valley Railroad crossed the Conococheague Creek. If the bridge there was destroyed, McClellan would lose the use of Hagerstown as a supply depot and would have to rely solely on the B & O. Such a venture might, Lee thought, buy some more valuable time from the already cautious Union commander. And Lee's Chief of Cavalry, Major General James Ewell Brown "Jeb" Stuart, was just the man to lead such an undertaking.

Lee summoned Stuart and Lieutenant General Thomas Johnathan "Stonewall" Jackson to a meeting on October 6th, where he outlined his plan. In addition to destroying the Conococheague Bridge, Stuart, with a force of between 1,200 and 1,500 veteran cavalrymen, would strip the Pennsylvania countryside of horses that might be used by the army. Also, Stuart was told that should he "meet with citizens of Pennsylvania holding state or government offices, it will be desirable, . . . to bring them with you, that they may be used as hostages, or (in exchange) for our own citizens that have been carried off by the enemy. Such persons will, of course, be treated with all the respect and consideration that circumstances will admit." Naturally, Stuart would also try to ascertain any information about the Army of the Potomac that he could.

To provide some initial cover for his operation, Colonel John D. Imboden would lead a force of cavalry west and threaten Cumberland, Maryland, hopefully pulling away some of the opposition Stuart might otherwise encounter.

Stuart returned to his own headquarters at "The Bower," the plantation home of A. Stephen Dandridge, west of Charles Town. In the week or so before, "Mr. Dandridge and his delightful family seemed to turn over the house to the army, and vacant rooms were crowded with young lady visitors who never complained for want of room." Captain W. W. Blackford, Stuart's engineering officer, wrote, "Every afternoon, after the staff duties of the day were performed, we all assembled at the house for riding, walking, or fishing parties, and after tea, to which we had a standing invitation which was generally accepted, came music, singing, dancing, and games of every description mingled with moonlight strolls along the banks of the beautiful Opequan or boating upon its crystal surface. The very elements seemed to conspire to make our stay delightful, for never was there a more beautiful moon or more exquisite weather . . . ." The war seemed very far away from "The Bower."

Now, all became hustle and bustle as preparations were made. Stuart allowed himself an extra 300 men for the raid (1,800 total) to be divided into three "divi-

"Jeb" Stuart
. . . legendary Confederate cavalry leader

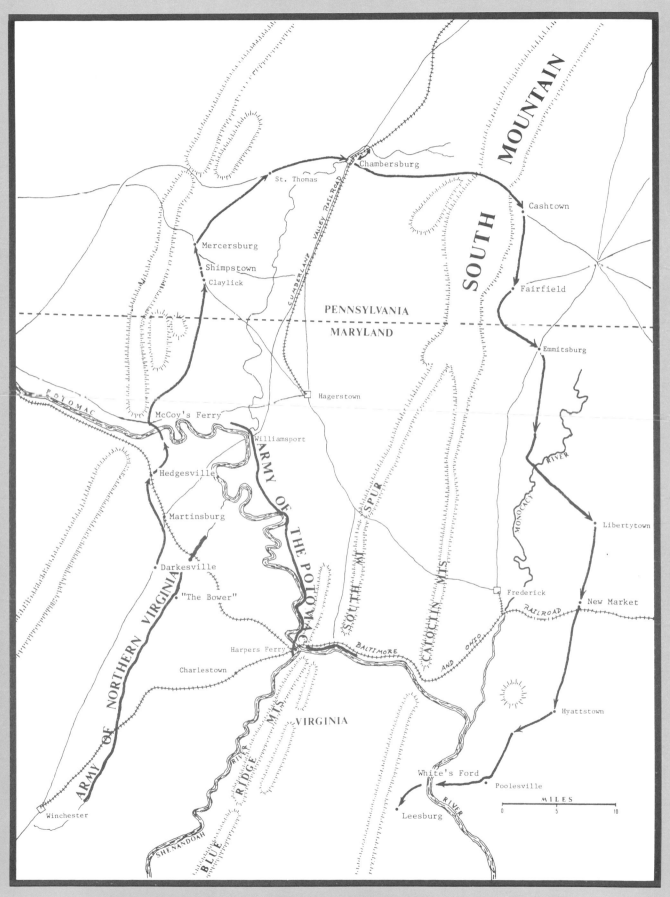

Route of Stuart's Chambersburg Raid

sions" of 600. These divisions would be led by General Wade Hampton, Colonel William "Grumble" Jones, and W. H. F. "Rooney" Lee. Four cannon, under the command of 20-year-old Captain John Pelham, would also be taken. These various commands were to meet at Darkesville, Virginia, at noon on October 9.

Stuart and his staff officers spent the evening of October 8 dancing and singing with the fine young ladies at "The Bower." After excusing himself for about two hours of office duties, Stuart returned at about 1 a.m. for a "farewell concert" before turning in. He and his staff could look forward to an eventful few days.

Meanwhile, life in Chambersburg had about returned to normal following September's threat of invasion. The Pennsylvania militia units that had poured into the area at the height of the panic had all gone home, and their commander, General John F. Reynolds, had returned to the Army of the Potomac. Martial law had been suspended. Store goods and personal possessions that had been hidden or sent away began to return to their proper places. Many local citizens even found the time to journey to the recently contested battlefields of Maryland.

Along the railroad, warehouses were being used by the army to store some of the excess goods that could not be kept in Hagerstown. Rifles and clothing articles of every sort were piled high in these buildings.

Hospitals were established in Franklin Hall, the schoolhouse on King Street, and in the Academy Building, and about 400 of the Union wounded from Antietam were sent to Chambersburg to recover. Members of the Christian Commission arrived. With the help of the Franklin County Ladies' Aid Societies, they provided what basic comforts to these men that they could. Relatives and friends came to Chambersburg from throughout the North, looking for maimed husbands, sons, and neighbors, not all of whom would survive their wounds. "Everyday we hear the sad strains of martial music as the hearses pass carrying the dead from some distant battlefield to be buried at their home. The hearses are draped with flags and the procession is partly military," wrote William Heyser.

Even with such sadness, the people of Chambersburg could again relax, knowing an invasion threat had passed and the Army of the Potomac stood between them and Lee.

On the afternoon of October 9, Jeb Stuart joined his assembled force at Darkesville and began the march to Hedgesville, some 17 miles distant. The men in the ranks knew nothing of their mission. Lee had ordered that to be kept secret. The men's spirits were high, though. They had never been beaten and didn't believe they ever would be. Four and a half months earlier, they had ridden around McClellan's army, north and east of Richmond, losing only one man and causing considerable panic throughout the Union Army. They might not know where Jeb Stuart was taking them, but they could still feel confident in the results.

Reaching Hedgesville, the column continued to the northeast another six or seven miles until it was a short distance from McCoy's Ferry on the Potomac River. Already dark, they would bivouac there for the night. There could be no campfires; they might easily be seen by the Federal signal station on Fairview Mountain just across the river. During the evening, Stuart had an address read to the men that would confirm their belief in themselves.

"HEADQUARTERS CAVALRY DIVISION
October 9, 1862

Soldiers: You are about to engage in an enterprise which, to insure success, imperatively demands at your hands coolness, decision, and bravery; implicit obedience to orders without question or cavil, and the strictest order and sobriety on the march and in bivouac. The destination and extent of this expedition had better be kept to myself than known to you. Suffice it to say, that with the hearty co-operation of officers and men I have not a doubt of it's success- a success which will reflect credit in the highest degree upon your arms. The orders which are herewith published for your government are absolutely necessary, and must be rigidly enforced.

J.E.B. STUART
Major-General, Commanding"

Stuart's additional orders detailed the seizure of property, especially horses, in which "a simple receipt will be given to the effect that the article is seized for the use of the Confederate States, giving place, date, and name of owner, in order to enable the individual to have recourse upon his government for damage. Individual plunder for private use is positively forbidden . . . . So much of this order as authorizes seizures of persons and property will not take effect until the command crosses the Pennsylvania line."

One-third of each division would be detailed to lead captured horses, and "the remaining two-thirds will keep at all times prepared for action."

About 3 a.m., Lieutenant H. R. Phillips of the 10th Virginia Cavalry led a party of 25 dismounted men into the Potomac River at McCoy's Ferry. Using the heavy morning mist as cover, Phillip's men fell upon the unsuspecting Federal pickets on the Maryland shore, and as the first shots rang out, 175 mounted troopers of the 2nd South Carolina Cavalry, under Colonel Matthew C. Butler, charged across the river. The fight was over in a few minutes, and with the small enemy force driven off, the remaining 1,600 Confederate cavalrymen splashed into the bridgehead.

Time meant everything now. With Hampton's troops in the lead, the long column struck north for the National Pike. Once there, Hampton detached a party of men to capture the signal station on Fairview Mountain. The officers there escaped, but a few men and all of the signal equipment were captured.

Stuart learned that his cavalry had just missed three Ohio infantry regiments marching west on the pike. He briefly considered turning his column toward Hagerstown, with its large stockpiles of Federal supplies, but "was satisfied from reliable information, that the notice the enemy had of my approach and the proximity of his forces would enable him to prevent my capturing it." The Confederate cavalry continued north.

Once across the Pennsylvania state line, the gathering of horses began. Hampton's troops led the column while "Grumble" Jones brought up the rear. "Rooney" Lee's 600 men branched out on both sides of the route, taking horses from the fields and farms of unsuspecting and astonished farmers.

Near Claylick, the first hostage was taken. Joseph Winger, the postmaster and owner of a small store, had the added injury of being paid in Confederate money for the goods the raiders took.

Shortly after noon, the column entered Mercersburg. Pickets sealed off the roads so no citizens could alert anyone to the north.

Captain Thomas Whitehead of the 2nd Virginia Cavalry remembered "the inhabitants of Mercersburg seemed terror stricken and paralyzed, and many ludicrous accounts were

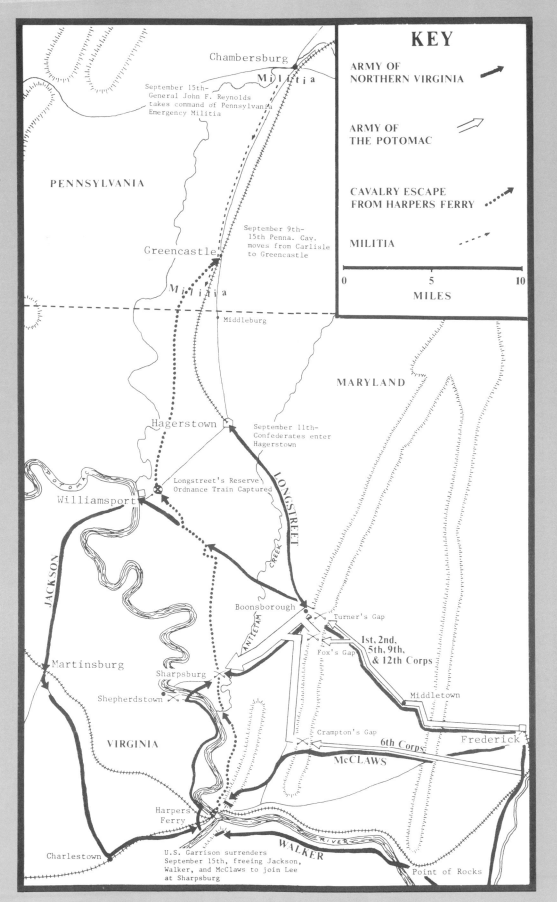

The Maryland Campaign of September, 1862

"Jeb" Stuart's men heading to the Potomac, as depicted in Harper's Weekly

given by the soldiers of their efforts to quiet their fears. I witnessed one: Private J. C. Pettit, of Company E, with a comrade, rode under the window of a house and proposed to buy some food of an old woman and her daughter. With pallid face bathed in tears the old lady said: 'Take anything, only spare the women and children'."

At J. N. Brewer's store, Colonel Butler's men helped themselves to the large stock of boots and shoes, nearly cleaning out the supply. Brewer, too, was paid with the nearly worthless Confederate banknotes.

Eight additional prisoners were taken: G. G. Rupley, Perry Rice, Daniel Schaffer, John McDowell, James Grove, William Raby, O. Louderbaugh, and George Steiger.

After making some inquiries, Captain W. W. Blackford was told he might find a county map at the home of a local family. Greatly in need of a detailed map, with its backroads and landmarks, Blackford proceeded to the house. Once there, however, "Only the females of the family appeared, who flatly refused to let me have the map, or to acknowledge that they had one; so I was obliged to dismount and push by the infuriated ladies, rather rough specimens, however, into the sitting room where I found the map hanging on the wall. Angry women do not show to advantage, and the language and looks of these were fearful, as I cooly cut the map out of it's rollers and put it in my haversack."

About 2:30, the long gray column started north for St. Thomas. Stuart and Hampton both hoped to get to Chambersburg before dark, and the raiders moved quickly. Horses were still being rounded up and brought in, and there were still 14 miles to cover.

Scouts were far in advance. At the hotel of Mr. Bratton, four miles west of Chambersburg, the proprietor entered into conversation with several blue-coated troopers, who had ridden up. When asked who he supported, the Union or Confederacy, Bratton generously offered to buy the boys a round of drinks if they would "keep old Jackson away."

"Are you afraid of old Jackson?" asked one.

Bratton replied that he wasn't, but the women were. After taking him up on the drink offer, the soldiers told Bratton the truth. They were Rebels; underneath the blue overcoats, they were wearing Confederate gray.

Wade Hampton . . . This South Carolinian led the advance of Stuart's column, accepting the surrender of Chambersburg

John F. Reynolds . . . He was detached from the Army of the Potomac to lead untrained troops at Chambersburg.

The church bells were ringing at St. Thomas as the column of raiders approached. A few scattered shots were exchanged with about 25 local militiamen, but no casualties occurred. David A. Fohl saw what looked like hordes of rebels as he looked west from St. Thomas. Turning his horse east, he was joined by Daniel Stitzel, and the two rode hard and fast for Chambersburg.

About 90 minutes after Jacob Hoke's first encounter with a Confederate, Samuel Etters came into the store and announced, "Well, the rebels are coming now for certain." This was met by disbelief from Anthony Haller, one of Hoke's employees. "Well, if you don't believe it, go over to Judge Kimmel's office and see for yourselves," retorted Etters. "There's two men from St. Thomas who saw the rebels, and were chased by them half ways to town."

Hoke, in spite of what he already had seen, did not want to believe the story. Slipping out the back door, he made his way to Kimmel's office, where Fohl and Stitzel confirmed it. Hoke hurried back and closed the store.

The ringing of the court house bell sounded the call to arms for the local home guard under the command of Captain John Jeffries. Muskets and ammunition were issued from one of the warehouses, and a column of 50 to 75 men started west on Market Street.

About the same time, a mile to the west, Wade Hampton sat on the heights overlooking the town. He had hoped to be in Chambersburg while it was still light. Now darkness had fallen, and he could see nothing but the lights of the town beneath him. Not knowing whether or not Chambersburg was defended, Hampton placed Captain Pelham's four cannon in position to bombard the town. He then detailed Lieutenant T. C. Lee of the 2nd South Carolina Cavalry, with an escort of 25 men, to go in and demand an immediate surrender, or Pelham's guns would bombard the town in 30 minutes.

Riding in the lead, with a large white hankerchief tied to a stick, Lee met the home guard near the bridge. "Halt. Who are you, and by what authority do you come here?" called Captain Jeffries.

"By the authority of the Confederate Army and General Hampton. He wants to see the authorities of the town," replied Lee.

After a few moments of discussion, Jeffries escorted the surrender party to Judge Kimmel's office. Realizing now that the odds were against them in a stand-up fight, the militia dispersed and returned to their homes. George Snyder lowered the United States flag on the Diamond; then he cut the rope so the Confederates could not raise their own flag.

Ushered into Judge Kimmel's office, Lieutenant Lee found an audience of Kimmel, Colonel Alexander McClure, Mr. T. B. Kennedy, and one or two others. He presented the surrender demand and told of the force that lay just to the west. Skeptical, or perhaps wishing to surrender the town to someone of higher rank, Kimmel accepted an offer from Lee to ride out and meet with Hampton.

Near the brow of the hill, the party met both Generals Hampton and Stuart (Stuart's name had apparently not been brought up before). "Well, General, what is it you want?" asked Kimmel.

Hampton did the dealing. "The unconditional surrender of the place," he replied.

After assurances for the safety of women and children and the protection of private property, Colonel McClure formalized the surrender, telling Hampton, "We are without protection, and of course can offer no resistance, and your terms must be accepted."

It was now about 8 p.m., and with the surrender concluded, the party started back into town, followed by the 1,800 man Confederate force. When the column came to the Diamond, they were dispersed to set about the various chores they had to accomplish. The telegraph lines were cut, and sentries were posted on all the roads leading into the town. "Grumble" Jones led his men north to destroy the railroad bridge, and Colonel Butler was sent to collect the money from the Bank of Chambersburg. When the vault was opened, however, only some small change was discovered on the shelf. The cashier had hidden the rest, when the first alarm had been rung.

The 280 Union wounded, still in the hospitals, were discovered and paroled.

Stuart, who had bequeathed the grand title of "Military Governor" upon Hampton, made his own headquarters at the Franklin Hotel. His mood was jovial in spite of the hard day's ride. While there, he was approached by a former Union officer, who had resigned his commission. Finding the man's papers in order, Stuart cheerfully told him that their relationship would have been quite different if they had not been in order. The former soldier had one request to make of Stuart - the return of his horse.

"We are not horse thieves, nevertheless we do want horses, and shall have to retain yours," he was told.

Soon Jones' men returned, disgruntled. They had discovered what Robert E. Lee's map could not have shown: the Cumberland Valley Railroad bridge was made of iron. Jones did not have the tools or explosives to destroy it.

Although a few bakery shelves were emptied of their contents, very little trespass of private property occurred. Some of the troopers took it upon themselves to seek handouts. Corporal Tip Tinsley of the 2nd Virginia, after knocking on a cottage door, was greeted by an old man carrying a lantern. After asking for bread, Tinsley waited at the door while the elderly

*The scenes above depict Chambersburg at the time of Stuart's raid:
Top, general view of Chambersburg (note county jail in the center
and courthouse at left); center, left, rebels exchanging rags for U.S.
Army overcoats; center, right, the burning of the engine house and
machine shops; below, Confederates raiding Mead's Warehouse for
U.S. Army material.*

The Rebel Chivalry

As the fancy of "My Maryland" painted them.   *As "My Maryland" found them.*

A newspaper cartoon shows two sides of Confederate horsemen.

gentleman gathered a baking sheet of rolls. When he returned, the old fellow asked Tinsley, "Who is your general - McClellan or Burnside?"

"Stonewall Jackson," replied Tinsley.

"Good God," the old man stammered, dropping the lantern and slamming the door. But Corporal Tinsley had gotten his bread.

Alexander McClure had any number of rebel guests spend the night at his farm house, north of town. They discussed politics, among other things, and drank up McClure's supply of coffee and tea. McClure was also out 18 horses.

Samuel Greenawalt was one of the few fortunate enough to escape the loss of his horses. In his hack, he had driven six members of the Chambersburg band to Marion for a political rally. The rain had made the meeting a washout, and none of the speakers had shown up. As they returned toward Chambersburg after dark, they met Frederick Walk, who told them that the town was occupied and horses were being taken. The band members told Greenawalt that they would walk into town and he should hide his valuable animals, but Greenawalt wouldn't hear of it and forged ahead.

A mile from Chambersburg, the hack was stopped by a Rebel picket. He soon let them pass, but shortly they were stopped again. Here they were met by Wade Hampton, who, after listening to their story, accompanied them into town. When they reached the Diamond, the men's names were taken, and they were paroled but told to be at General Stuart's headquarters at 6 a.m. Greenawalt was also told he would now have to give up his horses, but he talked Rebel officers into allowing him to give the animals one last good meal.

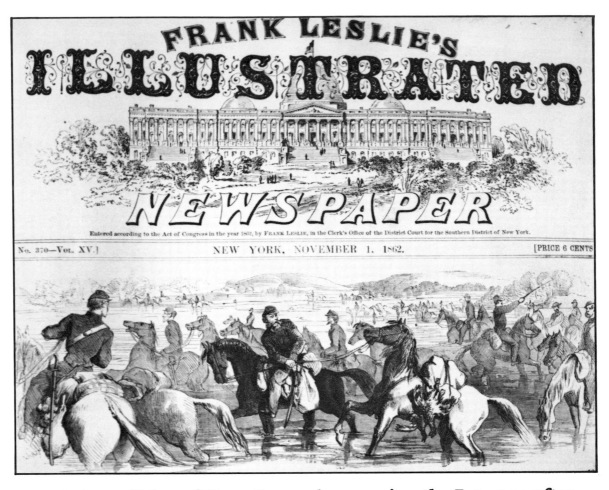

Artist's rendition of Stuart's cavalry crossing the Potomac after the Chambersburg raid.

The officers relented, but Greenawalt was to turn them in first thing in the morning. Once Greenawalt got his horses home, he unharnessed them and led them out German Street east of town and down a lane which remained unpicketed. Keeping the horses hidden until the raiders left, Greenawalt prevented them from becoming army property of the Confederate States. Greenawalt's friends in the band did not show up at General Stuart's headquarters either.

At 4 a.m. assembly was sounded, and the outlying pickets and bivouacs began to make their way back into Chambersburg. The railroad warehouses were looted, and large quantities of hats, boots, overcoats, and weapons were carried off by the rebels. Some wore as many as three hats, and they draped extra overcoats across their saddles.

In the Wunderlich and Nead Warehouse, the raiders found a bonus — the ammunition from Confederate General James Longstreet's reserve ordnance wagon train, captured nearly a month before, southwest of Hagerstown. Now, this ammunition would only help serve the coming conflagration.

Alexander McClure returned to Chambersburg at 7 a.m. He later recalled that "General Stuart sat on his horse in the center of the town, surrounded by his staff, and his command was coming in from the country in large squads, leading their old horses and riding the new ones they had found in the stables hereabouts." McClure also noted that, "His demeanor to our people was that of a humane soldier. In several instances his men commenced to take private property from stores, but they were arrested by General Stuart's provost guard. In a single instance only, that I heard of, did they enter a store by intimidating the proprietor."

Before leaving Chambersburg, all the hostages except Perry Rice, Joseph Winger, Daniel Schaffer, and William Connor were released. Rice would die in Richmond's notorious Libby Prison in January 1863. The others were afterwards exchanged.

Stuart led his men out of town almost exactly 12 hours after they arrived. They left not the way they had come but to the east. Stuart correctly suspected that his invasion route was by now sealed off by Union forces. This, he felt, left him no option but to continue to the east and then south to recross the Potomac River in the vicinity of Leesburg, Virginia. There the Confederates might use one of five fords along an eleven mile stretch of the river. The Union opposition at these fords would probably be light, and they would not be expecting Stuart at all.

The same Colonel Butler who had led the advance, now commanded the rear guard. Butler detailed Captain W. H. H. Cowles of the 1st North Carolina Cavalry to burn the railroad depot, the warehouses, machine shops, and several trains of cars, sitting on sidings. After informing residents in the immediate area, Cowles' men went to work. By 9 a.m., a great pillar of smoke rose above Chambersburg, and the last of Stuart's men were galloping eastward to catch up with their leader. Town residents attempted to put out the fires, but exploding shells kept them at a distance. This racket, however, didn't bother the ladies at the hospitals, for they had the usual noon dinner ready for their wards.

It didn't seem possible for Stuart's cavalry to get away. Pennsylvania Governor, Andrew Curtin, had telegraphed Secretary of War Edwin M. Stanton throughout the evening of October 10, informing him of events as they unfolded. General John Wool, commanding the Middle Department, started three regiments of infantry by train from Baltimore to Harrisburg. A fourth was to follow the next day. General George Crook's three Ohio regiments, which Stuart had so narrowly missed on the National Pike early on the 10th, were ordered to stay put in Hancock and be ready to intercept the raiders if they returned in that direction. General Ambrose Burnside was directed to send two brigades by rail from Weverton, Maryland, to Monocacy Junction, to protect Frederick from the east.

General Alfred Pleasonton, commanding the Cavalry Division of the Army of the Potomac, had the most difficult ride. Starting north from Knoxville, Maryland, at 4 a.m. on the 11th, Pleasonton arrived at Hagerstown about noon, where he received word that Stuart was moving back toward Mercersburg. After marching four miles west, Pleasonton learned he had been misinformed, and he began a countermarch to Mechanicstown (now Thurmont), 23 miles east. He would not arrive until 8 p.m.

At 12:30 p.m. on Oct. 11, General-in-Chief Henry Wager Halleck, in Washington D.C., received word from a confident George McClellan: "I have given every order necessary to insure the capture or destruction of these (Stuart's) forces, and I hope we may be able to teach them a lesson they will not soon forget."

As the Confederates rode east over South Mountain, the gathering of horses continued. At Cashtown, Stuart gave his men and mounts a half hour's rest before turning south to Fairfield and on toward Emmitsburg, Maryland. The collection of horses ceased when the raiders crossed the state line back into Maryland. Nearly 1,200 head had been taken, and Stuart's column stretched for almost five miles.

It was dusk when the Confederates entered Emmitsburg, and Stuart discovered he had narrowly missed 150 Union cavalrymen, heading northeast toward Gettysburg. A few miles further on, a messenger was intercepted, and Stuart learned that Frederick, Maryland, was heavily garrisoned. Also, Alfred Pleasonton's Federals were closing in from the west. Shifting the column eastward to avoid this new threat, Stuart chose a route that would take him south through Woodsborough, Liberty, New Market, Monrovia, and Hyattstown.

It was a hard, tiresome, moonlit night. The raiders had gotten very little sleep in the preceding 48 hours, and now many dozed in the saddle. At around dawn, the column reached Hyattstown and pushed on toward Barnesville. Stuart learned that Union Brigadier General George Stoneman had about 4,000 men, guarding Poolesville and the river fords.

Taking an old, out-of-use road to bypass the Federals at Poolsville, Stuart avoided a direct confrontation. But within a short distance of White's Ford, the Confederates came upon the advance of Alfred Pleasonton's cavalrymen, headed for Poolesville. The Confederates were still wearing their Federal blue greatcoats, and Pleasonton's troopers held their fire until it was too late. When almost on top of them, Stuart's men drew their sabres and charged, scattering the shocked Federals, who fired a few wild shots. Young Pelham brought up two of his guns, and with some of "Rooney" Lee's troopers, acting as skirmishers, held the Union troops at bay.

White's Ford was unguarded, and the 1,800 raiders and their nearly 1,200 extra horses plunged into the Potomac toward Virginia. Pelham's remaining two guns went into position on the Virginia side of the river to provide a covering fire for the withdrawing skirmishers and artillery, and soon Stuart's entire command was back in the Confederacy. Only two men had been slightly wounded.

Although the primary purpose of the raid had not been accomplished, the Confederacy could still take heart in the results. Some $250,000 worth of Federal and Cumberland Valley Railroad property had been destroyed, including 5,000 muskets. Thirty hostages and prisoners were brought back, and more than 280 more had been paroled in Chambersburg.

Twelve hundred horses were seized. Stuart himself reported that, "The results of this expedition, in a moral and political point of view, can hardly be estimated, and the consternation among property holders in Pennsylvania beggars description."

The Federal Government and the Army of the Potomac were left red-faced and angry. Secretary of the Navy Gideon Welles wrote in his diary ".... It is not a pleasant fact to know that we are clothing, mounting, and subsisting not only our troops but the Rebels also." Lieutenant Elisha H. Rhodes of the 2nd Rhode Island Infantry Regiment felt, "... very much ashamed that the Rebels were allowed to make their late raid into Pennsylvania. If this army cannot protect the loyal states we had better sell out and go home. I ought not to complain, but I am mortified to think that we did not catch some of the Rebel raiders." Samuel Cormany thought differently, though. The Chambersburg native and recent enlistee of the 16th Pennsylvania Cavalry thought that the destruction proved ".... strong incentive to boys with the stuff in them to enlist and help clean out the Rebel Hoards."

In Chambersburg, a kind of "raider paranoia" settled upon the town. Two weeks after Stuart's visit, reports were brought into the area that Confederate cavalry was again advancing from the west. Farmers hid their horses. Some unarmed soldiers, camping on the grounds, struck their tents and left town.

Worried citizens gathered in the Diamond, anxiously awaiting confirmation of this horrible turn of events. Within a few hours the truth was learned. A group of children near

Loudon had seen a party of Federal cavalry who were attempting to purchase what horses were left for the army. Youthful imaginations had turned these few troopers into a second raiding party.

Maryland Campaign

Stuart's Chambersburg Raid was really the final chapter of a series of events which began when Robert E. Lee's Army of Northern Virginia crossed the Potomac near Frederick, Maryland, on September 4, 1862. Lee fully planned to march North through the Cumberland Valley and take Harrisburg. However, he first had to eliminate the threat posed by the 12,000 Federal troops at Harpers Ferry. To do this he sent part of his army under General "Stonewall" Jackson to besiege the garrison which resulted in its surrender on September 15, 1862. However, the Union cavalry was able to escape. Near Williamsport, Maryland, it captured a Confederate wagon train loaded with ammunition, then headed north to Greencastle and eventually to Chambersburg.

At Chambersburg, the horsemen left their Confederate prisoners and train. The ammunition from the train was sorely missed by the Confederates at Antietam. Stuart would destroy the ammunition during his raid.

With Jackson in Harpers Ferry, Longstreet moved to Hagerstown, readying a strike into Pennsylvania. As the citizens of Chambersburg braced for an invasion, Union troops following the Rebels through Frederick would discover a copy of Lee's orders carelessly left at a campsite and Lee would then alter his plans to head north. He moved his forces to Sharpsburg, Maryland, thus setting up the great Battle of Antietam on September 17, 1862.

Just prior to that, on September 15, General John F. Reynolds came to Chambersburg to take charge of the "emergency" militia gathered there. Reynolds, a native of Lancaster, was detached from the Army of the Potomac. Eventually some 10,000 men would concentrate in and around Chambersburg. These citizen soldiers were ill-equipped, clothed and disciplined. When Reynolds ordered them to advance to Hagerstown after the Battle of Antietam, they balked, claiming they had signed on to defend Pennsylvania not Maryland. Not since the summer of 1861 had Chambersburg hosted such large troop concentrations.

The Battle of Antietam was the bloodiest single day battle in American history. Casualties topped 23,000. Although the fighting was 37 miles south of Chambersburg, many wounded soldiers were taken to Chambersburg on the Cumberland Valley Railroad. A number of buildings were converted to hospitals. Chambersburg merchant Jacob Hoke recalled the events in his book, Reminiscences of War.

"Immediately after the battle of Antietam many of the wounded who could bear transportation, were taken to the hospitals at Washington, Baltimore, Frederick, Hagerstown and this place. About four hundred were brought here, and quartered in Franklin Hall, the large school house adjoining the jail, and the Academy. A number of persons connected with the Christian Commission came to this place to look after the wounded. The ladies of the town, through their Aid Society, rendered invaluable services in distributing towels, handkerchiefs and delicacies. In this benevolent work they were aided by ladies from the country and adjoining towns. Fayetteville had a Ladies Aid Society which greatly assisted in caring for these wounded men, sending many delicacies. The Steward of the School House Hospital on King Street, Mr. George Bayne, made weekly acknowledgements, through the town papers, of articles of food, &c. Among the names of the donors thus acknowledged are Mrs.

Confederate dead along the Hagerstown Road following the Battle of Antietam. Hundreds of wounded soldiers were brought to Chambersburg.

Schofield, Mrs. Ebert, Mrs. Thompson, Mrs. Newman, Mrs. Nead, Mrs. Brewer, Mrs. Jordan, Mrs. Reeves, Mrs. Dr. Fisher, Mrs. Chambers, Mrs. Radebaugh, Mrs. Hutton, Mrs. Britton, Mrs. Hoke, Mrs. Trostle, Mrs. Sprecher, Mrs. Linn, Mrs. Long, Mrs. E.D. Reed, Mrs. Charles Eyster, Mrs. Wood, Mrs. Ritner, Lizzie Lester, Mrs. Banker, Mrs. Fry, Mrs. Lindsay, Mrs. W. Chambers, Mrs. Benj. Chambers, Miss Sarah Reynolds, Miss Sally Ann Chambers, Miss Susan B. Chambers, Mrs. Funk, Mrs. Embrick, Mrs. Miller, Mrs. Grier, Mrs. Auld, Miss Lizzie Flack, Mrs. Hull, Mrs. Grieve, Mrs. Montgomery, Mrs. Stumbaugh, Mrs. Wunderlich, Mrs. Beatty, Mrs. Eckhart, Mrs. Stine, Mrs. Gellespie, Mrs. Nill, Mrs. McGrath, Mrs. Dechart, Mrs. Huber, Mrs. Spangler, Mrs. Sewell, Mrs. Fahnestock and Mrs. Perry. The foregoing names I have copied from the Stewart's acknowledgements in the *Valley Spirit.* If any have been omitted, the fault is not mine. This, it will be recollected, is a list of donors to that one hospital alone. The other two fared equally as well. Affecting scenes were frequently seen when persons would visit these hospitals in search of friends and relatives. Fathers from a distance would find a son with arm or limb amputated, or otherwise wounded. Devoted wives would find their husbands maimed and suffering. A woman from Philadelphia came here to see after her husband. He was shot through the lung, and she found him in Franklin Hall Hospital. Situated next to the Hall we gave her a home. When her husband was able to be moved he was carried into our house, where his devoted wife cared for him. In a few weeks he was able to travel and his wife took him home. Some time after this my wife and I, while walking in Philadelphia, were somewhat surprised and confused by a woman rushing up and embracing and kissing us. She was that soldier's wife. We visited their home and saw her husband. He was able to work at his trade -- book binding, but had a cough. His physician said he thought his lung was affected, and he was going into consumption. We never heard of him afterwards. The scenes of suffering which occurred in these hospitals, and the tears which were shed over the wounded, sick, dying and dead soldiers, can never be told. They are parts of the price paid for the perpetuity of government. It was a fearful price, but the government is worth all the cost.

A gentleman came into our store shortly after the bringing of these wounded here. He was on his way to the battlefield. He requested me to go to each of the hospitals here and take down the names of all the Massachusetts soldiers, with the nature of their wounds, and send the list to the *Boston Journal*. Soon after its publication papers, letters, &c., came to me for some of these soldiers. About eight years after the war I was introduced to the President of the Young Men's Christian Association in Dayton, Ohio. He said he had been to Chambersburg once, but under the circumstances that he knew but little of the place. He said he was a member of a Massachusetts regiment, and he had been wounded at the Battle of Antietam and brought here. I referred to the circumstances of my visit, when he said he recollected it. Our acquaintance formed under such peculiar circumstances, was kept up for many years. He was afterwards transferred to Baltimore to take charge of the Association there. About two years ago failing health compelled him to resign his position, after which he went back to Massachusetts. Many occurrences of an interesting and touching character might be related, where scenes of suffering and death, amid the agonies and tears and prayers of newly arrived friends, took place in families throughout the town where wounded soldiers were taken and cared for. I have been present on such occasions, and have knelt around dying beds where departing heros were ebbing away their life while fathers, mothers and brothers wept and sobbed, and then, wrapped in the folds of the flag they loved so well, and for which they gave their lives, their lifeless bodies were borne back to desolated homes. Space however forbids details."

(William Heyser, a prominent Chambersburg citizen and businessman, kept a diary. Here are several days' excerpts from that diary recorded in the period of Stuart's 1862 occupation.)

SEPTEMBER 29, 1862

Clear and dry. Death of Matthew Gillan. One of the first volunteers to meet the call of arms, but remained a short time. Returned in worse shape, and declined thereafter. He was a kind, goodnatured man, and will be missed by his family.

Death of Jacob Oyster, a pillar of the Methodist Church, and a staunch citizen, much respected. One of our last citizens of the older generation.

OCTOBER 1

John Mull and I visited one of the hospitals of wounded soldiers in the Academy Building. About 100 of them, mostly wounded in their lower parts, but some with their arms and legs off. They are well taken care of and plenty of supplies for their wants.

OCTOBER 3

Rain, which we need badly. We see untold thousands of dollars drained from our Treasury by unscrupulous men using the war to further their personal affairs. We have several cases in our town that did not get their wealth honestly, but robbed by men in official stations.

OCTOBER 4

Out town has greatly changed by the events of the war -- business is so good, our town is taking on a city appearance of activity. We hear the Rebels plan a retreat from Staunton. McClellan at present has control of Winchester. Lincoln's Emancipation Proclamation denounced in Richmond. Some here do not think wisely of it as many abolitionists are so wild they would change our Constitution. Some of the wounded here

President Lincoln with Major Gen. George B. McClellan and his staff near Sharpsburg, Md., October, 1862. Near this scene, Lincoln reviewed the 5th Corps of which Franklin County's 126th Regiment belonged.

are Masons. One who died at the home of Burnet, I read the Masonic service for his burial. He and several others then taken to the cars where they will b transported home for interment. There was quite a number already received, filling up a car. Quite a rush of females to view the deceased, there being a glass opening in the box.

The crowd at the depot very large, from there to the hospital, near the jail which I visited to see some acquaintances, and perhaps offer a little help some way. To view this brings the war awfully near and deep sympathy for these poor suffering men.

To my farm, find it too dry to plant anything. It will be a loss this year, for a good crop if there is no immediate rain. The engines and cars are very busy taking supplies to McClelland (sic) on the Potomac. They are running night and day.

OCTOBER 7

Clear and pleasant. Every day we hear the sad strains of marshal music and the hearses pass carrying dead from the distant battlefield to be buried at their home. The hearses are draped with flags and the procession partly military. Every day the cars bring from 20 to 30 dead thru our town.

OCTOBER 8

Pleasant. Left to visit my mountain land. Saw many turkeys and partridges, but didn't have my gun.

OCTOBER 10

Rain today. A great saving for the farmers who were facing a great drought. Business is flourishing in town. The Rebels are in Mercersburg, and on the way to Chambersburg from St. Thomas. This evening they entered our town, demanding its surrender. Some 1500-2000 cavalry, with some artillery. They immediately took possession of the bank and telegraph office. Also requisitioned provisions, clothing, etc., as to their needs. It has all happened so quickly, we all felt safe knowing the Union Army was in Williamsport, MD., The Confederate troops all look well fed and clothed, and so far, conducted themselves orderly. They will be busy stripping our stores and gathering up horses. I have sent my three off with Proctor, I hope they got away safely. I did not go to bed until one o'clock, watching what may happen after all retire. So far, all quiet. Secreted some of my most valuable papers and went to bed, slept soundly until morning.

OCTOBER 11

Clear and pleasant. Rose early and to the square. Saw Major Gen. Stewart and Gen. Hampden (sic) in conference. The stores were all closed. Broke open Isaac Hutton's shoe store helped themselves freely. Then to the depot and confiscated a large shipment of arms and clothes. Afterwards, set fire to all the buildings and left town by the Baltimore Pike. They had fired the building of Wandelick and Nead which was used as a storehouse for government ammunition. The succeeding explosions of shells and powder was tremendous. The loss must be very great. All the machinery and present locomotives destroyed at the shops. This was all the fault of A.H. Lule, Supt. at the railroad shops. He should have sent the war supplies back to Carlisle, instead of keeping them here, being warned as early as three o'clock the past afternoon. However, this saved our stores from being pillaged as they got enough at the depot. Everybody out on the streets seeking news.

About mid-day, a large scouting party of our troops came thru producing a great sensation. We hear of another group at Waynesboro, marching towards Gettysburg hoping to head them off. All in all the invasion is a very orderly one. The troops were well disciplined and polite. Not a single house or person injured. They were more orderly than troops of ours that have passed this way. Outside of their plundering of Isaac Hutton's shoe store, nothing else occurred to criticize them. Many people from the country came into town in search of news and carried home relics of Rebel Invasion, as shells, balls, saberparts, parts of musquets, etc. Nearly every man and boy had some souvenir.

OCTOBER 12

Clear and pleasant, the Sabbath. All is calm, who would suspect that so much excitement had prevailed yesterday. However, there is much apprehension they will return. Some 2,000 troops from Maryland came this morning and encamped outside of town on the Baltimore Pike. I knew not of their coming and arrival until this afternoon. At three, attending a religious serivce at the hall among the wounded soldiers. Rev. Bausman conducted the services.

OCTOBER 13

Cloudy, a little rain. The encamped Rebels have moved on to Fayetteville, and across the mountain to Cashtown. There they went South thru Emmittsburg and Monrovia to the mouth of the Monocacy. Thus completely avoiding the searching Federal forces, and disappeared into Virginia. Their mission accomplished.

OCTOBER 14

Pleasant. Out to my farm to ascertain the damage done by the soldiers. Much fencing gone for fuel, and what corn they didn't use, tried to burn. Many farmers without horses and at a loss to do any work. We find no buildings burned or occupants harmed.

OCTOBER 15

Much apprehension about the Rebels returning as they have camped along the

Potomac. We can hear cannoning (sic) from the vicinity of Hancock, perhaps some skir-mishes.

The Rebels have found little at our bank of value, but did not complain. They were looking mainly for horses. I had previously sent mine to my man Proctor in Waynesboro, some 16 miles distance, for safekeeping. Many others not as fortunate as they delayed. They did take eight young colored men and boys along with them, in spite of their parents pleading. I fear they will never see them again, unless they escape.

OCTOBER 24

Our church has decided on the final adoption of the much discussed Liturgy as a book to be used in our church and family worship. I am glad this had been decided, we were much divided.

OCTOBER 25

Pleasant. Business at the bank, rode to my farm to inspect the new seeding. Home early in the evening to do some writing. Agreeable to the solicitation of Doctor Wilson, an artist, I sat for my portrait. He noticed some of my landscape work, which he commended. I suppose my work would improve with practice, but it is now too late in life to hope for much proficiency.

Some cavalry here this evening, to secure horses for Gen. McCelland's (sic) command. They hope to find two hundred by tomorrow morning.

I fear Lincoln is a tool in the hands of the Abolitionists. We need a man of Jackson's iron will in our present emergency to hold our National Government together.

OCTOBER 27

Cloudy. Our town filling up with drafted men to be sent to camp for training. Visited a wounded Mason (Captain Miller Moddy from Ohio) who lost one of his legs at Antietam. He is very low in spirits and much emaciated, his wife and son are visiting him. Spent some time with Wilson, the artist.

OCTOBER 28

Clear and pleasant. We had a sale of the Rebels worn-out horses, left here by Stewart's cavalry. Spent some time with Mr. Wilson, the artist.

OCTOBER 29

Beautiful weather. Out to my farm for inspection of the seeding. Nearly opposite there is an encampment of the drafted militia under Col. Geo. Wiestling, who is to get them in military trim. They are a raw set of men. It is hoped to get at least 600,000 men for another army together to crush the rebellion. Meanwhile our national debt is staggering, some 640,000,000 dollars. The expenditure of a million and a quarter a day to keep this war machine going.

CHAPTER 5

Prelude to Gettysburg

I n some ways, the invasion of Pennsylvania by the Army of Northern Virginia in late June and July of 1863 still had the innocence and romanticism which earmarked the beginning of the war. There was the grand gesture of the dashing general, General George Pickett, doffing his hat to a Northern belle on a street in Greencastle. There was the Confederate band playing "Bonnie Blue Flag" as the leading columns of the invading Rebel army marched up South Main Street in Chambersburg. There was the incident when a young farm girl stood at a water pump and offered a drink to a weary Robert E. Lee as he journeyed northward.

During these two weeks before the Battle of Gettysburg, the grim realities of war came to Franklin County. Merchants were cleaned out by an invading army. Farmers were "relieved" of their harvests and livestock. Chambersburg, even before the burning of its town a year later, would never be the same.

On June 15, 1863, hoofbeats were heard by residents coming up South Main Street. At approximately 11 p.m. that night, two young Rebel officers rode into the square and began shouting for the mayor.

Their shadows were cast ominously against the buildings around the square by the gaslights, which had illuminated the square for a few years. Men from the borough jumped the officers and placed them in jail. Within minutes, more of the Confederate forces, under the lead of General Albert G. Jenkins, moved through the

General Robert E. Lee arrived in Chambersburg on June 26, 1863 and made his headquarters east of town in Messersmith's Woods. His fateful decision on June 28, to move his Army east of the mountains, led to the Battle of Gettysburg.

Jenkins' brigade was assigned the task of scouting and gathering horses for the Army of Northern Virginia.

Brigadier General Albert G. Jenkins . . . he led the first Confederate contingent of Lee's invasion into Chambersburg on June 15. The following summer he was mortally wounded at the Battle of Cloyd's Mountain, Virginia. His successor, Brigadier General John McCausland, led his command back to Chambersburg on July 30, 1864 and burned the town.

square. Jenkins' brigade of Virginia cavalry, approximately 1,500 strong, was leading the advance of Robert E. Lee's invasion of Pennsylvania. Since Lee had sent his main cavalry force, under Jeb Stuart, on a raid 40 miles to the east, Jenkins' Brigade was assigned the task of scouting and gathering horses for the Army of Northern Virginia. Jenkins, who was at the front of his troops, moved northward to the residence of Colonel Alexander McClure, a noted politician and lawyer. McClure had already fled the area, fearing capture. Jenkins and his officers had a late night meal and spent the night.

When dawn broke on June 16, the first full day of the occupation of Chambersburg by Southern troops was underway. Jenkins decided to establish his headquarters in town. Before having his aides saddle his horse, he sent out troops about four miles north of town toward Harrisburg to take possession of Shirk's or Gelsinger's Hill.

He then sent a detachment of men armed with cans of black powder (called "torpedoes") to destroy the Scotland Railroad Bridge. Jenkins and his staff then moved to the Montgomery House just north of the square to set up headquarters. He immediately summoned the burgess and town council. When they arrived, Jenkins demanded that the two horses, pistols and equipment captured from his troops last night be returned.

The town fathers quickly produced the pistols needed as well as $900 in Confederate money, which was being circulated widely all morning by Confederate troops.

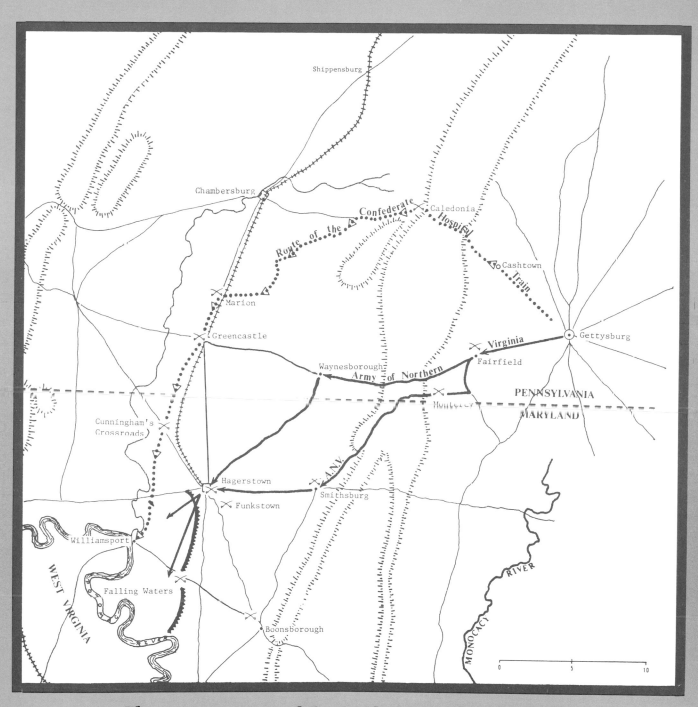

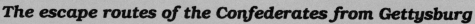

The escape routes of the Confederates from Gettysburg

These two sketches appeared in Frank Leslie's Illustrated Newspaper on July 11, 1863 by an artist named Mr. Law. The drawings show (top) Chambersburg (looking east) as a typical and tranquil town in central Pennsylvania and (bottom) Jenkins' cavalry galloping through the diamond during the early stages of the invasion of 1863. The buildings identifiable in the bottom picture are, left to right, Jacob Hoke's store, Franklin Hall, the courthouse, and the Crawford Building.

Jenkins' troops began crisscrossing the county throughout the day, confiscating what goods they could as well as searching homes for runaway slaves and Negroes. Many of the hunted blacks sought concealment in the high wheatfields in the area, but mounted Confederates began flushing out several.

During midafternoon, one Confederate party reached the Caledonia Iron Works, (where Caledonia State Park is today). The Confederates demanded all the horses and mules owned by the Honorable Thaddeus Stevens. In return, the Confederates said they would not burn the works. Stevens was at the works at the time and had to be spirited away to Shippensburg to avoid capture. He was belligerent and unwilling to leave.

On June 17, Jenkins appeared from the Montgomery House and issued a decree that all stores in Chambersburg be opened for two hours so that Jenkins' men could "purchase" articles. Merchants were well aware of what this order meant. Jenkins, in his attempt to be a humanitarian enemy invader, ordered his men to pay for what they wanted. Most often this meant worthless Confederate money.

Meanwhile, the pickets at Shirk's Hill noticed a large formation moving down the Harrisburg Pike toward them. It had been rumored that Federal troops were gathered at Harrisburg so the Confederates mounted up and returned to Chambersburg to spread the alarm of an apparent Union advance.

Jenkins issued orders as bugles blared and men hurried to their mounts. Part of the brigade rode north of the town, dismounted and formed a defensive line to meet the attack. In the meantime, several buildings in Chambersburg were made ready as temporary hospitals to treat the wounded from the forthcoming battle.

At noon, the Federals still had not attacked. Thinking cautiously, Jenkins withdrew to Greencastle where he could be near General Richard S. Ewell's Second Corps in Maryland. Jenkins' hasty retreat was unwarranted for the Union troops turned out to be a large gathering of area residents who were coming to Chambersburg to see the Rebels.

As war fever increased, Pennsylvania began to defend itself. On June 10 the War Department established a military jurisdiction to protect Pennsylvania — the Department of the Susquehanna. Commanded by General Darius Couch, who had asked to be relieved of his Army of the Potomac command under General Joe Hooker, the department recruited men for full-time and temporary duty.

Couch understood that he had to recruit these men, for the Army of the Potomac was in no hurry to rush to Pennsylvania. It had its orders to stay between Lee's army and

> **Jenkins' hasty retreat was unwarranted for the Union troops turned out to be a large gathering of area residents.**

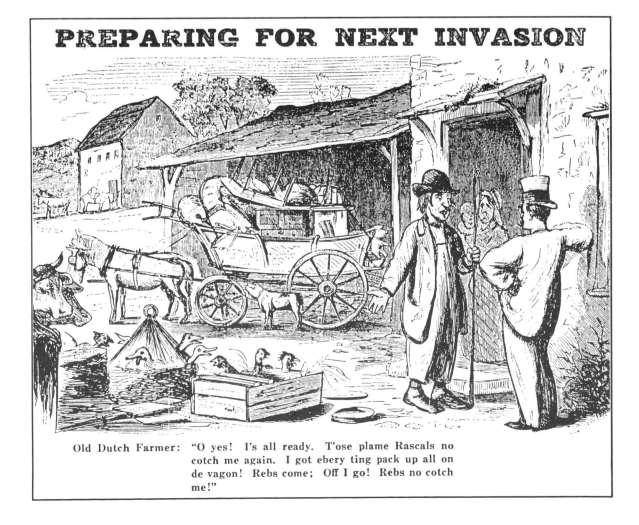

PREPARING FOR NEXT INVASION

Old Dutch Farmer: "O yes! I's all ready. T'ose plame Rascals no cotch me again. I got ebery ting pack up all on de vagon! Rebs come; Off I go! Rebs no cotch me!"

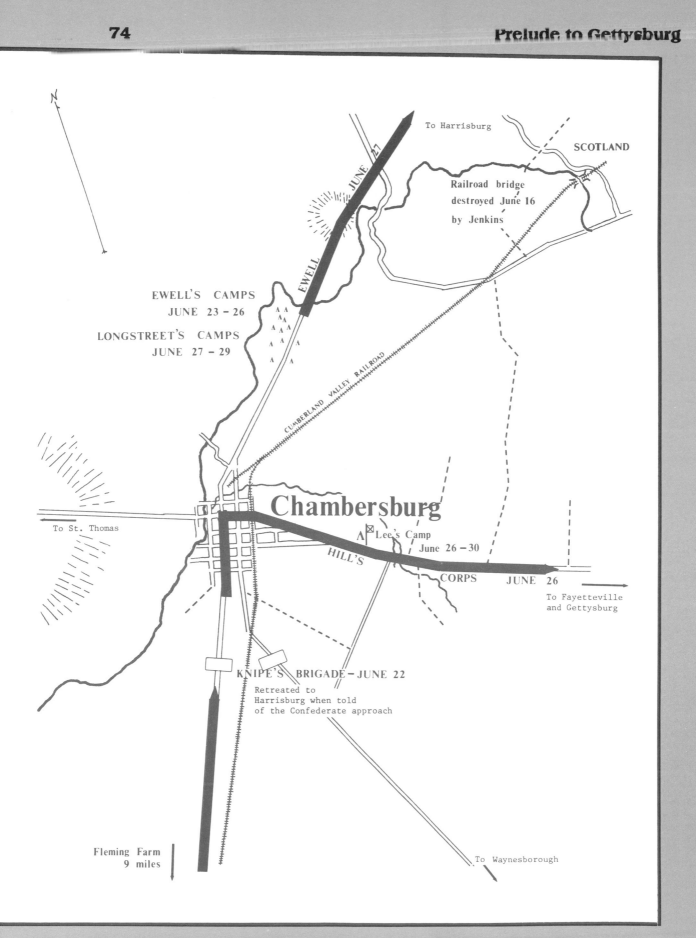

The military activity in and around Chambersburg in June, 1863

the nation's capital. Pennsylvanians were slow to respond to Governor Andrew Curtin's call for men.

On June 22, Rodes' Division of Ewell's Corps, Army of Northern Virginia, almost 8,000 strong, crossed the Mason-Dixon Line and camped at Greencastle. Close behind them was the rest of Lee's army. In all, nearly 70,000 men. To stop them, Couch had an invalid company, detachments of cavalry from Carlisle Barracks and the 1st New York "Lincoln" Cavalry, two regiments of New York State Militia and a naval gun battery from the Philadelphia Navy Yard. This inexperienced force was no more than 1,000 men.

Couch assigned General Joseph F. Knipe the thankless task of taking these troops and doing what he could to slow the Rebel advance. On June 21 he ordered the "Invalid" company to stay in Shippensburg, while he took the New York militia, naval battery and cavalry to Chambersburg.

Lt. General Richard S. Ewell, commander of the Second Corps, Army of Northern Virginia . . . he made his headquarters at the Franklin Hotel and later in the Mennonite Church north of town.

While the cavalry searched for the enemy, the infantry began setting up defenses for Chambersburg just to the south of the borough. The 8th New York defended the Greencastle Road (now Route 11) with the naval guns. The 71st was positioned on the Waynesboro Road, digging in with rifle pits backed up with two naval guns.

On June 22, Captain William Boyd, with 35 men from the "Lincoln" cavalry, was pursuing a small detachment of men from Jenkins' cavalry. Boyd, however, was leading his men into a trap set up by the Rebels in the fields just north of Greencastle. Boyd stopped his men behind the home of Archibald Fleming to survey the situation.

Two men, Sergeant Milton Cafferty and Corporal William Rihl, rode around to the front yard. Volleys of Rebel fire rang out, and Cafferty fell with a serious leg wound while Rihl dropped dead out of the saddle with a head wound. Corporal Rihl was the first Union soldier killed north of the Mason-Dixon Line.

Boyd beat a hasty retreat and quickly alerted Knipe to a large enemy force to the

Painting by nationally-known artist, Mark T. Noe, depicting the ambush at the Flemming Farm, June 22, 1863 (loaned by and displayed at the First National Bank in Greencastle).

immediate south.

About 3:30 p.m., Knipe and his staff rode out for a first-hand look. In Marion, he encountered a resident who had seen the skirmish and told Knipe that other roads existed from Greencastle to Chambersburg.

Knipe returned to his lines, and began mulling over the decisions that might await him if the Confederates were to encircle his troops. He did not have to make those decisions, however, because a message from Couch ordered him to have his men evacuate Chambersburg on a train north.

Panic ensued. Troops of the 8th New York literally left everything, from the cannons to personal effects, as the troops rushed pell mell to the train sta-

Brig. General Joseph F. Knipe . . . he was sent to Chambersburg with less than 1,000 men to stem the Rebel invasion.

Benjamin S. Huber, left, and Stephen Pomeroy . . . these two men and several others from the area were part of an espionage network that operated under the direction of A.K. McClure during the invasion. When telegraph lines were destroyed they carried messages to Harrisburg concerning the Confederate movements.

tion. Further panic developed when the 71st discovered in all the confusion they had been abandoned.

Apparently orders for their retreat never reached camp and only when they saw the clouds to the west of their counterparts' departure did they have an inkling as to what was taking place. Officers then sounded retreat, but the 71st never reached the train in time. After an all night march, weary and digusted, they joined the rest of the brigade in Carlisle.

No sooner had Knipe evacuated Chambersburg than the citizens started looting the camps. Clothing, equipment, including tents and food, notably cans of sardines, were among the articles taken.

One conscientious Chambersburg resident, Abram Metz, filled his wagon with all the equipment it would hold and took it to Shippensburg where Knipe's train had stopped temporarily. Metz was rewarded for his deed by having his horse confiscated by Confederates during his return home.

There was an air of undeniable triumph when Jenkins and his men returned to Chambersburg on June 23. They arrived in the diamond at about 10 a.m. As Jenkins' men followed him into the center of town, he signaled many of them to continue toward Harrisburg and occupy Shirk's Hill.

He ordered his chief of staff, Captain Fitzhugh, to place a demand on the town. Fitzhugh demanded that the townspeople once again come forward, as they did when Jenkins was there, with provisions for the Confederates. Fitzhugh threatened that if the citizens didn't respond, a general search of the town would be conducted.

By mid-afternoon, Rodes, who was still in Greencastle, began moving part of his 8,000 strong division toward Chambersburg.

They camped near Marion, while General Edward Johnson's division moved into Greencastle. Johnson ordered General George H. Steuart's 2,500-man brigade westward to conduct a huge horse and cattle raid in Mercersburg and McConnellsburg. Steuart also had 300 cavalry and a battery of six cannons at his disposal. Meanwhile, to the east and north, Jubal Early's division was moving through Way-

Troops of the 8th New York literally left everything, from cannons to personal effects, as the troops rushed pell mell to the train station

The look of a typical Johnny Reb marching through Franklin County in June, 1863.

nesboro, passing through Quincy and Mont Alto before reaching Greenwood (approximately where Rt. 997 intersects Rte. 30), where the troops spent the night.

If people were still sleeping by 9 a.m. on June 24, they were awakened as the Confederate band, marching on Main Street toward the diamond in Chambersburg, blared out the upbeat strains of "The Bonnie Blue Flag." Behind the band was the infantrymen of Robert Rodes' division, the first Rebel infantry to set foot in Franklin County.

The band then came to the diamond and moved to the side as the infantry continue northward to relieve Jenkins' horsemen at Shirk's Hill. A stream of men, estimated at upwards to 10,000 by local citizens, would pass through the diamond this day.

Huge trains of wagons and cattle poured through town, and the men, wagons and animals fanned out throughout the fields and open areas north of Chambersburg.

Around 10:30 a.m., a carriage accompanied by several riders, pulled up in front of the Franklin Hotel, which would become the Central Presbyterian Church in 1868. General Richard S. Ewell, newly-appointed commander of the Second Corps, alit gingerly from the carriage and walked stiff-legged with a crutch into the hotel. Ewell, now commanding many of the men who served the late Stonewall Jackson, had an artificial limb from a wound at Second Bull Run.

After Ewell set up his headquarters in the largest building in town, he assigned a Colonel Willis of the 12th Georgia Regiment as provost marshall. The colonel put his headquarters in the courthouse, and a Southern flag was displayed in the cupola. Willis then requi-

Lt. General A.P. Hill led his Third Corps into Chambersburg on June 26, 1863. To one observer he "seemed to be a man of splendid physique, of ordinary height, his figure was slight but athletic, and his carriage erect. His dress was ordinary Confederate gray and was plain and without ornament, except the stars upon the collar of his coat, which designated his rank."

Lt. Gen. Richard S. Ewell, now commanding many of "Stonewall" Jackson's men, set up his headquarters in the Franklin Hotel.

sitioned several hotels for mattresses and bedclothing so he could establish a hospital in the public school building on King Street. Before noon, Ewell issued a general order forbidding the sale of liquor. Ewell then demanded large amounts of supplies (like 5,000 suits of clothes, and 10,000 horseshoes) from the citizens.

On the morning of the 25th, Ewell moved his headquarters from the Franklin Hotel to the Mennonite Church north of town. Here he met with General Early, whose division was camped to the east at Greenwood. "Old Jube" was instructed to sever the Northern Central Railroad at York and burn the bridge across the Susquehanna at Wrightsville. He was then to march northwest through Dillsburg and rendezvous with Ewell at Carlisle.

It was raining heavily early on June 26 as Heth's Division of A.P. Hill's Corps entered the diamond by 8 a.m. The column turned east toward Gettysburg and did not continue northward. The troops eventually camped at Fayetteville.

An hour later Hill, along with a few staff, arrived in the diamond. He dismounted from his horse, hitched it in front of a grocery store, and began a conversation with a town resident. Hill once was stationed at the Carlisle Barracks, and he was asking about several people he knew. The rain slackened as Lee entered the diamond and was greeted by Hill, who had returned to horseback. Hill greeted him, and the two moved off for "a short, whispered consultation," noted one observer. The council between Hill and Lee ended, and Lee reined his horse, Traveler, to the east.

Lee then moved to a grove east of Chambersburg, just next to where the Chambersburg Hospital stands today. It was once known as "Shetter's Woods," but in 1863 it was named after the late George R. Messersmith and was called "Messersmith's Woods." It was the site of many town picnics, and celebrations such as the Fourth of July were held here. Lee remained here until he left on June 30 for Gettysburg.

To the east on this day, Early began his

Artist's rendering of the meeting between Lee and Hill in the town diamond on June 26, 1863.

march to York but not before putting the torch to Thaddeus Stevens' iron works at Caledonia. Early, along with the rest of the invading officers, had strict orders to treat the area humanely. Early, the headstrong and arrogant general, however, continued to stretch the rules, and burning the iron works was one example. After sending most of his supply train to Chambersburg, Early quickly reached Caledonia (now a state park. Evidence of Stevens' furnace still exists, and thousands of swimmers and visitors who come to the state park see it every summer.).

Early left the task of razing the enterprise of the famous Radical Republican Stevens to Colonel William H. French and his 17th Virginia Cavalry from Jenkins' Brigade. Early rationalized the burning by saying this was in retaliation for "deeds of barbarity" by Federal troops in the South and because Stevens had such a vindictive attitude toward the South. The works were just beginning to turn a profit for Stevens, and there was about $65,000 invested in the business. What went up in flames that day was a large charcoal-burning furnace, a forge, a rolling mill, a coal house, shops, stables, a sawmill, and a storehouse, as well as a cluster of cottages housing workmen. But Stevens took the loss fairly well, contending that someone must suffer from the ravages of war.

By June 27, thousands more Confederates were entering Chambersburg. Among them were General James Longstreet's First Corps and the remainder of Hill's Third Corps. Longstreet's men camped northeast of town, along the Harrisburg Pike and Conococheague Creek, near the Mennonite Church, where Ewell had his headquarters a few days before. Hood's Division was on the farm of Peter Lehman, Pickett's on the John N. Long farm and

General James Long-street (left) com-mander of the First Corps, Army of North-ern Virginia . . . One of his scouts, "Harri-son," brought word to Lee at Chambersburg that the Federal army was near Frederick, Maryland, that it had a new commander, Meade, and was head-ing for Pennsylvania.

McLaw's further upstream.

Meanwhile, Hill's divisions gathered around Fayetteville, and Ewell's Corps, with Jenkins' Cavalry was at Carlisle. Lee had issued orders for Longstreet to march north and support Ewell's movement on Harrisburg, while Hill was to follow the route Early had taken, cross the Susquehanna and disrupt the railroad between Harrisburg and Philadelphia.

The same evening (June 28) that Lee had issued these directions from his Messersmith Woods headquarters, something happened that forced him to send out couriers with instructions that countermanded his original invasion plan.

General Robert E. Lee was at work at his headquarters. Working closely with his military secretary, Colonel Charles Marshall, he had just sent an order to Ewell, who was in Carlisle to prepare to take Harrisburg the next day. He told Ewell that Longstreet's 1st Corps would support him. He instructed Hill to follow Early eastward. The rain forced Lee under his tent most of the day, and when nightfall came, he sat with his aides. Longstreet had arrived, and the two spent much of the evening chatting.

At 10 p.m., a Confederate spy arrived at Lee's camp, and the course of the invasion would change dramatically. A staff officer accompanied the spy to Lee's tent. The spy's name was Harrison, and he brought the news that not only had a change of command taken place (George Meade had replaced Joe Hooker) but also that the Army of the Potomac was in Maryland near Frederick. Harrison, who was not a military spy but a civilian spy, worked

Following Gettysburg, Lee's wounded were transported in a 17-mile-long train through Franklin County. During the stormy night of July 4, 1863, some of the wagons were separated from the main column and driven into Chambersburg by mistake.

through General Longstreet. Longstreet employed him, and Harrison worked the capital's bars and received information from army officers and government employees.

The next morning couriers fanned out across southern Pennsylvania with orders for the respective Confederate commanders to halt their movements to the Susquehanna and concentrate in the South Mountains near Cashtown.

Lee now knew he would have to do battle to keep the Yankees east of the mountains in order to protect his communication and supply lines back to Virginia. This command decision, made on the outskirts of Chambersburg on June 28, 1863, was one of the most momentous in American history. It resulted in the Battle of Gettysburg three days later.

The Retreat From Gettysburg

Gettysburg was the largest battle ever fought in the Western Hemisphere. Despite the tremendous din created by more than 150,000 muskets and 200 cannons hardly anyone in Chambersburg realized a battle was going on. Although a few residents on the eastern outskirts of town reported hearing what they thought was artillery fire, for the most part the mountains shielded the community from the noise of battle. This is interesting. Apparently

General John D. Imboden (right) . . . his Confederate cavalry occupied Chambersburg and guarded roads in Franklin County after Lee's main force moved to Gettysburg. Following the battle, Imboden escorted the Confederate wagon train of wounded.

during the Battle of Antietam in 1862 the battle sounds were more distinct.

On the evening of July 4, following an Independence Day ceremony at the County Courthouse a number of citizens heard a low rumbling noise to the east. This was Lee's wagon train of wounded. Escorted by the cavalry brigade of General John D. Imboden, the wagon train of misery was said to be 17 miles long. As it wound its way cross country through Franklin County from Greenwood to New Franklin, Marion, Greencastle and south to Williamsport, Maryland. In an article written after the war, Imboden remembered the horrors of this journey.

"About 4 p.m., the head of the column was put in motion and began the ascent of the mountain. After dark I set out to gain the advance. The train was seventeen miles long when drawn out on the road. It was moving rapidly, and from every wagon issued wails of agony. For four hours I galloped along, passing to the front, and heard more — it was too dark to see — of the horrors of war than I had witnessed for the Battle of Bull Run up to that day. In the wagons were men wounded and mutilated in every conceivable way. Some had their legs shattered by a shell or Minie ball; some were shot through their bodies; others had arms torn to shreds; some had received a ball in the face, or a jagged piece of shell had lacerated their

***Confederate prisoners at Gettysburg . . . following the battle,
hundreds of Rebel stragglers roamed Franklin County and many
were finally rounded up, processed at Chambersburg and sent to
prison camps.***

heads. Scarely one in a hundred had received adequate surgical aid. Many had been without
food for thirty-six hours. The irragged, bloody and dirty clothes, all clotted and hardened with
blood, were rasping the tender, inflamed lips of their gaping wounds. Very few of the wagons
had even straw in them, and all were without springs. The road was rough and rocky. The
jolting was enough to have killed sound, strong men. From nearly every wagon, as the horses
trotted on, such cries and shrieks as these greeted the ear:

"Oh God! why can't I die?"

"My God! will no one have mercy and kill me and end my misery?"

"Oh! stop one minute and take me out and leave me to die on the roadside."

"I am dying! My poor wife, my dear children! what will become of you?"

Some were praying; others were uttering the most fearful oaths and execrations that
despair could wring from them in their agony. Occasionally a wagon would be passed from
which only low, deep moans and sobs could be heard. No help could be rendered to any of the
sufferers. On, on; we *must* move on. The storm continued and the darkness was fearful.
There was no time even to fill a canteen with water for a dying man; for, except the drivers
and the guards disposed in compact bodies every half mile, all were wounded and helpless
in that vast train of misery.

The night was awful, and yet it was our safety, for no enemy would dare attack us
when he could not distinguish friend from foe. We knew that when day broke upon us we
would be harrassed by bands of cavalry hanging on our flanks. Therefore our aim was to go
as far as possible under cover of the night, and so we kept on. It was my sad lot to pass the

whole distance from the rear to the head of the column, and no language can convey an idea of the horrors of that most horrible of all nights of our long and bloody war."

While the wagon train of wounded passed just a few miles south of Chambersburg, the remainder of Lee's army was withdrawing through the South Mountains at Monterey Pass, just east of Waynesboro. There on the night of July 4 and early morning of July 5 part of the Confederate column was attacked by the Union cavalry of Kilpatrick's Division. Among them was the Michigan Brigade led by young General George Armstrong Custer. This confusing action took place on the mountain in a driving thunder storm and was the largest military engagement in Franklin County during the Civil War. Exact casualty figures for both sides are vague, however, Kilpatrick reported a loss of five killed, ten wounded and twenty-eight missing. His further claim of several hundred enemy casualties in addition to taking more than 1,000 prisoners is probably an exaggeration.

Lee was forced to entrench in and around Williamsport since the Potomac River was swollen by heavy rains and his pontoon bridges had been destroyed by Union Cavalry. Between July 4 and July 14, various Union forces, besides the Army of Potomac, were in motion to constrict Lee's movements. Among them, Pennsylvania's "Emergency" militia, which had been called out by Governor Curtin. Twelve thousand of these men camped at Chambersburg and then Greencastle during much of July and part of August. Once again Chambersburg citizens found themselves playing host to an army, this time a friendly one.

> **Lee was forced to entrench in and around Williamsport since the Potomac River was swollen by heavy rains and his pontoon bridges had been destroyed by Union Cavalry.**

Although the major battle of the invasion of 1863, Gettysburg, had by-passed Chambersburg by nearly 30 miles, the devastation wrought by the tramping of what would amount to more than 100,000 men through the area left many citizens destitute. Indeed many farmers who had their livestock taken and crops destroyed would end up leaving for better prospects in the west.

(The following are excerpts from the diary of William Heyser, prominent Chambersburg businessman)

JUNE 14

Our town in an uproar. Government property being loaded up and taken away. The drum calls for volunteers.

All the army stores have been packed up and sent to Philadelphia. Little attendance at church and Sabbath School. Much of the news is false we hear, but it serves to upset the people. We all feel Pennsylvania will be invaded. Many families are hiding their valuables, and preparing for the worst. Some preparing to leave town.

The stores are packing up their goods and sending them off, people are running to and fro. Cashier Messersmith is sent off with the books of the bank and its valuables. The cars are crowded to utmost capacity. The colored people are flying in all directions. There is a complete state of confusion.

After twelve we got word the Rebels have entered Hagerstown. The stores are all closed, and the streets crowded with those that can't leave. As President of the bank, might be held responsible for its assets, which I doubt, anyhow I shall stay to defend my property best

I can.

At 8 o'clock a number of contrabands entered our town, fleeing from Martinsburg with the Rebels not far behind. These were followed by a wagon train, many on three wheels, and less being dragged and pushed as fast as possible. The street is crowded with horses and wagons, all in the wildest state of confusion.

Suddenly about two hundred more wagons, horses, mules, and contrabands all came pouring down the street in full flight. Some of them holloring the Rebels are behind us. Such a sight I have never seen, or will never see again. The whole town is on the sidewalks, screaming, crying and running about.

The road into town is almost impassable by the teamsters cutting loose their wagons and fleeing with their horses. This further jammed up our town, some of the horses fall in the streets from sheer exhaustion. One soldier was killed by the fall. After the panic subdues, the teamsters that had cut loose their wagons went back for them. At twelve the excitement is beyond conception. I am again urged to leave. Mr. T.B. Kennedy sent me a message, feeling it was a good idea. I have consented against my will-packing up my valuable papers and at two, left with Mrs. Heyser in my buggy, for Carlisle, committing the house to William, Proctor my colored man, and girl. After I left they did not stay, but put off for the mountains. Had difficulty passing the wagon jam on the road and answering questions, arriving at Stoughs town about 6 in the evening, where I shall wait for news.

SABBATH, JUNE 21

Just about Sabbath School time, the town thrown into another state of confusion, that a column of Rebels were advancing. This proved to be just a poor man leading a few horses in town from his farm. So it goes, what is fact and fancey, we continued with our worship, the excitement subsided.

In the evening, troops came in from New York for our protection.

JUNE 22

Troops arriving from Harrisburg. Four Dalgreen pieces of ordinance arrive and taken out to the end of town and set up. The citizens have formed a few companies for defense, but how effective could they be?

More troops have arrived, perhaps a thousand here now. We breathe a little easier.

Our hopes are short lived. The troops have all been recalled to Shippensburg, the small battery is run out of town. Excitement is again intense in town.

A meeting is held of prominent men, to face the enemy, if they could come and surrender the town on the best terms we can get. Again there is a general stampede to leave town with valuables. The road to Shippensburg is again packed with fleeing citizens. There is not a Negro to be seen in town. At 11 o'clock, the streets are deserted. I did not go to bed till about one. All is quiet, but it is a sleepless town.

JUNE 24

The streets are crowded with Rebels who try to interrogate our lessor citizens as to where things are hidden or sent to, and also, as to the movements of the Federal troops that had left. By now, all of our stores have been ransacked.

My neighbor, Widow Murphy, who kept a small store, dispensing Queens Ware and shoes, nothing of value to the Rebels, did succeed in having her place exempt from being robbed. Some of the Rebel officers were very considerate.

My son's mill and warehouse has suffered much from confiscation for which they gave him $800.00 in Confederate script.

I hear my tenant farmer, Thos. Miller, was shot at while plowing his corn. I have felt much concern for him, but cannot get thru the line.

JUNE 25

All quiet until about 9 o'clock when the locusts begin to swarm again. On each side of the street, they stop and make further requisitions. There isn't much left to take.

All businessmen suffer — Eyster brothers, Myers and Brand, Huber and Tobert, Sol. Huber, Gelwix, James Shaffer, D. S. Fahnestock, Dittman, Metcalf, I. Hutton, and Hemsley, Nixon, these were the principal losers.

JUNE 28

Few soldiers seen on the streets until after breakfast, when the advancing corps of Gen. Johnston appears with waving flags and stirring music, as they approach the public square. Three cheers went up for Southern Confederacy. They passed on column after column, for hours.

At about three o'clock, the rear of Johnston's corps is passed, making about 125,000 men, rank and file, 72 pieces of ordinance, 350 wagons, about a regiment is left to guard the town. The large school building has been taken by them for a hospital.

Requisitions have been made on all the innskeepers for mattresses, blankets, quilts, sheets, etc., for the Rebel sick and wounded. It is expected the like orders will be given to the citizens.

SATURDAY, JUNE 27

About 11 o'clock Gen. Lee passed with his staff. He is a fine looking man, medium size, stoutly built, has the face of a good liver, grey beard, and mustache, poorly dressed for an officer of his grade. He wore a felt hat, black, and a heavy overcoat with large cape. His horse appeared to be rather an indifferent one, for a man who reputedly is fond of fine stock.

Occasionally a German would stop me and complain in his native tongue, as if I could help this situation, or was responsible for it.

Every brigade as it passed sent a file of soldiers around to examine the stores and places of business, requiring them to open up.

Rev. Schneck was relieved of his gold watch and $50.00. He complained to get it back, but to no use. Robberies are now common on the street, particularly where they are unguarded.

Decharts hat store was cleaned out today, not a single item left in stock. They opened up my son William's store today, and started to help themsleves. We are powerless to stop them, and can do nothing but watch and complain to commanding officers. They refer to the same treatment our soldiers gave the Confederacy in Virginia.

I finally found a Col. Greene that listened to some reason and had the men removed and the door shut.

JUNE 28

The troops are moving through town again. The drug store of J. Spangler was visited today by Lieut. Todd, President Lincoln's wife brother. He finally had to be ejected by the provost marshall as having no business being there. Reports come in our neighboring farmers are being robbed, one being shot. Many of these robberies are committed by vagabonds or camp followers in search of booty. The Rebels try to check them, but can't catch them all. One farmer was shot and the body hid in the manure pile. These robbers are mostly after money. The poor farmers are defenseless.

JUNE 29

Streets are clear until about eight. My son, Jacob, meets Robert Reynolds of Georgia. I knew his father well. Robert had his own horse and servant along. He is a conscript, wish I could have talked with him.

Stouffer's mill has been taken over by the Rebels and is running for their use. There isn't much food left in town now.

JUNE 30

The troops are busy destroying the Franklin Railroad at both north and south ends of the County. Along with sills of the road, they pile on all the fence they can find to heat and twist the rails.

Another force of about 500 men have been sent to destroy the railroad depot and buildings, starting with the large turntable. It is so soundly built of iron castings, their fires had little effect on it. The engine house was pulled down after an immense amount of work. So they went from building to building, a senseless thing to do, as the structures were of no importance to us as we could not use them. I tried to reason with a nearby officer about the wanton destruction. Their answers are always the same, "This is in retaliation for your troops' work on the South, particularly Fredericksburg."

Leaving this scene of destruction, which appears to be their last act. I went up to the belfry of the German Reformed Church to see if I could trace any damage to my farm, but could not, so much timberland intervening. You could mark the line of the railroad by the smoke of the burning ties. From what I can see, there is little damage to crops and grassland.

JULY 2

About 12, in the company of two other men, I walked out to my farm to assess the damage. Everywhere were holes cut in fences and grain trample down by the exercises of the cavalry. I sustained a great amount of damage, nearly 4,000 acres of oats and much damage to all other crops. My houses were robbed of clothing and any kind of gear with which to work. The report was circulated that I was a Colonel in the Union Army and now made to pay greater than my neighbors. How unjust even your supposed friends can be. In passing over the fields and woods where they encamped, there is already a great stench.

JULY 3

Very hot. Our streets are deserted. An occasional Rebel is seen, just a few stragglers. A Rebel soldier riding up Market Street was fired upon by Wm. Etter, one of our citizens. We feared a reprisal for this sort of thing and put a stop to it. We see more and more deserters. The town being clear of Rebels, the doors are opening again to promenading females. Nothing can stop them, many of them show little respect for their character and standing. They expose themselves, as if intentional, to be out late at night unprotected.

July 4

Showers of rain. Reports of terrible fighting at Gettysburg. We hear of a great battle at Gettysburg, but as yet no particulars, except the Union forces were victorious. Some public spirited citizens seized the mail (Rebel mail) going thru Fayetteville. Soon a detachment of cavalry was back looking for it, and took 18 prisoners locally for some hours before releasing them; on pain of death if it happens again.

JULY 5

Much rain. About three, 12 wagons of wounded from Gettysburg were routed by mistake thru our town, leaving them here at our hospital, a wonder they were alive, thrown in heaps in rough wagons. The wagons were captured by John W. Taylor and sent to Carlisle. This is the Sabbath, all is calm and still. Few persons on the streets.

I notice that most of our birds have gone since the appearance of the Rebels, and that flies and insects are more numerous.

JULY 6

As Lee withdraws towards the Potomac, we hear skirmishes along the way. One over near Waynesboro and Smithsburg. Reports that the Pine Stump Road is filled with broken Rebel wagons and caissons, filled with ammunition much of which is thrown in the mud with a view of destroying it. Also many dead and wounded lying by the roadside, indicating a hasty retreat.

There is a report the Rebels are forming at Marion to meet Pleasanter's cavalry which is expected to attack them. Also it is said a cannon was found buried by the Rebels near the place on the roadside.

JULY 7

Much rain. The grain is in danger of spoiling. About 200 Rebel prisoners were brought in today. Many are deserting. Lee is making a desperate attempt to escape Mead's army. Our stores are reopening and cleaning up.

My sons, Jacob and William, just returned from the battlefield. It is a fearful sight. The fields full of dead, by all the roadsides dead are hardly covered by a thin layer of mud. Wreakage everywhere, the implements of war fast disappearing by souvenir seekers.

JULY 8

Some companies of New York cavalry and infantry creating a disturbance by their drunkenness. We saw none of this among Rebels. Our town is now stirring with activity again. Many who left are returning and the stores re-opening with what they have left.

JULY 10

Some troops came in this morning and moved towards Greencastle. About 3,000 passed thru Mercersburg. The town in confusion. Many of our females show little self-respect. You see them bareheaded, mingling with the crowd, and a number of them hanging on the arms of strange soldiers. It is amazing that the parents allow this to take place. Perhaps it is condoned under the guise of patriotism, but this usually ends in the ruin of these daughters. Tonight, Gen. Couch arrived amid much cheering. The speeches they give are politically slanted and do nothing toward ending the war and healing our wounds.

SATURDAY, JULY 11, 1863

Many soldiers idle about town, laying on cellar doors and door steps. About ten o'clock nearly 7,000 troops passed thru town toward Maryland. Gen Couch orders the academy and Franklin Hall to be fitted up for a hospital.

MONDAY, JULY 13

Raining all day, Mrs. Fisher's hired girl accosted by a soldier in her room. Her screams brought help.

JULY 15

Clear. Lee has safely retreated over the Potomac.

JULY 16

How ironic, now we have plenty of troops around and not needed, before, in our hour of need, there were none.

(The following is an excerpt from the diary of Lieutenant Colonel A.L. Fremantle, a British Army officer traveling with the Army of Northern Virginia during the 1863 invasion)

JUNE 27

I entered Chambersburg at 6 p.m. This is a town of some size and importance. All its houses were shut up; but the natives were in the streets, or at the upper windows, looking in a scowling and bewildered manner at the Confederate troops, who were marching gayly past to the tune of "Dixie's Land." The women (many of whom were pretty and well dressed) were particularly sour and disagreeable in their remarks. I heard one of them say, "Look at Pharoh's army going to the Red Sea."

Others were pointing and laughing at Hood's ragged Jacks, who were passing at the time. This division, well known for its fighting qualities, is composed of Texans, Alabamians, and Arkansians, and they certainly are a queer lot to look at. They carry less than any other

(News clips from the *Franklin Repository*, July 10, 1863)

CAUGHT IN THE REBEL LINES -- A number of our citizens were caught in the rebel lines last week about Hagerstown. Among them were Rev. Jos. Clark, James and Geo. Watson, John P. Culbertson, F. Winter Tritle, Wm. Clugston, Wm. Hutton, Dr. Jas. Hamilton, Jacob N. Snider, Levi D.C. Houser and others. Most of them secreted themselves in Hagerstown or escaped through the lines; but Messrs. Dr. Jas. Hamilton, J.P. Culbertson, J. Porter Brown, Charles Kinsler, Allen C. McGrath, Thomas McDowell, Geo. A. Kaufman and Geo. S. Hack are reported to be across the Potomac and prisoners.

FRANKLIN COUNTY has contributed probably a dozen to the rebel army, and two have paid the penalty of death. James Allison, who studied law with Hon. Wilson Reilly some eight years ago, enlisted in Stuart's Cavalry a year or more ago, and was killed at Ball's cross-roads a short time before the battle of Chancellorsville. He was shot through the temple and died instantly. This information was given by the Rev. Charles Boggs, a native of this county, but now a chaplain in the rebel army, when the rebels occupied this place. Hugh Logan, formerly of this county, was a Captain in Stuart's Cavalry, and was here with him October last. He was overtaken in Hagerstown last Saturday by our cavalry, and in attempting to escape was shot in the back, the ball passing through the bowels. He was in Hagerstown and alive on Sunday, but no hopes were entertained of his recovery. They will not be widely regretted since they invited death by taking up arms against their government; but they, in their treason, preserved their manhood by openly espousing the traitors' cause.

General John Bell Hood (left) . . . his Texans "answered the taunts of the Chambersburg ladies with cheers and laughter."

troops; many of them have only got an old piece of carpet or rug as baggage; many have discarded their shoes in the mud; all are ragged and dirty, but full of good humor and confidence in themselves and in their general, Hood. They answered the numerous taunts of the Chambersburg ladies with cheers and laughter.

One female had seen fit to adorn her ample bosom with a huge Yankee flag, and she stood at the door of her house, her countenance expressing the greatest contempt for the barefooted Rebs; several companies passed her without taking any notice; but at length a Texan gravely remarked, "Take care, madam, for Hood's boys are great at storming breastworks when the Yankee colors are on them!" After this speech the patriotic lady beat a precipitate retreat.

Sentries were placed at the doors of all the principal houses, and the town was cleared of all the military passing through or on duty. Some of the troops marched straight through the town, and bivouacked on the Carlisle Road. Others turned off to the right, and occupied the Gettysburg turnpike. I found Generals Lee and Longstreet encamped on the latter road, three-quarters of a mile from the town.

(This is an excerpt from Colonel E. P. Alexander's recollections,commander of Longstreet's artillery in the field.)

JUNE 26

As we marched through Chambersburg, one of the houses with a little garden in front, not only had a U.S. flag hanging from a window, but a good looking stout dutch girl, on the porch, had a little one in her hand — she waving this defiantly and as I happened to be passing, in an access of zeal she came forward and stood in the front gate and began to wave it almost in the faces of the men marching on the sidewalk. One of the very first of these chanced to be a member of Parker's Battery with quite a reputation as a wag.

He stopped square in front of her, stared at her a moment, then gave a sort of jump at her and shouted, "Boo." A roar of laughter and cheers went up along the line, under which the young lady retreated to the porch.

CHAPTER 6

The Burning of Chambersburg

The Burning of Chambersburg, Pa. — July 30th, 1864

An artist's conception of the Burning of Chambersburg, July 30, 1864.

On July 30, 1864, Confederate cavalry under General John McCausland burned Chambersburg. The act was, at once, retribution and war gone mad - - war against civilians, an act of brutality that was regarded by people in the North as one of the most heinous in American history. Yet the principal Confederates in the raid, General McCausland and Jubal Early, would defend their actions to their deaths.

Events of that summer were muddled and urgent. All across the young nation Confederate troops were retreating. Sherman was advancing on Atlanta; General Franz Sigel was moving up the Shenandoah Valley; Mobile, Alabama was being threatened. And in eastern Virginia Robert E. Lee's ever diminishing Army of Northern Virginia was being pressed hard by U. S. Grant's insistence and the seemingly bottomless manpower of the Army of the Potomac. Lee desperately needed a way to reduce the heat, or his cause would collapse under the unbearable pressure.

On May 15, a very pivotal day, Franz Sigel's small army of 5,000 men was soundly whipped at the battle of New Market by Confederates under the command of former U. S. Vice President, John C. Breckinridge. General Grant relieved Sigel and appointed General David Hunter in his place. Hunter was one of the most abrasive men in the Union Army and would go down in history as one of the "Yankees" most hated by the South. The 62-year-old West Pointer was the son of a Presbyterian minister and a member of an old Shenandoah Valley family. He had, however, grown resentful of his background and vented much of his rage

The corner of North Main and East King Street

against Southerners and particularly against his Virginia relatives. His career prior to serving in the Valley was mixed.

After recovery from a wound received at 1st Manassas, he became commander of the Department of Kansas in 1861. One of his most controversial moves was as head of the Department of the South in 1862. In May of that year, he issued orders emancipating all slaves in Florida, Georgia and South Carolina and organized a regiment of blacks. An embarrassed Lincoln administration repudiated his actions. After this, Hunter spent most of his time in the West prior to his arrival in the Valley. Hunter's orders were to march up the Valley toward Staunton and disrupt supply lines that led eastward to Lee's army.

On May 26, 1864, he went south with his army of 8,500 infantry and cavalry and its 22 artillery pieces. Destroying public stores, warehouses, and miles of railroad, Hunter and his army swept away Confederate resistance. Considerable looting accompanied the destruction, and Hunter's reputation was galvanized.

Reinforced by another 10,000 men, Hunter marched into Lexington, Virginia on June 11 and immediately torched the Virginia Military Institute as punishment for the role that school's cadets played in Sigel's thrashing at New Market the previous month. He also torched the home of Virginia Governor, John Letcher. Other homes were burned as well, and Washington University was looted.

As the Union army ravaged Lexington and surrounding communities, Lee realized something had to be done to meet this threat. Indeed, Hunter would have to be driven from the Valley, and the force that did it would have to be strong enough to pursue him and, if possible, threaten Washington. The force chosen for the mission was the Second Corps of the Army of Northern Virginia. This was "Stonewall" Jackson's old command and was now led by General Jubal Anderson Early. "Old Jube," as he was known by his men, was as much of a "Yankee hater" as Hunter was a Southern detester. During the invasion of Pennsylvania the previous year, for example, Early had taken delight in ordering the destruction of the iron works owned by Radical Republican Thaddeus Stevens and had levied a tribute on the town of York, Pennsylvania, under threat of destruction. Although "Old Jube" was not a Jackson or Longstreet, he possessed an aptitude for strategy, knowledge of the Valley, and the confidence of Robert E. Lee.

Reinforcing Breckinridge on June 17 at Lynchburg, Virginia, Early's men easily defeated Hunter and drove him in a panic into West Virginia. A Union reserve force under Sigel was also driven back to Harpers Ferry, where it took refuge with the Harpers Ferry garrison on Maryland Heights. Early wasted no time attacking such a strong position; he sent troops under McCausland north of the Potomac to occupy Hagerstown. On July 6 McCausland levied

Major Gen. David Hunter . . . His destruction of private property in the Shenandoah Valley caused Jubal Early to order the burning of Chambersburg

a tribute of $20,000 on that city under threat of burning. He also demanded clothing and other supplies. After the ransom was paid, McCausland realized he had left out a digit.

He had misread Early's instructions for a ransom of $200,000 in "greenbacks." No matter, Early made up for this mistake on July 8 in Frederick. There he demanded $200,000, and the money was raised by the mayor through the town's five banks. The money from these payments was to be used for the relief of Staunton, Lexington, and other communities hard hit by Hunter's depredations.

Early then moved on Washington. On July 9 his advance was delayed by a much smaller Union force under Lew Wallace at the Monocacy River just south of Frederick, Maryland. For most of the day, Wallace's makeshift force held off Early's entire corps, disrupting his timetable.

That afternoon, as the Confederate infantry forced the withdrawal of their Union opponents, General Bradley Johnson, a Frederick native, set off on what could have been the war's most spectacular cavalry raid. Johnson, along with his second in command, Major Harry Gilmor of Baltimore, was to take his 1,500 man cavalry brigade and free the nearly 12,000 Confederate prisoners of war at Point Lookout Prison in Southern Maryland. To do

Bank of Chambersburg (building with pillars) and the Franklin House.

South Main Street, and the Zion Reform Church Steeple is on the right.

West Queen Street from Market House cupola; building, far left, is untouched.

South Main Street from the square. Zion Reformed Church Steeple is in the distance.

Lt. Gen Jubal A. Early (right) . . . at war's end he fled to Cuba, Mexico and Canada before returning to U.S. in 1868 after receiving assurances from the Federal government that he would not be sent to prison. He never regretted giving the order to burn Chambersburg.

this, the Confederates would have to ride 300 miles through enemy territory in a period of 96 hours.

Johnson took a circuitous route by way of Baltimore County. There he detached a small force under Gilmor to destroy railroads, bridges, and telegraph lines. A detail of the 1st Maryland Cavalry was also sent to burn the home of Maryland's governor, Augustus W. Bradford, in retaliation for the destruction of Governor Letcher's home in Lexington. When Johnson and his main force reached Beltsville in Prince Georges County, a courier met them with orders from Early to abandon the rescue effort. Confederate President Jefferson Davis had canceled the raid, fearing that the plans had been discovered by the Union.

Early himself reached the defenses of Washington on the 11th. For two days, the Confederates probed Fort Stevens. Early planned an all-out assault on the fort but was

Brig. General Bradley T. Johnson . . . This Frederick, Maryland, native was second in command on the Chambersburg raid and a critic of Confederate behavior. In his official report, he wrote . . . "every crime in the catalogue of infamy has been committed, I believe, except murder and rape."

Major Harry Gilmor . . . This dashing Baltimore aristocrat led his Maryland cavalry into the town early on the morning of July 30, 1864 to prevent the escape of townspeople to spread the alarm.

dissuaded by the arrival of veteran Union troops from the VI and XIX Corps. On July 14, "Old Jube" decided to break off the engagement and withdrew back into Virginia.

Although Early did not capture Washington, he did accomplish a number of things. The forces of Hunter and Lew Wallace were badly beaten; the Shenandoah Valley was cleared of the enemy at harvest time; the Union high command was thrown into confusion and was paralyzed for nearly two weeks; thousands of head of livestock were taken back into Virginia from Maryland; and Union troops had been diverted from the Virginia front to save Washington. Perhaps most importantly, "Old Jube" had shown the world that the Confederacy could still go on the offensive. His troops had gotten closer to Washington than any other previous Rebel incursions. The *London Times* summed up the raid by stating: "The Confederacy is more formidable as an enemy than ever." Democratic newspapers in the North criticized the Lincoln government's failure to stop such raids, and cynical headlines announced "The Annual Invasion." General Early remained philosophical about the whole matter, as he remarked to one staff officer, "Major, we haven't taken Washington, but we've scared Abe Lincoln like hell!" Indeed, he had, and he had done so in an election year.

Looking north on Main Street from the square. The left corner shows the remains of Miller Drugstore.

Back in the lower (Northern) Shenandoah Valley, Early would strike at the Federals at Kernstown, Virginia, beating them soundly and causing them to flee to Maryland.

Once again, Early was in control of the Valley. While at Martinsburg, the Confederates kept busy destroying the B & O Railroad, and General Early got word that Hunter had been on another pyrotechnic expedition. Hunter had chosen to burn a number of private dwellings in Jefferson County, West Virginia, that at best had only a tangential connection to wartime objectives. Among them were the homes of Alexander R. Boteler, an ex-member of the Confederate Congress, and Edmund I. Lee, a distant relative of General Lee.

Threats were also made to burn Charles Town if guerrillas were harbored there; and "Boydville," the home of Charles J. Faulkner of Martinsburg, was only spared by the personal intervention of President Lincoln. The most incredible incident of house burning involved the residence of Andrew Hunter, a first cousin of General Hunter. The Hunters were ordered out of their home and not even permitted to save clothing or any other personal belongings. Andrew was taken prisoner and held for a month in Harpers Ferry without charges. When he was arrested, he wore a gold ring that his cousin, David, had given him as a token of affection before the war.

Hunter's overzealous behavior clearly exceeded Grant's instructions. The Union commander had instructed Hunter on July 17 to make "all the valley south of the Baltimore and Ohio road a desert as high up as possible. I do not mean that houses should be burned, but every particle of provisions and stock should be removed, and the people notified to move out." He went on to explain that the job should be so thorough that "crows flying over it for the bal-

From Washington Street looking toward the "diamond."

ance of the season will have to carry their provender with them." Hunter's intense hatred of his native South drove him to acts that the Union would regret.

The Union commander's arsonist activities in Jefferson County, coupled with his prior behavior toward civilian property during the Lynchburg campaign, forced Early to make a grim decision. After the war he wrote in his memoirs: "I came to the conclusion it was time to open the eyes of the people of the North to this enormity, by an example in the way of retaliation." Chambersburg was selected as the target. A mounted Confederate raiding party

A North Second Street view from the Market House (now Borough Hall). The unburned Masonic Temple is shown in the foreground at right.

The burned shell of the Bethel Church as it was viewed on the Lincoln Way West Bridge across the Conochocheague Creek.

The Franklin County Courthouse on the diamond was gutted.

King Street Bridge looking northeast. The cupola of the Falling Spring Church is in the distance. The foot trail is now a railroad track.

Another view from the market house exposes the 120-foot flag pole (at left) still standing.

The Rosedale Seminary for Girls following the Raid.

was to demand $100,000 in gold or $500,000 in U.S. currency as compensation for the destruction of the private dwellings in Jefferson County. A written demand was to be presented to the municipal authorities in Chambersburg, which included the provision that failure to comply would result in the burning of the town.

Late on the evening of July 28, 1864, a courier rode into the cavalry camp of General John McCausland and handed that officer Early's orders to strike at Chambersburg. McCausland's brigade of Virginia cavalry, two guns from Braxton's battery, and Bradley Johnson's brigade, which included Maryland and Virginia units, along with two guns of the Baltimore Light Artillery, would conduct the raid. The combined units numbered approximately 2,800 men. McCausland would be overall commander. On the evening of July 29, the two brigades assembled near Hammond's Mill, in Berkeley County, West Virginia. Within hours they would be crossing the Potomac.

McCausland's Raid, and all other Southern incursions north of the Potomac for that matter, cannot be fully understood without examining the role of the Baltimore and Ohio Railroad and to a lesser degree its sister transportation networks, the Chesapeake and Ohio

A view from Queen Street toward the diamond.

Canal and the Cumberland Valley Railroad. The late James Murfin, a noted historian on the Maryland Campaign of 1862, described the B & O this way: "As the Mississippi River was to the Confederacy, so the Baltimore and Ohio Railroad and the Pennsylvania Railroad were to the Union. They were not only main lines of supply to the west but vital lines of communication. The B & O, although, running on the border, as it were, was solidly controlled by strong Union support. Its vast potential of 4,000 locomotive and cars, and its capabilities of supplying 10,000 troops daily, made it a prime target."

The B & O was indeed Washington's main transportation link to the West. Sever it and all rail transportation would have to move north by northwest through Philadelphia and Harrisburg. Its importance as a means of transporting troops cannot be exaggerated. In September 1863, for example, some 25,000 men were transported

General John McCausland

The Courthouse LWE (formerly Market Street) entrance. The side entrance was eliminated when rebuilt.

A view from the cupola of the King Street School. Market House cupola is at the far left.

on it to the West to break the siege of Chattanooga. In addition, the railroad had seen a steady increase in traffic as it carried supplies for the army and western farm produce destined for European markets that needed American foodstuffs because of poor crops abroad in the 1860's.

Perhaps the B & O's most important function was the role it played with the C & O Canal as a carrier for the coal industry. By the mid-nineteenth century, coal was becoming important in the American economy, both as a fuel and as a source of power. The Federal government, itself, increased its consumption from 200,000 tons in 1861 to more than a million by 1864. The bulk of the coal carried by the B & O in the 1860's came from the mines of western Virginia and Maryland. When the war broke out, the Baltimore and Ohio was the only line operating in this region. Labor strife in the Pennsylvania coal mines helped business in western Virginia and Maryland. Despite constant Confederate threats, approximately 318,000 tons of coal were shipped east from the Cumberland region in 1862. The following year this increased to more than 748,000 tons and in 1864 was around 650,000 tons. The C & O Canal also played a major role in transporting coal. By March 1864, its boats were

A close-up view of the charred remains of the Bank of Chambersburg.

loading and leaving Cumberland at the rate of 15 or 20 per day.

A letter from Lincoln to B & O president, J. W. Garrett, on January 10, 1865, exemplified the desperate need for coal in eastern cities. "It is said we shall soon all be in the dark here, unless you can bring coal to make gas. I suppose you would do this, without my interference, if you could, and I only write now to say, it is very important to us, . . ." If President Lincoln felt this way in 1865, it is a logical assumption he felt even stronger about it being "important to us" several months earlier during election time. Would not lack of heat in Northern homes be one more point of frustration to make even the strongest Unionist lean toward George B. McClellan, Lincoln's Democratic opponent?

The Confederates were aware of the importance of disrupting the B & O Railroad and C & O Canal from the early days of the war. In June 1861, "Stonewall" Jackson received orders to destroy all the B & O property at Martinsburg. Nearly 400 cars and 42 engines were destroyed, along with shops, depots, and machinery. During the Maryland campaign of 1862, Robert E. Lee directed Colonel John Imboden to disrupt the B & O by destroying bridges and tunnels. In doing so, Lee hoped "their destruction would tie up the railroad for the winter."

Local townsfolk amid the rubble. The Bethel Church shell is in the right background, located at West Queen Street and Water Street.

Four buildings remain surrounded by the debris of burned buildings. Local folklore says that the buildings were owned by townspeople who performed a superstitious ritual which would protect their homes from fire. The buildings stand today.

A view of the east side of North Main Street.

Late in April 1863, Confederate cavalry under Generals "Grumble" Jones and Imboden conducted a joint raid into West Virginia and western Maryland again to try to wreck the B & O. This resulted in the destruction of two trains, sixteen railroad bridges and one tunnel. In concert with his invasion of Pennsylvania in June 1863, Lee had Imboden strike key railroad depots and bridges in West Virginia and western Maryland, and was "very much gratified at the thorough manner in which your work in that line has been done."

Now in July 1864, prior to crossing the Potomac on his raid to Washington, Early was ordered by Lee to tear up a good portion of the B & O track and wreck as much of the C & O Canal as possible. Once back in the Valley, "Old Jube" found that Hunter had repaired the railroad, so he put Breckinridge to the task of tearing it up again. Besides levying tribute on Chambersburg, McCausland was to "if possible destroy the machinery of the coal pits near Cumberland and the machine shops, depots and bridges on the Baltimore and Ohio Railroad as far as practicable."

At Chambersburg, McCausland would also be able to destroy an important rail head of the Cumberland Valley Railroad. This line, although not as efficient as the B & O, spanned the Cumberland Valley from Harrisburg, where it met the Pennsylvania Railroad to Hagerstown. In 1861 part of Union General Robert Patterson's army moved south on the railroad. In both the 1862 and 1863 Confederate invasions, it was an important link in moving troops, supplies and wounded soldiers to or from the front for the Union. Troops from the major rail center of Harrisburg could be transported on this line to the Shenandoah Valley within 24 hours. In 1862, following Antietam, Lee sent Jeb Stuart on the first Chambersburg Raid with the destruction of the Cumberland Valley Railroad as a major goal. The railroad was also important to the economy of south-central Pennsylvania. Grain carried over it went to markets in Baltimore, the major center of commerce and trade for the region.

View of the remains looking north toward Lincoln Way West up the Conococheague from Bethel Church.

The Signal Corps

The U. S. Army Signal Corps has its origins in the Civil War. Prior to that, the only form of signals used were short range commands by drum or bugle. Although the system of flags and torches to send messages was developed under the leadership of Union officer Albert J. Myer, the first use of such signals under combat conditions was done by the Confederates at First Bull Run.

An act of March 3, 1863 officially created the Signal Corps and authorized officers for it ranging in rank from lieutenant to colonel and enlisted men in the grades of private and sergeant. By the end of the war the Signal Corps numbered more than 300 officers and 2,500 enlisted men.

By 1864 most of the major military departments either had or were organizing signal detachments. The Department of the Susquehanna's was organized in February, 1864 and trained in Chambersburg. After duty at Hagerstown and Cham-

bersburg, the detachment was temporarily assigned to the Department of West Virginia at Harpers Ferry in July, 1864. Incredibly, this is when they were most needed in the Cumberland Valley, since McCausland's Raid took place at the end of the month. Following the burning of Chambersburg, the detachment was sent back to Franklin County where a system of signal stations, based in Greencastle, provided an early warning against any further Confederate excursions.

Many men from Chambersburg and the surrounding area were members of the Signal Corps detachment, One of them was James H. Montgomery of St. Thomas. The son of a tanner, he was a school teacher when the war began. His diary provides a detailed account not only of army life but also of happenings around Franklin County. Excerpts from the Montgomery diary and rare photos are located in Appendix 1.

A new floor was added to a Second Street building after the burning at the site of the today's Chamber of Commerce.

Disruption of these transportation networks was vital for the Confederate war effort in the East. Washington would be isolated, the Northern economy would be crippled, Union morale would be damaged, and Federal control of the Shenandoah Valley would be compromised. Both sides recognized the high stakes in raids of the sort Early wanted McCausland to conduct.

That part of the Northern border most susceptible to direct Confederate incursions was an area running roughly between Baltimore, Maryland, on the east and Morgantown, West Virginia, in the west. The lines that these transportation networks traversed were protected by five different military jurisdictions or departments. This overlap of military departments almost assured Confederate success. Independent of each other and unable to coordinate efforts effectively, the Union forces were dramatically vulnerable.

The weakest link in this confusing chain of overlapping Union military departments was the Department of the Susquehanna. It was created in June 1863 to organize the various "emergency" militia forces raised by Pennsylvania and adjoining states during Lee's invasion and was commanded by General Darius N. Couch. This 42-year-old New Yorker had led the Union II Corps at Fredericksburg and Chancellorsville. Disgusted with Hooker's poor performance at the latter battle, he requested a transfer and was made commander of the new department at its inception.

Headquarters of the Department of the Susquehanna was at Chambersburg, located in the center of the strategic Cumberland Valley. This valley, the northern extension of the "Great Valley" of which the Shenandoah also was a part, formed a natural corridor connecting the North and South. It ran for approximately 100 miles from Harrisburg on the Susquehanna River, southwest to Williamsport, Maryland, on the Potomac. As the Shenandoah Valley was a "breadbasket" for the Confederacy, so was the Cumberland Valley for the

The Assembly Reform Church shell is shown in the center. The King Street School stands intact in the background.

North. The Cumberland Valley Railroad ran from Harrisburg to Hagerstown via Chambersburg, where railroad warehouses and shops were located.

Although Couch was authorized in early July to recruit 24,000 "volunteer militia" for 100 days' service, Pennsylvania's response was slow. Most of the units raised were sent out of state to Maryland and Washington, D.C. Mounted units had to provide their own horses and equipment. To further frustrate matters, a signal corps detachment that could have tracked McCausland's precise movements had been sent to Maryland Heights at the beginning of the month. Now as the threat of another Confederate raid loomed, Couch's request to have this detachment returned to his department was refused.

To defend Chambersburg and the Cumberland Valley, Couch had a meager force of probably fewer than 400 men. These included the Patapsco Guards, an independent company of Maryland infantry under the command of Capt. Thomas S. McGown. This unit had been the main garrison at Chambersburg through much of the war. At least two companies of mounted militia were in the area, probably at Greencastle and other points along the state line. These troops would prove ineffective. Couch also had a section (two guns) of Battery A, 1st New York Light Artillery in Chambersburg. On July 26, Couch received an important addition to his small command: 45 men from the 6th U.S. Cavalry, under Lt. Hancock T. McLean. These men would prove invaluable in slowing McCausland's advance long enough to allow the evacuation of military supplies from Chambersburg.

Former hotel, located at Second and Queen Streets, receives a new third floor in the reconstruction period.

A view of the devastated South Main Street.

A front view of the Bank of Chambersburg with local townspeople.

From McCoys Ferry Ford to Chambersburg

McCoys Ferry Ford near Clear Spring, Maryland, was one of the principal fords along the upper Potomac. The primary Federal units picketing the area were elements of the 12th and 14th Pennsylvania Cavalry and probably some of Cole's Maryland Cavalry, perhaps 400 to 500 men scattered at posts for more than fifteen miles. Jeb Stuart had crossed there in October 1862 on his "Chambersburg Raid." Now less than two years later another mounted Confederate column, even larger than that of Stuart's 1,800 men, would use the ford and many of the same roads to Chambersburg.

Late on the night of July 28, McCausland ordered Major Harry Gilmor to send men from his two Maryland Cavalry units to scout other fords along the river as possible alternate crossings and to determine Union strength in the vicinity. At 1 a.m., Gilmor was directed to take the rest of his men and secure McCoys for the main column. For some unexplained reason, the Marylanders did not reach the ford until daybreak at about 6 a.m. With Gilmor in the lead, the Maryland Cavalry made short work of the small picket post at the ford, and after a brief exchange of fire, they scattered the Yankees and gained control of the C & O Canal of the Maryland shore.

Before McCausland led his main column across the river, he ordered Gilmor to send out patrols on the nearby National Road toward Cumberland and Hagerstown. At Hancock, Maryland, a patrol captured a company of dismounted Union cavalry. Another group met stiffer resistance when it encountered part of the 14th Pennsylvania Cavalry at Clear Spring. After an unsuccessful charge which cost three Confederate dead, the patrol, under Lieutenant Jeff Smith, fell back to await reinforcements from Gilmor.

McCausland's plan was to march from Clear Spring to Chambersburg through Mercersburg, Pennsylvania. While he did this, Gilmor was to create a diversion by pushing the Union cavalry across the Conococheague Creek, thereby creating the impression that the main strike would be against Hagerstown. Simultaneously, Early was making other feints toward Hagerstown, Shepherdstown and Harpers Ferry to confuse the Federals.

Gilmor's movement on the National Road soon met stout resistance. After driving ele-

The remains of the Golden Lamb Hotel remains in the northwest quadrant of the diamond. The 120-foot flagpole is at right.

ments of the 12th and 14th Pennsylvania Cavalry out of Clear Spring, with the assistance of the 36th Virginia, the Marylanders continued chasing the Federals east toward Hagerstown.

Following a running fight, Gilmor ran into an ambush. The Yankee cavalrymen, armed with breach-loading carbines, made good use of the woods, stone walls, and sturdy rail fences as they poured a heavy fire into the Confederate ranks. Before dispersing them, Gilmor lost 17 men, who were either killed or wounded. The major then "impressed" some carriages to take his wounded back to Virginia. Some of the wounded, unable to travel, were treated at the homes of local citizens. Gilmor continued the chase until the afternoon, probably taking the Williamsport/Greencastle Road to Cunningham's Crossroads (known as Cearfoss today) to present-day Pennsylvania Route 416 to join McCausland at Mercersburg.

While Gilmor was busy creating the impression that the Confederates were headed for Hagerstown, McCausland's main body was crossing the "deep and wide" Potomac. By 11:00 a.m. the men were across and in Clear Spring "as thick as flies." One citizen, Otho Nesbit, wrote in his diary that squads of soldiers started to enter homes and businesses taking what they pleased. "The stores were all robbed. 'Tis estimated that Edlin lost from 2,500 to 3,000 dollars. Loose near the same. Houck 7 or 8 hundred, Snyder and Miller 3 or 4 hundred. David Houck, postmaster, 600." Mr. Nesbit also noticed that the Confederates were actively rounding up livestock, particularly cattle. "'Tis said they drove about 400 across the river . . ." In more than three years, the people of the Clear Spring area had suffered depredations at the hands of both Confederate raiders and unruly Union troops. Nesbit's diary recorded the frustration of the local citizenry. After listing what he and his neighbors had lost on the raid, he noted that "many are talking about stopping farming or farming less."

As the head of McCausland's column, with the 36th Virginia as point, wound its way north into Pennsylvania, they pushed McLean's regulars before them. Drawing in his available pickets, fewer than 30 men, McLean fell back to Mercersburg leaving a few soldiers in ambush about a mile south of town. When the gray horsemen approached, the Federals fired, then fell back, set up another ambush, fired again and repeated these tactics several times, creating the illusion of greater strength than they actually had. This went on for about an hour.

Following a final stand in the town's Diamond, the little band of regulars was driven out by the 200 man 36th Virginia around 3:00 p.m. McLean's actions had bloodied the nose of McCausland's advance; upwards of 16 Confederates were casualties, as opposed to two of the regulars. The Confederate advance had been slowed down, buying time for Couch.

Looking to the center of town from the Market House. The street to the left is Queen Street.

Approximately 5 p.m., the main Southern force started to enter the town, and by 8 p.m. the entire column had closed up and prepared to rest, feed their horses, and let stragglers catch up. Most of the raiders camped just north of Mercersburg, but local civilians noted the whole length of Main Street was filled with soldiers lounging about eating, smoking, and "making themselves comfortable generally." While some rested, others started breaking into stores and robbing citizens. By 10 p.m., Gilmor's tired command arrived and to their dismay found that McCausland was ready to mount up. They were to be the rear guard. By midnight the last Confederates were leaving Mercersburg.

McCausland hoped to reach Chambersburg by going through Bridgeport (now known as Markes) and St. Thomas before daybreak. He did not reckon, however, with McLean and his detachment of regulars, who harassed the head of the column as it inched its way through the darkness of the Pennsylvania countryside. At 12:30 a.m., McLean's pickets were driven in at Bridgeport, and by 2 a.m. the Confederates were pushing the regulars out of St. Thomas. In Chambersburg, herds of livestock and wagon loads of goods were leaving the city, headed toward

Looking toward the square up South Main Street from the Zion Reform Chruch Steeple.

Shippensburg and points north.

Couch, meanwhile, was directing the evacuation of quartermaster supplies and the department headquarters by way of the railroad. From St. Thomas, McLean withdrew to a hill along the Pittsburgh Pike, a few miles west of Chambersburg. There he was reinforced by about 35 men of the Patapsco Guard and one gun of the 1st New York, the other being used to cover the rear of the evacuation.

As the Confederate force continued its nighttime ride, one soldier remembered the column was greatly "strung out" and that many of the men were riding in their sleep. Any sleep was soon broken when McCausland's point unit, the 36th Virginia, blundered into McLean's position at 3:00 a.m. and were met point blank with a blast of cannister from the field piece, killing one and wounding several. This jolt sobered the advancing raiders and held them up for another two hours as the Federal gun peppered the area at intervals with five additional rounds to keep the Confederates at bay.

After a time, McCausland realized that once again he had been deceived by a numerically inferior enemy and directed his units to flank McLean's position. By now it did not matter; the regular officer had bought time in order for the last train to leave with General Darius Couch and the headquarters of the Department of the Susquehanna. As this train rolled out of Chambersburg, McLean took the small force under his command and headed for Shippensburg. The time was 5 a.m.

Dawn, July 30, 1864, saw the Confederate cavalry grazing their horses in fields adjacent to the Henry Greenawalt residence a mile west of Chambersburg. At the Greenawalt house, McCausland had held a meeting with his officers and probably revealed to many of them for the first time the plan to ransom or burn the town. In Washington, President Lincoln would soon be boarding a steamer for Fort Monroe, Virginia, where he would confer with General Grant. At Petersburg, a mine had just exploded under a Confederate fort, and ironically, the 2nd Pennsylvania Heavy Artillery, a unit that contained men from the Chambersburg area, would be taking part in the "Battle of the Crater."

But back home the early morning calm was broken around 5:30 a.m. by the belching of Confederate cannon that sent perhaps a half dozen rounds over the town. Residents who would have peeped out of the windows would have noticed Confederate cavalry lined up on a hill west of town. The 8th and 36th Virginia were sent on foot into the town to reconnoiter, followed by Gilmor's cavalry to assist in blocking exits out of Chambersburg.

When the word was passed that all was secure, Colonel William Peters' 21st Virginia Cavalry was ordered to occupy the town. Soon McCausland, Johnson, Gilmor, and other officers were sitting down to breakfast at the Franklin Hotel. After

> IT DID HAPPEN HERE -- Buried deep in Jacob Hoke's "Reminiscences of War" is a paragraph which corroborates the report of an unnamed English military observer that a flag-draped woman confronted Confederate troops when they burned Chambersburg during the Civil War. The paragraph read: "On the morning of the fire, Mr. David Brand, brother of our townsman, Mr. Jacob L. Brand, took the flag which hung in front of Col. Rutherford's headquarters in the Mansion House and carried it to his home on Queen Street. While the rebels were firing Queen Street, Miss Louisa Brand, his sister, took the flag, and, wrapping it around her, and with revolver in hand, stood in the front door of their house and dared any rebel to fire the house or disturb the flag. She passed unmolested and the house was not burned." So there you are. Daniel Henderson, the poet, was on sound historical ground when he chose the English officer's report for the basis of a poem in a recent issue of the Saturday Review of Literature.

eating, McCausland ordered Harry Gilmor to "arrest" 50 or more of the town's leading men. Meanwhile, one of McCausland's staff, Captain Fitzhugh, recognized J. W. Douglas, a local attorney, from his visit the previous year with Jenkins' brigade.

After showing him a copy of Early's orders demanding a ransom on threat of destruction, Fitzhugh instructed Douglas to "go immediately and see your people and tell them of this demand and see that the money is forth coming, for I assure you that this order will be rigidly enforced."

The general response of the Chambersburg population to the Confederate threat is well documented. "I then went up Market Street," Douglas wrote, "and told everyone I met of the rebel demand. They generally laughed at first, and when I spoke earnestly about the terrible alternative, they said they were trying to scare us and went into their houses. I then went up Main Street in the same manner and with the same result." Confederate participants remembered vividly the attitude of the citizens. "They seemed to think we were jesting and bluffing," wrote J. Scott Moore of the 14th Virginia. "It seemed impossible to convince your people that we were in earnest," Fieldor Singluff of the 1st Maryland remembered; "they treated it as a joke, or thought it was a mere threat to get the money, and showed their sense of security and incredulity in every act." Gilmor, in his memoirs said, "the citizens . . . . positively refused to raise the money, laughing at us when we threatened to burn the town."

The behavior of Jeb Stuart's cavaliers in 1862 and Lee's army, under his strict charge in 1863, had lulled the people of Chambersburg into a false sense of security. After all, the New York militia the summer before had probably caused more vandalism to private property than the previous Confederate raids. Why should anything have been different this time around?

When Douglas returned empty handed, he was confronted with the uncomfortable task of explaining to General McCausland that all the bank funds had been removed when word of a possible Confederate raid had been announced. An impatient McCausland then ordered the Court House bell to be rung in order for the

Many individual citizens were robbed, like S. M. Royston, the barkeeper at Montgomery's Hotel, of their life savings.

The Franklin County Courthouse shell. A section of the corner wall of Franklin Hall stands to the left.

citizens to gather on the town Diamond. By now, Gilmor had been able to round up a number of prominent citizens who, after being read General Early's ultimatum, could only plead that the town had no money available to give.

At this point arises one of the greatest controversies surrounding the burning of Chambersburg. How long did McCausland wait after announcing his demands before torching the town? McCausland claimed that after reading Early's order, he gave the community six hours to comply. Although his force stayed in Chambersburg 5 to 6 hours, sufficient evidence exists to refute his claim that he waited six hours.

On the other end of the spectrum are accounts by local civilians who claimed that the fires were started within 15 minutes after McCausland addressed the citizens' delegation that Gilmor had gathered. Jacob Hoke, a local businessman, stated that the buildings were on fire as early as 7:30 a.m. This charge is not only refuted by Bradley Johnson, a McCausland critic, who stated that "after remaining in the town some three hours, he (McCausland) ordered it to be fired," but also by a Union soldier who was an eyewitness.

> **"Every crime in the catalogue of infamy has been committed, I believe, except murder and rape."**

Sgt. William S. Kochersperger of the 20th Pennsylvania Cavalry was on detached duty at Couch's headquarters and was "unavoidably detained" in Chambersburg following the Union evacuation. Disguised in civilian clothing, he claimed to have been present when Early's order was read to the citizens in the town Diamond and that "at 9:00 o'clock McCausland ordered the town burnt." Based upon the fact that the Confederates entered town between 5:30 a.m. and 6 a.m. and that McCausland took time to eat breakfast, track down prominent city fathers, and announce his ultimatum, it is safe to assume that at least one hour had gone by.

If Kochersperger is right, some two hours elapsed between issuing the ransom demand and the actual burning. All the accounts agree that the town's core was in flames. "The most usual method of burning was to break the furniture into splinters, pile it in the middle of the floor and then fire it," wrote one soldier. "This was done in the beginning but as the fire became general, it wasn't necessary as one house set fire to another." The comparison of the various accounts, both civilian and military, leads to two conclusions.

First McCausland exaggerated his leniency toward the town in the account he wrote after the war. He obviously did not wait six hours before ordering the town burned. Second, the reports of military men, one Union, another Confederate, agree that the town was not fired immediately either. Several hours elapsed before the final order to burn was issued. Numerous civilian charges that the burning started sooner can either be attributed to confusion and hysteria; or consistent with other Confederate behavior that day, it may be true that individual soldiers acted on their own and set fires prior to official direction.

There is, however, abundant evidence that chronicles a general disintegration of discipline and an orgy of looting and other misbehavior by the Confederate soldiers. Apparently this commenced soon after the Confederates entered Chambersburg that morning. According to a local newspaper, "While McCausland and Gilmore (sic) were reconnoitering around to get a deal with the citizens for tribute, his soldiers exhibited the proficiency of their training by immediate and almost indiscriminate robbery.

Hats, caps, boots, watches, silverware, and everything of value were appropriated from individuals on the streets without ceremony, and when a man was met whose appearance

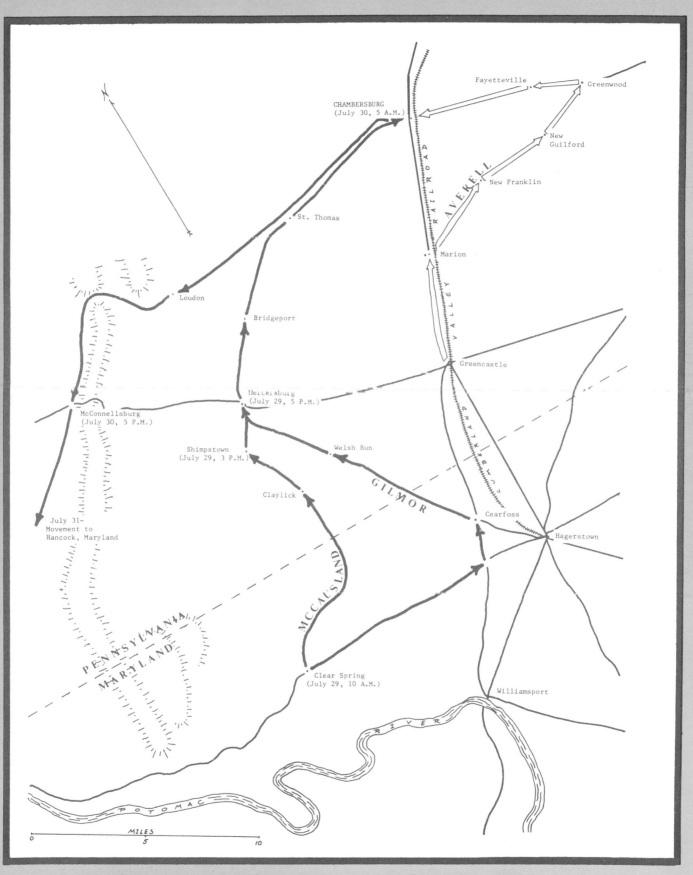

Confederate and Union movements, July 29-31, 1864

The charred town as viewed from the Market House cupola.

Some (Rebel) officers instructed their men to assist the civilians in retrieving as much of their household goods as possible.

indicated a plethoric purse, a pistol would be presented to his head with the order to 'deliver,' with a dexterity that would have done credit to the free-booting accomplishments of an Italian brigand."

Soon Confederate soldiers were seen breaking into shops and coming out with bonnets, hats, feathers and other articles. Others were seen carrying jars of candy and handfuls of cinnamon. Squads of soldiers entered private dwellings prior to setting them on fire and rifled cabinets and bureau drawers in search of money, jewelry and other valuables. All was mass pandemonium as citizens dragged trunks, sewing machines, furniture and anything else they could save from the flames.

Many individual citizens were robbed, like S. M. Royston, the barkeeper at Montgomery's Hotel, of their life savings. Father McCullum, the local Catholic priest, had been robbed of his watch the previous summer when the same troops, then under Jenkins, had entered town. Now as he sat on his front porch, a squad of soldiers demanded his new watch, which he promptly delivered to them.

In some instances people paid ransom to individual soldiers or groups of them to spare their homes. Often the Confederates took the ransom money and burned the house anyway. Johnson, in his report of the raid, noted, "while the town was in flames a quartermaster, aided and directed by a field officer, exacted ransom of individuals for their houses, holding the torch in terror over the house until it was paid. These ransoms varied from $750 to $150, according to the size of the habitation. Thus, the grand spectacle of a national retaliation was reduced to a miserable huckstering for greenbacks."

Liquor was acquired by many of the Confederates, and drunkenness was quite prevalent. Numerous eye witness accounts substantiate this charge. Jacob Hoke wrote that "the street was filled with the drunken and infuriated soldiers." Sgt. William Kochersperger reported that "when they left nearly two thirds of their party were in a state of intoxication, hardly capable of sitting on their horses."

Bradley Johnson wrote "after the order was given to burn the town of Chambersburg and before, drunken soldiers paraded the streets in every possible disguise and paraphenalia, pillaging and plundering and drunk." George Booth of the 1st Maryland Cavalry told of commanding one of the last details to leave the town "in the effort to clear the town of those who were under the influence of liquor."

As a result of this breakdown in discipline, Confederate officers "begged" local men to "get the women out of town as fast as possible, as many Rebel soldiers were intoxicated and they feared the worst consequences." Although there are no substantiated accounts of sexual assaults upon women, the August 8, 1869 *Baltimore American*, in an article protective of the role Maryland troops played in the raid, stated: "It was the Virginia Cavalry that burned Chambersburg. They have in several cases ravished women on their route." Despite the sensationalism of the newspaper, even Johnson in his severely critical report of the raid said, "Every crime in the catalogue of infamy has been committed, I believe, except murder and rape."

> **Averell immediately set out to track down the raiders and found their trail out of Chambersburg easy to follow.**

Probably the worst case scenario in the treatment of women was revealed by John K. Shyrock, a bookseller in Chambersburg. "Bundles were fired upon women's backs, ladies were forced to carry back into the houses articles of clothing they had saved from the flames; drunken wretches danced upon the furniture and articles of value and ornament, women's person were searched in the most undecent manner; oaths and foul language abounded . . ."

In an age when 16-year-olds wrote the number 17 on the soles of their shoes when swearing to Army enlistment officers that they were over 17 and when combat veterans threw away decks of playing cards ("instruments of the Devil") prior to entering a battle, rape would have been beyond the pale even for much of McCausland's force that had degenerated into a drunken armed mob. Indeed, the mindset of the Victorian era was so compelling, that even Quantrill and his guerrillas, who are generally agreed upon as one of the most bloodthirsty bands in history, bragged following the Lawrence, Kansas raid, where over 150 civilian men and boys were gunned down, that they had not molested women.

Not all the raiders were in favor of the burning or misconduct displayed by others. One officer was said to have wept publicly and denounced McCausland. Some officers instructed their men to assist the civilians in retrieving as much of their household goods as possible. According to a local newspaper, "one whole company was kept by its Captain - name unknown - from burning and pillaging, and the Southeastern portion of Chambersburg stands to-day solely because an officer detailed there kept his men employed in aiding people out of their burning houses, and did not apply the torch at all." A Confederate officer recognized the Masonic Temple and being a fellow Mason, posted guards to prevent it from being burned, along with nearby buildings which, if fired, would have threatened it.

The most notable case of dissension in the ranks occurred with the 21st Virginia. Colonel William Peters led his regiment into Chambersburg that morning, apparently not knowing about the plans to burn the town. When McCausland gave the order to begin burning, the young colonel refused to obey and threatened to break his sword. Johnson then

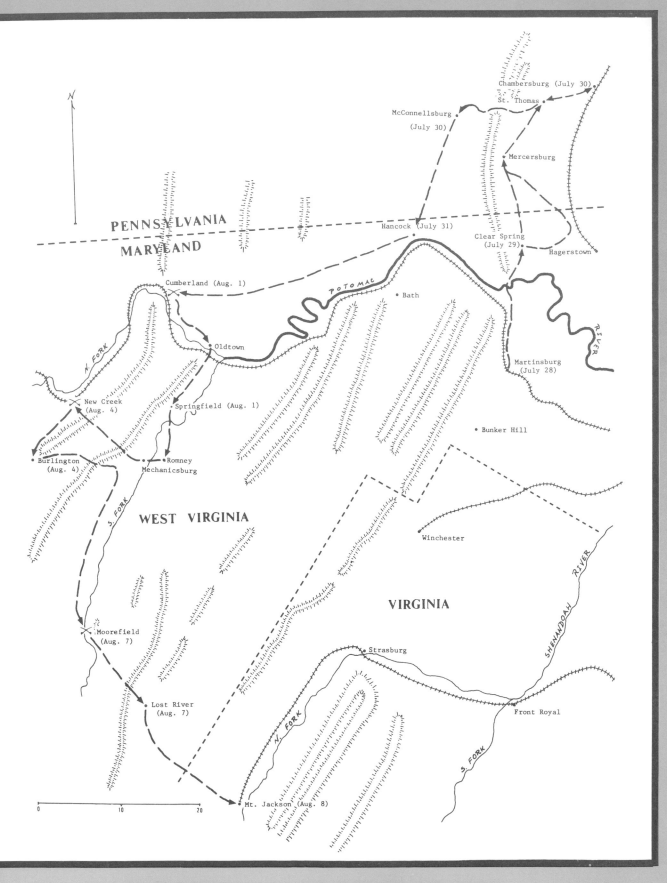

McCausland's route July 29-August 8, 1864

ordered him to collect his entire regiment and withdraw them to the edge of town. Although McCausland had Peters placed under arrest for insubordination, the charges were dropped the same day when he was returned to command in order to cover the retreat of the raiders.

While it would have been futile for the citizens of Chambersburg to resist the Confederates via guerrilla warfare as some critical New York newspaper editors were to suggest afterward, there were several notable examples of individual civilian resistance. One elderly lady attacked a soldier with her broom, giving him a "sound drubbing." Two soldiers entered the drugstore of Andrew J. Miller to loot and burn it, but in their haste and excitement they inadvertently locked themselves inside. Miller, standing in the adjacent hallway, filled both men with blasts from his double barrelled shotgun. Either killed outright or disabled, both died in the fire.

The highest ranking Confederate casualty at Chambersburg was Captain Caulder A. Bailey, adjutant of the 8th Virginia Cavalry. Bailey apparently got very drunk and was separated from his command. Several citizens captured him; he escaped and was shot and wounded in the process. Then he took refuge in the cellar of one of the burning homes. When the heat got too intense, he came out and begged for his life but was shot down by members of the crowd that had gathered. He was placed in an unmarked grave and a few days later reinterred in the Methodist cemetery.

> **The Confederates entered Hancock about 1 p.m. on July 31. Incidents there reflected the poor state of morale and discipline in the Southern ranks.**

Accounts vary as to the actual time the Confederates left Chambersburg, but it was somewhere between 11 a.m. and noon. What they left behind was an inferno of blazing houses, with several thousand numbed or crying men, women, and children cowering in vacant lots and in the town's cemetery. As the Confederate column departed, a squad of soldiers was sent to burn the home of County School Superintendent Andrew J. McElwain. The reason? He had taught Negroes.

The burning of Chambersburg had been, for most of the men in Johnson's and McCausland's brigades, the most dramatic event of their wartime experience. Fieldor Slingluff of the 1st Maryland placed the burners into three categories. First were men who had suffered directly from Union depredations and were driven by a spirit of revenge. Second, and largest was that portion of Confederates who simply obeyed orders as soldiers. These, he claimed, were often as not, also involved in humanitarian efforts to save personal property.

The third class he listed were "the men to be found in all armies who looked upon the occasion as an opportunity to plunder, and who rejoiced in wanton destruction." Lt. James D. Sedinger of the 8th Virginia summed it up best in his diary entry for that day: "Then we witnessed to the fullest extent the horrors of war."

McCausland's Departure from Chambersburg

While Chambersburg burned, a division of Union cavalry, approximately 2,500 men, under General William Averell, was camped north of Greencastle. Early on the morning of July 30, these troops mounted up to intercept the Confederate raiders. As McCausland's column headed west from Chambersburg, Averell's cavalry moved east toward Greenwood. Although this was nearly 10 miles east of Chambersburg, the Federal commander, no doubt, hoped history would repeat itself, for Jeb Stuart had passed this way on his 1862 raid. When informed by his scouts that the Confederates had moved west on the Loudon Road, Averell turned his column toward Chambersburg, arriving there around 2:00 p.m.

The Federal cavalry was not prepared for what they saw in Chambersburg. C. M. Newcomer of Cole's Maryland Cavalry wrote: "Those of us, who were in the advance, went through the burning town, bending forward upon our horses' necks, as fast as our faithful steeds would carry us. We had no knowledge of the great destruction and devastation that we should witness, and when we had once started, it was necessary to continue through the burning streets. Houses on fire on both sides, it was no time to turn back, and to stop was to be burned up; our poor horses were mad with fright. Each and every one of us felt relieved when we got to the outer edge of the town. The atmosphere was stifling, with the smoke that settled over the earth like a pall. The citizens were gathered in groups; strong men with bowed heads, women wringing their hands and the little children clinging to their mothers' dresses and crying. Desolation on all sides! It was a sad picture, long to be remembered."

Averell immediately set out to track down the raiders and found their trail out of Chambersburg easy to follow. According to Newcomer, "merchandise of every description was strewn along the road, boots, clothing, window curtains and even infants' shoes and little slips, and women's dresses, that had been stolen from the houses in Chambersburg and along the route, were now thrown away by the raiders, no doubt not wishing to be captured with stolen plunder on their possession." The raiders also left a trail of burning barns along the way. When officers from the 1st Maryland Cavalry (Confederate) confronted two enlisted men, who had just torched a barn, as to their rationale for such uncalled- for vandalism, one of the soldiers replied, "Why damn it, they burnt our barn," and rode away. Soon the head of the Union column was trading shots with elements of McCausland's rear guard.

> **McCausland's Raid of July 29 and Early's movement across the Potomac on August 5 created anxiety throughout the Cumberland Valley that resulted in a tremendous refugee problem.**

With Johnson's brigade in the advance, the column of gray horsemen entered McConnellsburg, Pennsylvania, in the late afternoon between 3 and 5 p.m. Upon entering this community of 556 people, the Confederates immediately cut the telegraph wires and destroyed the instruments in the telegraph office. McCausland then levied a demand for 2,600 rations under threat of burning the town. Although this large demand for such a small town was not met in full, the citizens supplied what they could. After eating, the Rebels started to plunder stores and private dwellings.

The only establishment to escape considerable loss was the dry good firm of Hoke and Nace. Upon hearing rumors and reports of a possible raid several days earlier, they had removed most of their goods to a safer place. Private homes were entered and robbed. According to the local newspaper, "Citizens were stripped and robbed in the streets. In almost every instance money was demanded and secured through threats of burning, or by a cocked revolver pointed at the citizen's head." Squads of soldiers also fanned out in the neighboring countryside to rob farms.

That evening the Confederates went into camp. McCausland's brigade probably camped in McConnellsburg or just east of it to guard the road from Chambersburg. Johnson camped south of the town. Johnson and his officers camped on the John B. Patterson farm about a mile south of McConnellsburg. The Maryland general pitched a tent under a large tree just behind the barn. Mrs. Patterson was instructed to cook them dinner, and Johnson and 25 other officers enjoyed fried chicken, hot biscuits, and rye coffee in the Patterson dining room that evening.

Because of the unexpected guests, only one of the Patterson's chickens survived the day. As the officers ate and conversed, Mrs. Patterson overheard Johnson complain about the Confederates' behavior at Chambersburg. Outside, Confederate soldiers slept on the ground of the Patterson farm. Guards were posted around the farm house and yard to keep the soldiers off the premises. These Confederate camps on the night of July 31, 1864, were the last Southern bivouacs in Pennsylvania during the war.

Next morning the men arose and made plans to re-enter Maryland. By this time Averell's column of bluecoats was crossing the mountains, having, no doubt, considered it wiser to wait until daylight before continuing pursuit of the raiders. Meanwhile, civilians from Franklin County were streaming up the mountain to view what they expected to be a large battle in which Chambersburg would be avenged. At 8 a.m., Averell's advances drove McCausland's pickets off the mountain and out of McConnellsburg, killing and capturing several. Averell's appearance preempted a planned movement of Gilmor's Marylanders and Dunn's 37th Virginia toward Bedford. Instead, the entire Confederate force headed for Hancock, Maryland, and the Potomac River.

When the Confederates destroyed the telegraph equipment at McConnellsburg, they failed to reckon with the ingenuity of the telegraph operator, 15-year-old Thomas F. Sloan. Anticipating such a move by the raiders, young Sloan had hidden an extra set of telegraph instruments in the home of the local judge. Now Averell was able to use the repaired line and telegraphed to General B. F. Kelly at Cumberland to aid him in stopping a probable Rebel crossing of the Potomac at Hancock.

The Confederates entered Hancock about 1 p.m. on July 31. Incidents there reflected the poor state of morale and discipline in the Southern ranks. The Confederates rested at Hancock and fed their horses and themselves. Once again, the more unruly raiders set about robbing and looting. It was a bad week for Catholic clergy, for as in Chambersburg, this town's priest was also robbed of his gold watch. One officer robbed a citizen of $1,000 in greenbacks, and a Maryland trooper was "nearly brained" for trying to prevent the robbing of a woman by a soldier. Particularly hard hit were the town's stores, which faced the C & O Canal. These were all robbed and vandalized. The raiders also burned several canal boats.

While this was going on, McCausland issued another of his ransom demands. In this case the town authorities were to pay $30,000 and provide 5,000 cooked rations, or Hancock was to meet the same fate as Chambersburg. This was too much for Johnson and the other Marylanders. After consultation with several prominent citizens, who were Southern sympathizers, Johnson argued with McCausland that the town of 700 people could not afford to pay and furthermore was partially Southern in its sympathy.

Johnson also advised the town leaders to gather as much money as they could and pay McCausland. Meanwhile, fearing the worse, he ordered Gilmor to post town men at the door of every home and store to prevent any further looting. What might have followed could have been the mutiny of the Maryland troops, but around 5:00 p.m. a now heated argument between McCausland and Johnson was interrupted by firing.

Averell had made contact with McCausland's rear guard on the high pine hills northeast of the town. While the main Confederate column mounted up and headed west toward Cumberland, Gilmor's Marylanders and other elements of Johnson's brigade served as a rear guard and battled Averell first on the hills, then in the streets of Hancock. An iron-clad train was brought up to support the Federal cavalry, fired two rounds, then was hit twice by counter

PORTION OF CHAMBERSBURG BURNED
DURING THE CONFEDERATE RAID
LED BY JOHN MCCAUSLAND,
JULY 30, 1864

Legend of Burning

1. Court House (3-story brick)
2. Mansion House
   Reformed Publication House (Etter & Hamilton)
3. John Jeffries (2 story stone & brick)
4. Hiram White building (new 3-story brick)
5. A. J. White (2-story stone & brick)
6. Gilmore Building
7. Chambersburg Bank (2-story brick)
8. Franklin Hotel (C. M. Duncan)
   (3 story brick Arcade)
9. John Noel's Building
10. R. Austin (2-story brick)
11. James Watson (2-story brick)
12. A. J. Miller (2-story stone)
13. Jacob Hoke & Co. (2-story brick)
14. Town Hall (3 story brick) (Franklin Hall)
15. Rosedale Seminary (3-story stone)
16. Judge George Chambers
    (office & residence)
17. C. Stouffer Machine Shop
18. M. P. Welsh (2-story brick)
19. J. Schofield
20. C. Flack
21. Allen Smith
22. Mrs. C. Snyder
23. W. G. Reed (2-story brick)
24. Benjamin Chambers
25. Benjamin Chambers
26. Col. A. K. McClure
27. Mrs. Geo. Goettman' Shop
28. A. S. Hull, (2-story brick)
29. A. P. Frey, Coachmaker Shop
30. Miss Susan B. Chambers' residence
31. Daniel Trostle (National Hotel)
32. Mrs. Montgomery's Hotel
33. Dr. Langenheim
34. P. Brough (3-story brick)
35. James King
36. S. M. Shillito
37. Lambert & Huber (4-story stone & frame paper mill)
38. Eyster (brick flouring mills)
39. Paper Mills & Brewery
40. Paper Mills & Brewery
41. John Miller, Hotel
42. Mrs. Jacob Smith
43. G. W. Brewer, brick building
44. Mrs. Joseph Chambers residence
45. Mrs. Radebaugh
46. D. Trostle. (2-story brick)
47. John McDowell
48. Samuel Brant
49. C. Stauth. 2, 2-story log
50. Mrs. Bard (row of law offices)
51. E. Culbertson (2-story brick)
52. C. M. Duncan (law offices, etc.)
53. Lyman Clark (2-story frame)
54. Mrs. Jordan
55. J. A. & J. C. Eyster
56. Martin Brown (frame & log)
57. J. W. Douglas
58. Jacob Sellers (2-story brick)
    stables, ice-house, hotel
59. James M. Brown
60. Wm. H. McDowell (2-story stone)
61. J. C. & R. Austin (2, 2-story brick)

62. Patrick Campbell's heirs
63. Jacob Wolfkill
64. Chambersburg Academy
65. Engine-House (2-story brick)
66. D. O. Gehr
67. Benjamin F. Nead
68. A. D. Caufman
69. Mrs. Goettman
70. Peiffer's Heirs (Old Jail)
71. T. B. Kennedy (Large 2-story brick)
72. Rev. B. S. Schneck (2-story stone)
73. L. Humelshine
74. S. Etter
75. Brank & Flack, (2-story stone & brick, ware-house)
76. Eyster & Bro. (3-story brick)
77. Eyster & Bro. (2-story brick & Stone)
78. James Eyster, (2-story brick)
79. Eyster (Nixon's Drug Store)
80. D. Reisher (2-story brick)
81. Wm. Wallace Hotel (3-story brick)
82. Mrs. R. Fisher
83. Dr. J. Lambert (2-story brick)
84. John P. Culbertson
85. I. Hutton (2-story brick)
86. M. Kuss, (2-story brick)
87. D. Reisher
88. H. H. Hutz
89. George Ludwig, Tin Shop
90. J. W. Taylor Hotel
91. David L. Taylor
92. Samuel M. Perry
93. John A. Lemaster
94. Miss Hetrick's Hat Shop
95. F. Spahr
96. Jacob B. Miller
97. Dr. Richards
98. C. Burkhart (3-story brick)
99. J. M. Cooper (3-story brick)
    "Valley Spirit"
100. James L. Black
101. Dr. J. Hamilton
102. John A. Grove - Shop
103. Jacob Hutton (3-story brick)
104. John McClintock
105. Lewis Shoemaker
106. Samuel Greenawalt
107. J. Allison Eyster
108. Wm. Heyser Heirs
109. Row of 2-story brick bldgs.
110. Aug. Duncan (3-story brick)
111. Edgetool Factory
112. Edw. Aughinbaugh
113. Dr. Wm H. Boyle
114. Mary Gillan (3-story brick)
115. T. J. Wright (3-story brick)
116. S. F. Greenawalt (2-story brick)
117. A. H. McCulloh
118. Rev. Mr. Nelson (2-story)
119. J. P. Culbertson (3 brick bldgs.)
120. W. F. Eyster & Bro. Foundry
121. Mrs. Riddle (2-story brick)
122. Mrs. Frederick Smith
123. J. Burkholder Heirs
124. Hunter Robison
125. Jacob B. Miller Hotel
126. All properties to Franklin Street burned

battery fire.

One Confederate ball went through the engine's firebox and another tipped its smoke stack. The engine was hurriedly reversed and steamed back toward Cumberland. Averell claimed in his official report that the Confederates suffered 15 killed and wounded at Hancock. He did not mention his own losses, nor do Confederate reports discuss casualties there. Gilmor himself was slightly wounded and was one of the last Southern horsemen to leave town.

Satisfied with driving the Rebels out of Hancock, Averill did not pursue. The nearly 20 mile chase from McConnellsburg to Hancock had cost him 300 horses that collapsed from exhaustion.

After an unsuccessful attempt to take Cumberland, McCausland withdrew to the presumed safety of the South Branch Valley of West Virginia.

Aftermath

As the fire died down at Chambersburg, the people who had sought refuge in the cemetery and surrounding fields filtered back to view the remains of the town. Some went into the countryside and neighboring towns to stay with friends or relatives. Others spent the night crowded into whatever buildings were left standing.

Around 550 structures had been destroyed. These included some 278 homes and businesses and 271 barns, stables, and other out buildings. This loss of real estate exceeded $783,000.00. Over 2,000 people were left homeless, and the entire inner core of the town had been leveled. Miraculously, only one fatality resulted from the terrible conflagration. Daniel Parker was a former slave who had, in his youth, traveled the "underground railroad' and settled in Chambersburg. Enfeebled by "age and infirmities," he was either impaired by the flames, overcome with smoke or so distraught at the destruction of his home that he died that evening.

McCausland's Raid of July 29 and Early's movement across the Potomac on August 5 created anxiety throughout the Cumberland Valley that resulted in a tremendous refugee problem. People as far north as Carlisle were packing up and leaving. Although the Cumberland Valley Railroad offered free rail service following the burning of Chambersburg, this, in some ways, exacerbated the situation. Harrisburg was reported to be filled with people who had fled the Rebel threat. Many of them were blacks quartered at the train depot.

Although civilian life had been greatly disrupted in and around Chambersburg, the military situation had improved. Recruiting was reported to be up all across the state. Confederate operations had spurred extensive construction of defensive positions, not only in Harrisburg but as far west as the Pittsburgh area, where rumors of a possible raid lingered. Probably the most significant military movement in the Cumberland Valley was the return of the Susquehanna Department's Signal Corps detachment on August 10. Signal stations were erected near Greencastle, Mercersburg, Hancock and Williamsport. These stations covered area that McCausland's raiders had traveled and provided an early warning system for the valley.

More significantly, McCausland's Raid forced U. S. Grant to finally bring all Union forces in the area under one unified command. That command was given to the competent and aggressive Phil Sheridan. The promotion of Sheridan to command Union efforts in the Valley sealed the fate of Jubal Early and his little army. Fighting overwhelming odds, Early was successively defeated at Fisher's Hill, Third Winchester and Cedar Creek. On March 2,

1865, Early and the remnants of his Valley army, now numbering fewer than 2,000 men, tried to retreat but to no avail. More than 1,600 Confederates were captured along with nearly 200 wagons, 14 cannons and 17 flags.

With this defeat, there was a loud outcry in the South for Early's removal to which Lee was forced to yield. With the news of Appomattox and of parties of Federal soldiers searching for him, "Old Jube" decided Virginia was not a safe place any longer. Accordingly, the general traveled to the Trans-Mississippi Theater with hopes of joining Kirby Smith's Confederates who had not yet surrendered. On route, Early learned of that commander's capitulation and moved on to Galveston, Texas.

From there he boarded a steamer, ending up in Cuba. From Havana he sailed to Mexico with hopes of joining Maximillian's army. Dur-

Brigadier General William Averell . . . While Chambersburg was burning, his cavalry division was camped just nine miles south. On Aug. 7, 1864, he caught up with the raiders in Moorefield, W. Va. There the Confederates were routed with heavy losses. Chambersburg was avenged.

ing this period, Early spent his time writing his memoirs of the Shenandoah Valley campaign. After three months, "Old Jube" saw that the French intervention was not supported by the Mexican people and was doomed to failure. He, therefore, moved to Canada. There he joined John C. Breckenridge and other former Confederate leaders who had fled the country.

General John McCausland would command Confederate cavalry until Lee's surrender at Appomattox after which he would return home, his only desire being to lead a peaceful life. Soon, however, the officer who had ordered the burning of Chambersburg found he was a wanted man. In June 1865, the U. S. War Department issued the following directive to Major General Winfield Hancock, who then commanded the Middle Department: "The President directs that you cause the rebel General McCausland to be arrested and held until application is made for his person by the civil authorities of Pennsylvania. . ."

Following the example of his old commander, General Early, McCausland fled the country first to Canada, then to England and Scotland to visit relatives. After a short time he went to France. While there, he joined the French Foreign Legion and served with it in Mexico. McCausland even remained south of the border after Maxmillian's fall.

Like most Confederates who went into exile, McCausland soon longed to return to the States. Even though indictments had been issued for his arrest in Franklin County, Pennsylvania, he had one ace in the hole. According to one interview, Grant, prior to the war, had been his neighbor in St. Louis, and several accounts suggest this resulted in the quashing of the indictments and led to assurances that if McCausland returned, he would not be molested. McCausland returned in 1867 and settled in Mason County. His estate covered several thousand acres in the Kanawha Valley. In 1878, he married Charlotte Hannah, a union which produced four children.

> By now, Averell was in full charge, rolling back the Confederates pell mell in the fog of the morning into and across the river.

For most of the remainder of his life, McCausland lived an almost reclusive existence at the fortress-like residence he named "Pliny." Although rarely leaving his farm, he did attend one Confederate reunion in Richmond and ironically wrote his own account of the burning of Chambersburg for the *Philadelphia Times*. The newspaper was owned by Alexander McClure.

"Tiger" John, like "Old Jube," remained an unreconstructed rebel and never regretted his part in the Chambersburg affair. As he told one interviewer, "I don't feel that I did anything to disgrace the uniform. If I had do you suppose Lee would have let it go unreprimanded?" Another time he was heard to exclaim proudly, "By Jesus Christ I burned her to the ground!" in reference to Chambersburg.

McCausland survived all the other major figures in the Chambersburg raid. He died at his home on January 23, 1927, at the age of 90. He holds the distinction of being the next to the last Confederate general to die. Brigadier General Felix Robertson of Texas was the last. Even in death, McCausland could not escape the bitter feelings that existed 65 years after the war. Some obituaries in Northern publications referred to him as the "Hun of Chambersburg."

Where was Averell?

While McCausland's force headed for Chambersburg, "Old Jube" sent other columns out to divert attention from the raid. Confederate strikes were made toward Harpers Ferry, Shepherdstown, Williamsport and Hagerstown.

At Hagerstown, on July 29, the Union cavalry division of General William Averell fought Confederate cavalry in the streets. After several hours of fighting, Averell withdrew his men north across the state line. Around 8 p.m. they set up camp north of Greencastle on the Fleming farm. This was the scene of the skirmish in the year before where Captain Boyd's 1st New York Lincoln Cavalry was ambushed and Corporal Rihl met his death.

Averell and some of his staff ate supper with the Fleming family. Afterwards the general laid down in the front yard to rest. A controversial aspect of the Chambersburg Raid was Averell's response or perceived failure to respond. Throughout the day and night of the 29th and early on the 30th, Couch and Averell communicated over the telegraph. Couch's last messages to Averell read: The enemy are just at the edge of town. Let me know what you intend doing"; and "The enemy are advancing down Loudon pike. Let me know what you intend doing. I will endeavor to hold the town until daylight."

Thomas Bard, an official of Cumberland Valley Railroad, fled to Hagerstown on a handcar when the Rebels took Greencastle. Bard was in the town's telegraph office and saw Couch's messages going unanswered. Bard then sought Averell, finally finding him asleep. Some two decades later Bard recalled the incident and described Averell as unresponsive and unconcerned. Jacob Hoke reinforced Bard's feelings, with the implications being that Averell was drunk. Hoke's reactions are understandable, given that he was one of the many merchants victimized by the burning.

H.R. Fetterhoff, the Greencastle telegraph operator, stated that Averell kept in touch with his office throughout the evening of the 29th, and said communcations ceased on the 30th. Greencastle newspaper editor, William Reid, recalled 20 years later, that William Fleming informed him that Averell and his troops were up by 3 a.m. and that the commander was viewing a map in the Fleming hallway. Reid remembered that Fleming said Averell expected the Confederates to leave Chambersburg on the Gettysburg Turnpike. He and his troops were also seen around New Franklin on the morning of the 30th.

When Averell headquartered at Greencastle late on the 29th, he contacted Couch. He reported of Confederate troop movements and asked of similar information from Couch concerning Federal troops. By about 10:30 p.m., Averell probably knew the occupation of Mercersburg. Averell then reportedly laid down to rest.

Thus, it is reasonable to assume Averell knew Chambersburg was at risk from troops in Mercersburg as well as being threatened from Hagerstown. Yet, Averell telegraphed to Couch that he expected a Confederate retreat or movement on Bedford.

With that in mind, Averell is perhaps judged too harshly for not saving Chambersburg. He also assumed that any Confederate activity near Chambersburg, if history could be trusted, would continue to be a string of irritations. Averell then could intercept the raiders along an escape route on the Gettysburg Turnpike.

As Averell's "intercepting" column marched eastward through New Franklin, a resident recalls that "smoke and flames" clearly were evident in the direction of Chambersburg and many of Averell's men were upset at moving away from the action.

Chambersburg avenged: Moorefield

Averell had remained at Hancock following his engagement there with McCausland's rear guard on July 31. He listed several reasons for remaining there: Rebel raiders blocked the route to Cumberland; his mounts were weary; Hancock was the best location to move from if the raiders attempted a strike on Bedford or a movement south toward Winchester; and stragglers from McConnellsburg could easily be captured around Hancock as they fled south. The most logical of all those reasons was probably that his horses needed rest, since Averell's men had covered 1,400 miles in three months.

On August 3, General Alfred Duffie's brigade reported to Averell. Still fighting fatigue, Averell's men could only provide 1,300 men to resume a chase, so Averell took 500 men from Duffie. It included about 200 men from the 1st New York "Lincoln" Cavalry, 100 from the 22nd Pa. Cavalry, and more from other units.

The following day Averell crossed the Potomac in Hancock, moved through Berkeley Springs, West Virginia,

All of Averell's men had sabers and revolvers, usually the Colt Navy model. In addition, every regiment had the latest breechloading carbines such as Sharps, Smith and Burnside.

and continued to Springfield, but not before 100 mounts broke down. At Springfield, Averell learned that Rebel raiders were headed for Moorefield. On August 6, after receiving rations late the previous evening, Averell moved to Romney and then on to Moorefield. Meanwhile, a detachment, mostly from the 22nd Pa., was sent to block a retreat across the mountains east of Moorefield. Along the way, a dispatch was captured confirming that Moorefield was where the Rebels were headed.

Averell moved his troops within four miles of Moorefield, halted for the evening and planned an early attack on August 7. But Averell did not go undetected. By midnight of the 6th, McCausland was informed of a pursuing enemy force. By 3 a.m., his men were ordered to be ready for an attack.

At around 3 a.m., two Rebels were captured by men led by Averell himself, and then more than a dozen men under Captain T.R. Kerr of the 14th Pa. were sent to probe deeper into enemy lines. Kerr and his men easily captured several Rebels, but by then it was apparent to each side that no surpirse attacks could be launched.

At daybreak, Averell moved his men out, and some penetration into enemy lines was made easier by having the gray-colored "Jesse Scouts" under Kerr lead the way. Many of the 1st and 2nd Maryland were captured still asleep. When firing began, Harry Gilmor remembered, " I was roused by a shot in the direction of the 1st Maryland, and so near that I took it to be someone cleaning his pistol. Even a second shot hardly caused me to open my eyes, for our men had a bad way of firing whenever the fancy struck them."

By now, Averell was in full charge, rolling back the Confederates pell mell in the fog of the morning into and across the river. From time to time, short stands were made by pockets of Rebels, giving McCausland time to seek a better position. McCausland formed a line and wheeled the remaining cannons in place. Those cannon ripped the Union lines, fording the stream, and one Rebel recalled, "in five minutes the water was blue with floating corpses."

After three assaults, the 14th Pa. and the 1st and 3rd Virginia carried the ford, with cavalry crossing the steam above and below the main ford threatening the Rebel flanks. Downstream, some of the "Lincoln" cavalry and the 3rd W. Va. found themselves facing the brunt of McCausland's 1,000 men.

Though outnumbered, the Federal troops attacked and broke the Rebel line. The Rebels retreated hastily through Moorefield, much to the disgust of most of the townspeople who were Rebel sympathizers. Meanwhile, the 22nd Pa. was capturing Rebels and their horses eight miles east of Moorefield.

The engagement at Moorefield ranks with Trenton and San Jacinto among the most complete surprise attacks on a military force in the history of North American warfare. Averell reported taking 420 prisoners, including six field and staff and 32 company officers. Probably 150 Rebels were killed or wounded. In the days and weeks following the disaster at Moorefield, McCausland regrouped near Mt. Jackson. "Old Jube" wrote of Moorefield: "This affair had a very damaging effect upon my cavalry for the rest of the campaign."

Who or what was responsible for the Confederate rout at Moorefield? As is the case in most historical events, a multiplicity of factors, both objective and subjective, converged to bring about the defeat. The Federals were better trained for the kind of warfare on the flat lands around Moorefield.

All of Averell's men had sabers and revolvers, usually the Colt Navy model. In addition, every regiment had the latest breechloading carbines such as Sharps, Smith and

Burnside. The 1st New York, and 2nd and 3rd W. Va. had companies armed with the Spencer seven-shot repeaters. In contrast, the Rebels were basically mounted rifle units. Few riders had revolvers or sabers, and most had muzzleloading rifles, primarily the Enfield.

Union horsemen were trained and experienced in conventional mounted tactical situations. The 1st W.Va. had fought in the Gettysburg Campaign and the 3rd W. Va. had fought "Jeb" Stuart at Brandy Station. The 1st New York was the first volunteer cavalry regiment raised in the north and had experience in the Peninsula and Gettysburg campaigns. Except for the 1st Md., most Rebel troops lacked conventional combat experience.

Another reason for Rebel failure could be traced to command delinquencies. McCauland's communcations with his officers have been described as spotty. And McCausland's failure to take adequate measures to meet the Federal threat were inexcusable.

But how did a numerically inferior Union force, in enemy territory, roll back the Confederates? Commented McCausland, "They (his men) had the makings of fine soldiers . . . but they were undisciplined." Bradley Johnson recalled, "I had about 800 half armed and badly disciplined mountaineers from southwest Virginia, who would fight like a veteran when they pleased, but had no idea of permitting their own sweet wills to be controlled by any orders."

Accounts by Union soldiers and citizens along the retreat trail from Pennsylvania to Moorefield bolster claims that not only were the Confederate troops undisciplined. Add to that the fatigue factor (the Rebels were in the saddle for more than a week during the raid in Chambersburg, and a month overall) and one could see that they were plainly exhausted at Moorefield.

Regardless of valor, any successful military venture requires competent organization, discipline, teamwork, and the firearms and equipment to make it work. The Confederates were clearly deficient on all those areas at Moorefield. They were fatally vulnerable to a major setback by the time they faced the well-equipped and efficient fighting force under Averell in early August, 1864.

BY M'CLURE & STONER.   CHAMBERSBURG, PA., THURSDAY, AUGUST 25, 1864.   VOL. 1.—NO. 3.

INCIDENTS OF THE BURNING

We find it impossible to make room for all the many touching incidents which occurred in the burning of the town. The house of Mr. James Watson — an old and feeble man of over eighty, was entered, and because his wife earnestly remonstrated against the burning they fired the room, hurled her into it and locked the door on the outside. Her daughters rescued her by bursting in the door before her clothing took fire. Mrs. Conner, the widow of a Union soldier, who has no means of support, got on her knees and begged to save her and her little one from the fury of rebel wrath; but while she was thus pleading for mercy, they fired her little home, and stole $10 from her — the only money she had in the world. Mr. Wolfkill, a very old citizen, and prostated by sickness so that he was unable to be out of bed, plead in vain to be spared a horrible death in the flames of his own house; but they laughed at his terror and fired the building. Through the superhuman efforts of some friends he was carried away safely. Mrs. Lindsey, a very feeble lady of nearly eighty, fainted when they fired her house, and was left by the fiends to be devoured in the flames; but fortunately a relative reached the house in time, and lifting her in a buggy in the stable pulled her away while the flames were kissing each other over their heads on the street. Mrs. Kuss, wife of the Jeweller on Main Street, lay dead; and although they were shown the dead body, they plied the torch and burned the house. Mrs. J.K. Shyrock was there with Mrs. Kuss' dying babe in her arms, and plead for the sake of the dead mother and dying child to spare that house, but it was unavailing. The body of Mrs. Kuss was hurriedly buried in the garden, and the work of destruction went on. The next day it was taken up and interred in the Catholic graveyard. When the flames drove Mrs. Shyrock out with the child, she went to one of the men and presenting the dying babe, asked — "Is this revenge sweet?" A tender chord was touched, and without speaking he burst into tears. He afterwards followed Mrs. Shyrock, and

asked whether he could do anything for her; but it was then too late. The babe had ceased to be motherless, for it shares a mother's sepulchre. The houses of Messrs. M'Lellan, Sharpe and Nixon were saved miraculously. They are located east of the railroad, and out of the business part of town. They were not reached until the rest of the town was in flames, and the roads were streaming with homeless women and children. Mr. M'Lellan's residence was the first one entered, and he was notified that the house must be burned. Mrs. M'Lellan immediately stepped into the door, and laying one hand on the rebel officer, and pointing with the other to the frantic fugitive women and children passing by, said to him — *"Sir, is not your vengeance glutted? We have a home and can get another; but can you spare no homes for those poor, helpless people and their children? When you and I and all of us shall meet before the Great Judge, can you justify this act?* He made no reply, but ordered his command away, and that part of town was saved. Mrs. Louis Shoemaker rushed up stairs when they fired her house to save some valuables, and returned with some silver spoons in her hand. She found the rebels quarreling over a valuable breast-pin of hers — several claiming it by right of discovery, and the dispute was ended, for the time at least, by one rudely taking the spoons from Mrs. Shoemaker and dividing them among the squad. Mrs. Denig escaped by wetting blankets and throwing them around her, thus enabling her to get out through the burning buildings in the rear of her house. The residence of Mrs. McElwaine was burned by a squad of rebels, who first demanded and procured their breakfast from him, because he was guilty of teaching colored children, and he was fired at as he made his escape. S.M. Royston, bar-keeper at Montgomery's Hotel, was robbed on his way down stairs of $700 — all the savings of his life. He was met by a squad of rebels, and dexterously relieved of his money and all valuables. Mr. Holmes Crawford was taken into an alley while his house was burning, and his pockets rifled. All he had about him was $1.60, and that was ap-

propriated. He was thus detained until it was impossible for him to get out by the street, and he had to take his feeble wife and sit in the rear of his lot until the buildings burned around him. Father M'Cullom, Catholic Priest of this place, was robbed of his watch. He was sitting on his porch, and a party of rebels came up and peremptorily demanded his watch, which he delivered. He was also robbed of his watch last year by Jenkins' men — the same command that burned Chambersburg. Col. Stumbaugh was arrested near his home early in the morning, and with pistol presented to his head ordered to procure some whisky. He refused, for the very good reason that he had none and could get none. He was released, but afterwards re-arrested by another squad, the officer naming him, and was insulted in every possible way. He informed the officer that he had been in the service, and that if Gen. Battles was present, they would not dare insult him. When asked why, he answered — "I captured him at Shiloh, and treated him like a soldier." A rebel Major present, who had been under Battles, upon inquiry, was satisfied that Col. Stumbaugh's statement was correct, ordered his prompt release, and withdrew the entire rebel force from that part of Second Street, and no buildings were burned. Col. Boyd's residence — "Federal Hill," was also put under guard, when Mrs. Boyd informed them who lived there. They had some recollections of Col. Boyd occasionally penetrating the Shenandoah Valley, at it was not deemed wholesome to burn his property. Mr. John Treher, of Loudon, was robbed by the rebels of $200 in gold and silver, and $100 in currency. The money was in a bureau drawer, but it was most dexterously appropriated by the scienced light-fingered gentry of M'Causland. The also stole all his liquors. Mr. D.R. Knight, an Artist, started out to the residence of Mr. McClure when he saw Norland on fire, and on his way he was robbed off all his money by a squad of rebels. He reached the house in time to aid in getting the women away. Rebel officers had begged of him before he started to get the women out of town as fast as possible, as many rebel soldiers were intoxicated and they feared the worst consequences.

BURNING OF NORLAND

Soon after the work of destruction had commenced, a squad was detailed to burn "Norland," the residence of A.K. M'Clure. It is situated a mile from the centre of town, and no other building was fired within a half mile of it, although fifty houses stand between it and the burnt portions of Chambersburg. The squad was commanded by Capt. Smith, son of Gov. Smith (Extra Billy) of Virginia, whose beautiful residence near Warrenton had ever been carefully guarded by Union troops when within our lines. The mother and sisters of the officer who fired "Norland" have lived in peace and safety in their home, under federal guards, since the war commenced. With the cry of "retaliation," Captain Smith proceeded to Mr. M'Clure's residence. Passing the beautiful mansion of Mr. Eyster, he supposed he reached the object of his vengeance, and he alighted and met Mr. Eyster at the door. "Col. M'Clure, I presume," said the chivalrous son of Virginia. "No sir — my name is Eyster," was the reply. Where is M'Clure's house?" was the next interrogatory. As the property was evidently doomed, and in sight, Mr. Eyster could only answer that it was further out the road, and the noble warrior passed on. He found Mrs. M'Clure quite ill — having been confined to her bed for ten days previous. He informed her that the house must be burned away by retaliation — for what particular wrong, he did not seem anxious to explain. He magnanimously stated that she should have ten minutes to get the family out of the house and away; and to prove his sincerity, he at once fired the house on each story. To convince Mrs. M'Clure that he was a chivalrous foe, he ordered her to open her Secretary while the house was in flames around her, and, evidently ambitious to show his literary taste, and acquirements he commenced to read her private letters. Mrs M'Clure informed him that he would doubtless be disappointed in her assortment of literature, as her husband had no papers of letters in the house; but as he seemed desirous to read something, she would commend to him a letter she had just received the day before from a rebel prisoner, invoking the blessing of Heaven upon her and hers for her kind ministrations to a foe. The writer had been here with Lee, in June, 1863, and was on guard at the house, and was of course treated kindly. The sick of the same command, as well as those of M'Causland's forces — then under Jenkins — were all humanely cared for by Mrs. M'Clure; and the author of that letter, having since been captured, and suffering from sickness and destruction, wrote her some time before stating his condition. That she had not turned a deaf ear even to a foe when suffering, is evidenced by the acknowledgement presented to Capt. Smith, which was a follows:

PRISONER'S CAMP,
PT. LOOKOUT, Md.,
July 20, 1864

Mrs. M.S. M'Clure.

Madam: — It is with feelings of intense gratitude I acknowledge the receipt of your letter under date of 21st June, enclosing — dollars. Words are inadequate to express my gratitude for so kind, so benevolent and unexpected a favor. I can only simply say — many thanks, and may God bless you. I have a mother and sisters; and your letter I shall retain and convey to them in order that they may see the christian kindness of one who is against us, and urge that they may emulate your example, and never be backward when an opportunity is offered in giving aid to a needy Federal soldier.

As it may be never in my power to reciprocate the favor received at your hands, my prayer is that God may reward you for it * * * With best wishes for your health and happiness, and trusting this dark war cloud may soon be dispelled and peace and happiness and prosperity once again smile upon us,

I am Madam with much Respect
Your Obedient Servant
JAMES B. STAMP
Co, C, 9th Division

Such a letter was not just the entertainment to which the imperious son of the South considered himself invited. Instead of retaliating for wrongs done, he found himself about to apply the torch where friend and foe had found solace in distress — even his own men having been mercifully ministered to there by the one over whose aching head and enfeebled limbs he was inviting the fury of the flames. He read the letter and answered — *"This is awful — it is awful to burn this house."* — and in vindication of his contrition, he left Mrs. M'Clure to escape from the fire while he proceeded to the adjoining room and, in a fit of remorse, stole M'Clure's gold watch and other articles of value which might adorn the elegant mansion of the Governor of Virginia at Warrenton. Fortunately Mrs. M'Clure had some of her own clothing in a trunk, and one of the squad kindly aided her in getting it out of the house, and it was saved, but nothing belonging to Mr. M'Clure was allowed to be removed. Mrs. Rev. Niccolls, who had rushed to the house, was caught on the stairs with a coat on her arms, and it was rudely taken from her with the remark — "saving anything belonging to *him* is expressly forbidden." In five minutes the house was inveloped in flames, and Mrs. McClure, and the other members of the family at home, started on foot, in the heat of the day, to escape the vengeance of the chivalry. The torch was thrust into the large, well-filled barn, and in half an hour a few charred walls was all that remained of "Norland." Capt. Smith could conceal the watch and other articles he purloined at "Norland" as trophies of his valor, but the silver pitcher was unwieldy, and could not be secreted from profane eyes as he rode back through town from the scene of his triumph. He resolved therefore to give a public display of his generosity. He stopped at Rev. Mr. Kennedy's, and handed the pitcher to his wife, with the request-"please deliver this to Mrs. Col. McClure with the compliments of Capt. Smith." The goblets were strapped to the saddle of one of his squad, and the watch could be pocketed to prevent the tell-tale qualities of the pitcher, and they were borne off to the land of heroic warriors and noble blood. The watch stolen by Capt. Smith was presented to Mr. McClure by some friends as a testimonial for his services as Chairman of the State Committee in 1860; bears as engraving to that effect, and is worth $500.

CORRECTION

The following card explains itself fully:

To the Editor of the New York Times:

Your correspondent writing from the southern border of Pennsylvania, says in the *Times* of the 4th inst:

"I was informed by a gentleman on the train that Col. McClure paid $5,000 as a ransom for his threatened property, and after all the scoundrels set the torch to his house, and it now stands a smoking ruin."

The foregoing statement has not the shadow of truth. I paid no sum of money to ransom my property, nor did any one for me; and although my loss is scarcely less than $50,000, not one dollar of tribute would have been paid to barbarous freebooters to save it. I was not present, but no member of my family would have entertained a proposition of any kind to ransom anything belonging to them or me.

A.D. McClure.
Chambersburg, Friday, Aug. 5, 1864.

CAPT. SMITH'S IDENTITY.

Capt. Smith, the worthy son of a noble Virginia sire, now Governor of what treason has left of the Old Dominion, gave his home and parentage at "Norland," and also at Rev. James F. Kennedy's. It seems that the residences of ministers were not to be burned, and he gave the following order to Mr. Kennedy:

Chambersburg, July 30, 1864.

Rev. James F. Kennedy's house is not to be burned-positively prohibited. By order of Brig. Gen. M'Causland.

F.W. Smith, A. A. D. C.

The order was hastily written with lead pencil, but in a very legible hand, while he was delivering Mrs. M'Clure's pitcher to Mrs. Kennedy, and declaring by way of justification of his conduct, that his father's house had been burned by our troops-a statement he knew to be false.

HUMANE REBEL OFFICERS.

Fiendish and relentless as were

M'Causland and most of his command, there were notable exceptions who bravely maintained the humanities of war in the midst of the infuriated free-booters who were plying the torch and securing plunder. Surgeon Budd was conversing with several citizens when the demand for tribute was made, and he assured all present that the rebel commander would not burn Chambersburg. In the midst of his assurances, the flames burst forth almost simultaneously in every part of the town. When he saw the fire break out, he wept like a child, and publicly denounced the atrocities of his commander. He took no part in it whatever, save to aid some unfortunate ones in escaping from the flames. Capt. Baxter, formerly of Baltimore, peremptorily refused to participate in the burning; but aised many people to get some clothing and other articles out of the houses. He asked a citizen as special favor to write to his friends in Baltimore and acquit him of the hellish work. Surgeon Richardson, another Baltimorean, gave his horse to a lady to get some articles out of the burning town, and publicly deplored the sad work of M'Clausland. When asked who hes commanding officer was, he answered-"Madam, I am ashamed to say that Gen. M'Clausland is my commander!" Capt. Watts manfully saved all of Second street south of Queen, and with his command aided to arrest the flames. He said that he would lose his commission rather than burn out defenceless people, and other officers and a number of privates displayed every possibel evidence of their humanity. One whole company was kept by its Captain-name unknown-from burning and pillaging, and the South-eastern portion of Chambersburg stands today solely because an officer detailed there kept hes men employed in aiding people out of their burning houses, and did not apply the torch at all. After the rebels had left, the following note was received by Rev. S. J. Niccolls, Presbyterian Pastor, written on an envelope with a pencil:

Rev. Mr. Niccolls: Please write my father and give him my love. Tell him, too, as Mrs. Shoemaker will tell you, that I was most strenuously opposed to the burning of the town.   B.B. Blair,

Chaplain and son of Thos. P. Blair, Shippensburg, Pa.

That there was a most formidable opposition to burning the town in McCausland's command was manifested in various ways. In the morning before daylight, when McCausland was at Greenawalt's on the turnpike west of Chambersburg, a most boisterous council was held there at which there were earnest protests made to McCausland against burning anything but public property. McCausland was greatly incensed at some of his officers, and threatened them with most summary vengeance if they refused to obey orders. Many, however, did openly disobey, and went even so far as to give the utmost publicity to their disobedience.

Excerpt from a Philadelphia newspaper, The Sunday Record, in 1889

BORDER RAIDS RECALLED

MEASURES TO PREVENT SPECULATIONS ON CLAIMS.

How McCausland and Early Burned and Pillaged Chambersburg—Claims Still to be Deferred.

Chambersburg, Pa., April 27. - The Pennsylvania Border Raids Claim bill, now before Congress, and which provides for the payment of losses amounting to nearly $3,500,000, sustained by citizens of the border counties of this State from Union and Confederate troops during the rebellion, will hardly be considered at this session, but its friends are hopeful that the bill will pass at the next session of Congress.

The counties affected are those of Adams, Franklin, Cumberland, Bedford, Fulton, York and Somerset, and the total of the adjudicated claims amounts to $3,447,945.94. The people along the southern tier are very anxious for the bill to become a law. They say they are entitled to the money, and that the Government has been cruelly neglectful in keeping them out of it for the past twenty-five years.

Speaker Reed has requested the promoters of the measure not to call up the bill this session. The reason for this is explained in the extravagant appropriations that have already been made at the present session. The Congressional elections will be held next fall, and Speaker is anxious that the Republican majority shall make as good a showing as possible to the people of the country in the approaching campaign.

WHEN IT MAY BE PASSED

Attorney General Kirkpatrick, who has labored long and earnestly in behalf of the bill, says that the information he has leads him to believe that the bill will pass at the short session. However, there is sure to be a tremendous fight on the floor of the House over the bill.

Majority and minority reports have been submitted by the Committee on War Claims which had the bill under consideration. The Chairman of the committee, Ormsby B. Thomas, together with J.P. Dolliver, W.H. Gest and B. A. Enloe, has presented the minority report. Mr. Maish, of York county, who introduced the bill, is a member of the Committee on War Claims, and is the most active man on the committee in its favor.

A proviso has been attached to the bill as originally introduced which reads as follows:

"That where any claims embraced within this act have been assigned or transferred by the original claimants the assignee or prisent owner of the same shall receive no more than was actually paid therefor, and the remainder of such claims shall be paid to the original claimants or their heirs or legal representatives."

This was added with the hearty approval of the representatives of the State and the Border Claims Commission in order to prevent the certificates of the adjudicated claims being bought up by speculators.

STORIES OF SPECULATION

But even this proviso is thought in some quarters not strong enough to prevent speculation in the certificates, and stories are rife that this business has been attempted. However, the representatives of the State Border Claims Commission and the claimaints themselves indignantly stamp these stories as being utterly without foundation in fact. They say the certificates have never had any market value, and that the only cases where they have been transferred have occurred where a claimant has failed in business and the certificates have gone in with the assets at a nominal valuation. According to the proviso the present holders can receive only what has been paid for the certificates, and the remainder must either go to the original claimants or their heirs or legal representatives.

In view of the present status of the bill and the attention it is bound to attract throughout the whole country when it is discussed in Congress, a resume of the facts connected with the raids along Pennsylvania's border becomes of much interest. The counties that were invaded extend from Somerset on the west, to and including York county on the east, are included in the southern tier. They lie near the Potomac River, in some places probably not more than two miles distant. They are on the north side of what was known as Mason and Dixon's line in the olden time. Realizing that that section would be exposed during the war, the State took early steps to protect it, and as early as May, 1861, organized fifteen regiments, and these were known as the Pennsylvania Reserve Corps.

CALLED TO UNCLE SAM'S SERVICE

The exigencies of the National Government were such after the battle of Bull Run that the Government called upon the State for these troops, and they were turned over to the authorities at Washington. Again, in 1862, when General Lee first invaded Pennsylvania, during the Antietam campaign, the State organized twenty-seven or twenty-eight more regiments of militia, with the express understanding that they were not to be marched beyond the State line. But the National Government made another appeal for these troops and followed in the wake of the first fifteen regiments to the front.

Twenty-five more regiments organized in 1863, during General Lee's second invasion of Pennsylvania, and they were also turned over to the general direction of the United States. Finding that any force that Pennsylvania might organize for her own protection would be called upon by the Government, the State authorities turned their attention to re-enforcing the army of the United States, and allowing the General Government to take care of the Southern border. In addition to these troops Pennsylvania contributed 362,284 men under the several calls made upon her to the general armies of the Union.

It was in this way that the counties lying near or adjacent to the Potomac were left exposed to the marauding expeditions of Confederate troops with ferocious Southern brigadiers at their head. The first invasion occurred in 1862, when General Stuart penetrated quite a distance into the counties of Adams and Franklin. The region traversed by Stuart and those who led subsequent raids was one of the richest and most inviting portions of the State, and the trend of the valleys leading into the State from Northern Virginia was such as to afford easy access and open avenues for retreat.

WHOLESALE PLUNDER

Stuart took out of Franklin county alone 1500 horses, and the other losses he inflicted in that county by burning buildings and otherwise destroying property amounted to $120,000. They plundered what they found of supplies and committed other depredations. The rebels went out of the State by crossing the South Mountain, and thus reaching the Potomac below Harpers Ferry. Governor Curtin called into service the Anderson Cavalry, then encamped at Carlisle, and two companies of regulars at the barracks at that place. Major General Wood took command of these

forces, but the rebels marched with so much celerity that they escaped without being overtaken by Wood.

In a message to the Legislature of 1863 Governor Curtin recommended that application be made to Congress for an appropriation to compensate our citizens for the damages which they suffered by the raid.

In the summer of 1863 occurred the great invasion of General Lee at the head of oner 70,000 men, which culminated in his defeat at Gettysburg and his retreat across the Potomac. Much damage was done by these troops, as they confiscated everything that was useful to them. The claims for damages in Adams county by reason of this invasion amount to nearly $500,000.

But the crisis of misfortune came when Generals McCausland and Johnson, at the head of 3000 rebel cavalry, dashed across the border and into Chambersburg, the county-seat of Franklin county, on July 30, 1864, and burnt the town, causing a loss of over $1,600,000. The incidents connected with this calamity make a terrible story.

OVER THE RIVER TO TOWN

The rebel brigades of Johnson and McCausland crossed the Potomac at Clear Spring Ford at 10 o'clock on the morning of July 29, 1964. The head of this column reached just outside of Chambersburg at 8 o'clock on the morning of July 30. The citizens planted three guns on a hill near the entrance of the town, but this availed them only to check the rebels until daylight. Then some 800 penetrated the outskirts, their skirmishers simultaneously investing every street and alley, gradually moving forward, and then halting until the signal or forward command was again given.

The people were fully aware of their peril, and even at that early hour, 6 o'clock in the morning, the main street was filled with them. General McCausland lost no time in summoning the principal citizens together, with the view of levying tribute. The Court House bell was rung for this purpose, and when they had gathered McCausland presented a written order from General Jubal Early, directing the command to demand a tribute of $100,000 in gold or $500,000 in Northern currency, and on failure to secure this sum to proceed to burn the town at once.

The citizens hardly believed that McCausland would carry out his threat. It was felt that the most they would do would be to pillage the place. They little feared that their homes would be reduced to ashes within a few hours. The citizens replied that they were neither willing nor able to pay the sum demanded.

Instantly orders were given to fire

the town. The rebels entered a paint shop across the street from the Court House, seized two barrels of turpentine, rolled them into the Court House, knocked in the heads and applied a match. The building was roaring in flames in a few minutes. Every store in the business section was entered and fired.

The soldiers moved about in squads. They went about their work of destruction like demons eager for the fray. From the stores they moved on to the private swellings. General McCausland entered the drug store of J.S. Nixon and demanded to know if there was any inflammable material to be had to hasten the work of demolition. Mr. Nixon's store was next set on fire, and together with all its contents was completely destroyed, causing a loss of $7000.

HOW IT STRUCK COLONEL M'CLURE

The Chambersburg *Repository*, then edited by Colonel A. K. McClure, who lost heavily by the conflagration, thus describes the scene at that time: "The main part of the town was enveloped in flames in ten minutes. No time was given to remove women or children, the sick or even the dead. No notice of the kind was communicated to anyone; but the work of destruction was at once commenced. They divided into squads and fired every other house, and often every house, if there was any prospect of plunder. They would beat in the door with iron bars or heavy planks, smash up furniture with an ax, throw fluid or oil upon it and ply the match. They almost invariably entered every room of each house, rifled the drawers of every bureau, appropriated money, jewelry, watches and other valuables, and often would present pistols to the heads of inmates, men and women, and demand money or their lives.... Many families had the utmost difficulty to get themselves and children out in time, and not one-half had so much as a change of clothing with them. Thus the work of desolation continued for two hours; more than half the town was set on fire at once, and the wild glare of the flames, the shrieks of women and children, and often louder than all, the terrible blasphemy of the rebels, conspired to present such a scene of horror as has never been witnessed by the present generation."

HIS OFFICE AND HIS HOUSE.

Not content with burning Colonel McClure's printing establishment in the town of Chambersburg, a squad of soldiers marched out of the town, a distance of over a mile, and burnt down the Colonel's beartiful residence, causing a loss of over $26,000.

McCausland and his men remained in Chambersburg until 11 o'clock that morning, when they heard that some Union troops were pushing on to Chambersburg to punish the rebels for their work. They lost no time in beating a retreat. General Averill, with a small force, pursued and overtook them at McConnellsburg, in Fulton county, in time to save that place from pillage and destruction. He promptly engaged and defeated them, driving them to Hancock and across the Potomac. The total number of buildings burned in Chambersburg was 559, divided as follows: Residences and places of business, 278; barns and stables, 98, and outbuildings of various kinds,173. There was $912,177 worth of personal property and $713,258.50 worth of real estate destroyed in Chambersburg, making a total of $1,626,435.

The condition of the people of Chambersburg was so deplorable that the State made an appropriation of $100,000 to relieve immediate distress there. This was a gift on the part of the Commonwealth. Subsequently $800,000 additional was among the sufferers. This appropriation was made with the understanding that when the United States advanced money to cover these losses that this sum should be deducted from the claimants and covered into the State Treasury.

After the war Commissioners were appointed in the border counties to adjudicate all claims for losses sustained in these raids. It is claimed that every effort was made to mimimize these losses as far as possible. All the records are now on file in the Auditor General's Office at Harrisburg.

There is still lying among the dust-covered records of the District Attorney's office of Franklin county a document which recalls in a strange way the story of Chambersburg's baptism of fire. Public feeling was so intense against McCausland that when the Grand Jury of Franklin county assembled after the fire one of their first acts was to return a true bill of indictment against General McCausland for arson. If they could have gotten McCausland in their grasp at that time they would have made things hot for him.

EARLY OFFERED 75 PER CENT

Congressman Levi Maish, of York, tells an equally amusing story in connection with these raids. The rebels once invaded Carlisle and demanded $100,000 ransom to save that town from being burned. The citizens made up a big pot of money, and the deficit was supplied in the shape of notes of business men who agreed to pay the sums named therein when peace should be declared. These notes afterward got into the possession of General Early, who had directed the raid. Meeting Maish in Washington some years after the war, Early said:

"Mr. Maish, I have a little business that I would like you to transact for me in your section of Pennsylvania?"

"All right; what can I do for you?"

responded Maish.

"I have some business paper I would like to collect, and if you get the money I will allow you 75 cents on the dollar." Here he drew forth a fat wallet, and from its inner recesses pulled forth the notes that had been given by Carlisle's business men to save their homes from destruction. Maish looked them over, and returning them to Earley, admitted that all the Sheriffs in the United States would not be able to collect one penny on the notes. Early thought it was a good joke, and walked off with a grin that spread all over his face.

THE TWO CONFLICTING REPORTS

The majority report of the Committee on War Claims recommends the passage of the bill as an act of simple justice to the citizens of a State whose militia, though raised for the defense of the State only, was called away by the President, and is entitled to whatever benefit and indemnity results from the constitutional covenant which guarantees to the States "protection against invasion."

The minority report contains some stunning figures of the cost, as an argument agaisnt the passage of the bill. It says that if these claims are paid Congress will quickly be asked to pay like damages sustained in the boarder loyal States, which would amount to about $500,000,000. "But this is not all," says the report.

"If loyal men in loyal States are to be paid for the damage caused by the ravages of war, loyal men in former disloyal States certainly have as good, or even better, claim for lide compensation. Taking the same basis of losses for all the States as first above indicated, and the amount rises to something beyond any accurate computation, but it will probably not be less than $1,000,000,000, and, indeed, this may increase to proportions which equal the entire cost of the war of the rebellion.

"The conclusion of the minority of the committee is that there is no rule of law under the Constitution or otherwise which requires the Government to pay this claim. By the passage of this bill the door will be opened to and the precedent set for the satisfaction of what is strictly known as 'ravages of war,' not only destruction of property by the forces of the United States, but also by the enemy. There is no possible means of stating or calculating the amounts which will be required to pay such losses, but there is no doubt that the same will be so great as to make it burdensome to the people of the country."

(The following excerpt is from *Four Years in the Saddle*, the memoirs of Major Harry Gilmor.)

When the town was no longer tenable, I took two men with me to fire a fine brick dwelling beautifully situated on an eminence northwest of the town. Dismounting, I went in, and told the lady who came to the door that I was there to perform the extremely unpleasant duty of burning her house, which I much regretted; that we were obliged to resort to such extreme measures in order to prevent or check the terrible devastation committed by such men as General Hunter. I told her that the people of that town had seen us twice before, and that all had spoken in the highest terms of our behavior, saying that our soldiers had behaved better than their own. She was weeping, evidently much distressed, but she acknowledged the justice of my remarks, and declared that she blamed none but the administration for allowing such horrible acts of cruelty to go unpunished. She was in deep distress, and shed many bitter tears; did not beg me to spare her house; only asked time to remove some articles of value and clothing. This was readily granted. Breakfast was on the table, and she asked me to eat something while she was getting her things together. Being hungry, I accepted the invitation, and drank a glass of wine before sitting down. I delayed as much as possible, in order to afford her more time, and when I rose from the table I had half a mind to disobey orders in regard to this house. She then came in, and entered into conversation. I asked her the name of her husband. She replied, "Colonel Boyd, of the Union Army." "What! Colonel Boyd, of the 1st New York Cavalry?" "The same, sir." "Then, madam, your house shall not be destroyed."

I now understood why she had not pleaded for it. The reader will recollect that this officer has been already mentioned as operating in the Valley. He had ever been kind and lenient to the citizens, men, women, and children, warring only against men in arms. The fact of her being the wife of Colonel Boyd decided me at once. I told her that I knew her husband, and had fought against him for two years

Legislators Visit Ruins Of Burned Chambersburg

CHAMBERSBURG, PA., Aug. 11 — Pennsylvania legislators from Harrisburg and the President of the Cumberland Valley Railroad arrived here at 10:30 a.m. today to view the ruins of the town, which was burned last month by Rebel troops from the command of Maj. Gen. Jubal A. Early.

A committee of citizens escorted the lawmakers through the downtown area, where all the buildings, both private and public, had been destroyed.

"The order of the invaders had been to spare the churches," the *Washington Evening Star* said, "and none of these was destroyed, except those in close proximity to residences. The fact that a Catholic church joined the depot was the means of saving the latter structure.

"The total loss to Chambersburg will be $3,000,000," the *Star* said.

"The records of the court were nearly all preserved, and are now being arranged in a new structure.

"The people of Chambersburg are now returning, and commencing to rebuild their dwellings. All are well supplied with the necessaries of life."

The *Frederick Examiner* yesterday printed an editorial that labeled the leader of the Rebels, Brig. Gen. John McCausland, "an uncivilized ruffian" and said his men were "despicable robbers and thieves."

"The scene that followed the turning loose of these hell-bound specimens of humanity can be more easily imagined than described," the Frederick paper said.

"Amid the crackling flames, crashing walls, falling timbers and screaming women and children, the sight presented was terrific and appalling in the extreme. The conflagration is described by eye witnesses as being horrible beyond conception.

"If anything can swell the list of crimes committed by these drunken vagabonds and scoundrels since the inception of the rebellion, surely the huge monument of ashes now in the Cumberland Valley will add ineffaceable infamy to the black hue of their guilt as thieves and traitors.

"At the present period of civilization and enlightenment, respect for private property has been the boast; it was thought that the savage customs of heathen nations had yielded to the mild and more humane usages of modern warfare. But in Chambersburg, the passions of the untutored savage most forcibly exhibited; the torch was applied indiscriminately, without notice and without warning.

"Squads of infuriated inebriates, incited by their leaders, proceeded from house to house plundering and burning.

"The aged and decrepit, helpless women and children alike with the young and strong, were ruthlessly expelled from their homes, with barely clothing enough to screen their persons.

"When such examples of cruelty as characterized the burning of Chambersburg by the Rebel forces are forced upon a reflective mind, it is hard to conceive how any other than the armed traitors themselves could have the audacity to offer anything in extenuation of such gross irregularities of conduct. Yet, strange to say, and we blush to own it, with the tales of fiendishness still fresh in our ears, and the smoke of ruin still hanging in clouds over hundreds of desolated homes, we have in our very midst, under the protection of the Government, in full possession of the immunities and privileges of society, men and women who insult loyal Marylanders by seeking to justify and palliate the shocking outrages that sicken us as we record them.

"When approached upon the subject, they flippantly allege that Gen. Hunter committed many excesses in Virginia, that the Union forces destroyed a great deal of Rebel property, and wind up with the insolent declaration that the burning of Chambersburg was nothing more than a bit of retaliation.

"The man who shall attempt to justify the destruction of Chambersburg on any score whatever, should be kicked beyond the lines without a moment's delay."

Several days ago citizens of Baltimore met to organize a relief committee for the stricken city.

The committee was assigned to collect food, clothing and other contributions for the people of Chambersburg. More than $1,000 was collected at the initial meeting of the relief group.

Other cities in Maryland and Pennsylvania are organizing relief committees to aid the residents of the burned town.

An unidentified Chambersburg newspaper account, circa 1864.

in the Valley of Virginia; that he had gained a high reputation among the citizens for kindness and gentlemanly conduct; that while we were there for the purpose of punishing Vandalism, we were ready and anxious to repay acts of kindness done to our people, who, when unprotected, had been exposed by the fortunes of war to the mercy or harsh treatment of our foes. I told her that her house should not be burned, blame me for it who would, and that I would leave a guard for her protection till all were gone. She seemed to be completely overwhelmed, as though she did not comprehend what I had said; but when I assured her again that neither her house nor anything that belonged to her should be molested, her gratitude knew no bounds. To the picket near by the house she afterward sent baskets filled with nice eatables, hot coffee, and as much wine as they desired.

I left a guard; and well I did, for an officer who had been drinking too much came up soon after, and tried to force the guard and burn the house.

CHAPTER 7

The Post War Years

As veterans of the Union armies returned to their homes, their immediate concern was to get back to their former jobs or to find employment in other places. Those whose homes were in cities and the larger communities, learned that the wartime economy they had left had collapsed, and that there was widespread unemployment through most of the North.

Although written before the war had ended, Stephen Foster's plaintive song, "Hard Times Come Again No More," could have been an anthem for the poverty thousands of families faced. It was in this post war depression that Horace Greeley gave his oft quoted advice. Contrary to the belief that to "go west" was his primary counsel, he actually said, "The best business you can get into, you will find on your father's farm or in his workshop. It you have no family or friends to aid you, and no prospect opened to you there, turn your face to the great West, and there build a home and a future."

Many, thousands actually, joined in the western movement to find employment on farms or in the plants engaged in making farm equipment or machines. Chicago and St. Louis also became centers for an ever expanding food market that dealt in beef, pork, and grain.

Some county people, often those who had suffered bankruptcy through loss of animals and the inability to farm their land after the invasion of 1863, did go to the West to join those who were taking advantage of the Homestead Act. A grant of 160 acres became theirs after occupying and cultivating land for a period of five years.

Looking up north Main Street, an early view (before 1876) of the square as it was rebuilt following the burning.

The Franklin County Courthouse less than ten years after the burning . . . the Lincoln Way East pillars and side entrance were eliminated in the reconstruction.

In Franklin County immediate employment could be found in Chambersburg as rebuilding the town continued after the McCausland Raid. A July 22, 1866 copy of a local paper, *The County Merchant,* revealed the remarkable pace with which the town was returning to normalcy. The Court House, although not yet completed, had been occupied for about eight months by county officers. The new town hall being rebuilt by the Repository Printing Company was yet to be finished, but was far enough along to be printing the town's leading journal, *The Franklin Repository.*

Houses and commercial buildings along the principal thoroughfares of Main and Market Streets and around the Square had either been replaced or were under construction. Evidence of a change in architecture could be seen by the appearance of more three-storied structures which were replacing the one and two tiered buildings of an earlier time. By the summer of 1866, the town's principal hostelries were back in business. These included the Union Hotel on South Main Street, the Washington House at the corner of Second and Market Streets, the National and Montgomery Hotels on North Main Street, and the Indian Queen, referred to as headquarters for the Dutch Settlement, on South Main Street. All of the hotels featured the latest in dining rooms, bars, and overnight facilities along with ample livery service.

There also arose, from the ashes of the 1864 fire, a new building for the Bank of Chambersburg, which became known as The National Bank of Chambersburg; the town's Academy for boys; an Opera House where the Rosedale Seminary for girls had stood; railroad shops and other buildings; numerous mills and factories; and several hundred homes, stables, and other outbuildings.

A listing in a Franklin County Atlas for the year 1868 shows that within the borough there were sixteen mills and industrial operations. Included among these were paper and strawboard mills (Strawboard was a forerunner of today's cardboard). Also, there were several

Peace

April 1865 brought joy and sorrow to both Chambersburg and the nation as people rejoiced over the Confederate surrender and mourned President Lincoln's death. The following updated items appeared in April 1865 issues of the Chambersburg *Valley Spirit*.

"Up With the Flag"

A beautiful Union pole surmounted by stars and stripes was erected in West Market Street, opposite the residence of John M. McDowell, on Friday last. As the flag was being run up and given to the breeze the huzzahing from the crowd that surrounded the pole made the welkin ring again. The pole was erected in honor of our recent great victories and fall of the Rebel capital.

"Rejoicing"

The news of Lee's surrender reached this place, by telegraph, on Sunday night between nine and ten o'clock. The whole community was at once thrown into a state of wild excitement, the like of which was never before witnessed here. Everyone left their beds and gathered on the streets. The bells were rung, guns, pistols and cannon fired and bonfires blazed at every corner. The excitement continued all night and increasing to a perfect panic about morning. The speech makers were called out and mounting the store boxes haranged the crowds in the most excited strains -- our friend of the Repository leading off in a blaze of glory. The rejoicing continued through the whole next day. The troops stationed here turned out and made a grand parade. The artillery company fired a salute of two hundred guns. We feel assured that no community exceeded ours in its demonstrations of joy over Grant's glorious victory.

"The Murder of the President"

The news of the murder of President Lincoln was received in this place on Saturday morning last and was so astounding as to seem almost incredible. The news spread with great rapidity causing universal gloom and sorrow. The chief burgess at once passed a recommendation that all business be suspended and that bells be tolled from 11:00 o'clock for the rest of the day. In the evening a meeting of citizens was held in the Methodist Church at which arrangements were made to give a fitting expression to the public servant at this great national calamity. The several chruches on the Sabbath were clothed in sable drapery and the services were of the most solemn and imposing character. All the sufferings of our citizens since the outbreaking of the rebellion are of nothing compared with this crushing affliction by which the whole nation suffers.

carriage shops, numerous harness and saddle operations, and woolen mills. Through the decade that followed, industrial expansion brought flouring mills, a planing mill and door factory, a furniture factory (said to be the largest in the Middle States), and an industry that still operates today - the T. B. Wood's Sons Company, maker of power transmission appliances. This company goes back to 1840 when it was established by William Gilman and Charles Eberley. The Wood's ownership came in 1872.

> **T. B. Wood's Sons Company goes back to 1840 when it was established by William Gilman and Charles Eberley.**

Industries of the post-war period were operated by water power from the Conococheague Creek or the Falling Spring Stream or by steam power, a source that permitted greater flexibility in locating plants for rail service or highway transportation.

This industrial growth of Chambersburg was matched in other parts of the county. The period also saw Waynesboro and Quincy develop as centers for producing steam engines, grain separaters, carriages, tools, and woolen goods. The mills or factories of the area were mainly powered by steam, yet water power continued to run the grist or flour mills and the wool factories.

Greencastle's economic life, at this time, was enhanced by factories producing farm related machines such as grain and fertilizer drills, hay rakes, and wagons. Steam power

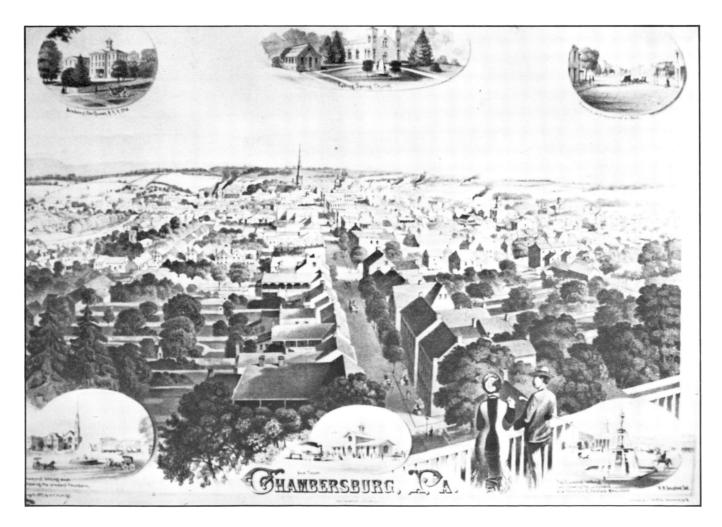

An 1876 lithograph panoramic view of Chambersburg just 12 years after the burning. Note the left corner inset rendering of the first fountain placed in the square of Chambersburg.

dominated the town's plants with the exception of a woolen mill powered by water from Moss Spring.

Mercersburg continued to be a market town while its industrial economy lay in the production of milling equipment, carriages and leather goods. A tannery that served the community through the war period continued to develop and eventually became the town's principal industry.

The Franklin County Courthouse (center) and the Repository Hall (left), as they looked approximately five years following the burning.

Perhaps the operation most essential to the economic needs of the entire county was the iron industry. Although iron furnaces and forges had been in the Path Valley region of the North Mountain since colonial times, the largest producer of iron was the Mont Alto Iron Company. Not only the industries of Franklin County but those in the southern parts of Pennsylvania and nearby Maryland were served by it through the Civil War years until its demise in the 1890's.

Supporting the county's industrial growth was the increase of financial institutions through the remainder of the post war years. The National Bank of Chambersburg, founded in 1809, continued to serve not only that community but many business and industrial operations throughout Franklin County. This began to change when, in 1865, another bank came into existence. This was the Franklin County Bank, later becoming the Chambersburg Deposit Bank in 1880. In 1863, Waynesboro's Savings Fund Society became the First National Bank, and twenty years later another Savings Fund Society came to the town. In Greencastle, the First National Bank was established in 1865, while the Mercersburg Farmers' Bank came into existence in 1874, establishing the financial foundations of the business, industrial, and agricultural prosperity that came to the county through the remaining years of the century.

Perhaps the operation most essential to the economic needs of the entire county was the iron industry.

By 1900, Chambersburg's major industries included the T. B. Wood's Sons, the Chambersburg Woolen Mill, the paper mill of earlier years, along with the Cumberland Valley Railroad shops and the numerous craft businesses, all of which were manufacturing operations that were part of the industrial scene during the war and the years following the war's end.

However, beyond these traditional firms several new enterprises had come into the corporate life of the community. One was the Wolf Company, which, in its beginning years, was the region's principal maker of flour mill machinery. By the close of the era, it was also producing machines for feed mills and food processing operations. The plant was located along the Conococheague Creek in the northeastern part of the town.

Another company, which was still part of the borough's industrial picture, was the Chambersburg Engineering Company located on lands along the southern edge of the town. Its roots lay in earlier operations of the Taylor Manufacturing Company, which began business in 1882 as producers of locomotives, stationary engines, sawmills, and general machine work. By the end of the century, it was a leading manufacturer of drop forging equipment and hydraulic machinery, and it accommodated customers throughout the nation and in Europe, South America, and the Far East. This was the last large industrial operation to come out of the post war era. It represented the transformation of the county seat's localized industrial economy into one that extended throughout the nation and markets of the world.

Farming

Throughout the county's pre-war period, farm life was dominated by families of German origin, who followed the widely accepted pattern of traditional farming that featured production of wheat and corn as the two principal crops and rye, oats, and barley as secondary grains. As they had done prior to the war, farm people continued to supply the cattle, sheep, and hogs for the county's meat suppliers, and they produced potatoes, eggs, butter, and cheese for town grocers or household customers.

Fresh farm produce found a ready market in most towns. Chambersburg's most elaborate outlet for this kind of merchandising was a borough hall with a market house located at the southeast intersection of Second and Queen Streets. This center was built in 1831. After the war, in 1874, minor alterations were made, and through the remainder of the century, it was said to be the marketing center of the valley. (Today's structure, with its clock tower, continues to serve the borough as its council hall, police headquarters, and municipal office building.)

Rural living patterns found little change through the remaining years of the century. Most farm families were large with all members, old enough to work, engaged in planting, cultivating, and harvesting crops and caring for the animals essential to successful rural living.

Beyond family workers, there were extra hands that came from a kind of bondage where children of poor families were bound over to farmers for a given period in return for payments to their parents, ranging from fifty cents to a dollar a week. Farm laborers from the villages or towns also worked for wages as low as fifty cents a day. Such practices continued until labor-saving machines came to agriculture in the late years of the 1800's and early decades of the twentieth century.

An 1870s view of Chambersburg's rebuilt South Main Street . . . Many of the beautiful buildings with unique architecture remain on South Main Street today.

Specialized agriculture such as orcharding, dairying, cattle raising, or chicken and egg production began developing in the late post war period to become a principal aspect of farming in the present century.

Prior to the Civil War, Franklin County had an Agriculture Society which sponsored annual Farm Fairs held in October. Although disrupted by the war, these fairs continued when peace came. Early fair grounds were located in the western end of town beyond the tollgate on the "south side of the pike." (This reference is to the Pittsburgh-Philadelphia Turnpike which not only led to markets in Philadelphia but to those in Baltimore.) Later years found the fairs being held on an eight- acre plot along the Conococheague Creek in the northwestern part of the town. The site was changed in 1882 when grounds, now occupied by the Chambersburg Engineering Company, were used. This area continued to be used until the annual event was moved to Red Bridge Park in the early years of the 20th century.

Rail Service

The county's growing economy of the post war era was due, in part, to the expansion of rail service. This began with the Cumberland Valley Railroad Company rebuilding the machine shop, round house, warehouse, and depot destroyed during the McCausland Raid. These improvements were accompanied by the construction of a new roadway from Harrisburg to Hagerstown. This included replacing old war-torn rails with new iron and steel ones laid upon a new bed of limestone ballast. Wooden bridges were replaced by iron structures while new depots were built in the line's major towns and stations at important rural points along the way.

Expansion of rail service was another part of the economic growth during this era. In 1871 the Southern Pennsylvania Railroad was built from Marion to Richmond Furnace to accommodate the agriculture and iron production of the western regions of the county. This was followed, a year later, by a line connecting Scotland to Mont Alto. This provided more efficient transportation for lumber companies and for grains from farms of the eastern part of the county. However, a major reason for this line came from the ever expanding production of the Mont Alto Iron Works. Later, in 1879, the line was extended to Waynesboro, a transportation boon to the industries of that community. These extensions were leased by the Cumberland Valley Company, and this network continued to be an important element in bringing greater economic stability to Chambersburg and the rural regions it served.

Expansion did not stop with extending service to parts of Franklin County. In 1873 a line known as the Martinsburg and Potomac Railroad was completed, and within a matter of weeks this line was leased by the Cumberland Valley Company. Then, in 1882, a Shenan-

Chambersburg, looking North on Main Street . . . Left of the Courthouse, the Repository Hall was removed; the Chambersburg Trust Building was erected in 1904. (The Eastern third of the Trust Building was erected first, then the Repository Building was torn down and the Trust Building construction completed.) The Chambersburg Trust Building remains standing.

A view of reconstructed Chambersburg looking East on Queen Street from South Main Street. The Market House cupola can be seen in the right background.

doah Valley line was opened from Hagerstown to a connection with the Norfolk and Western Railroad at Roanoke, Virginia.

In 1876 the Western Maryland Company brought rail service that connected Franklin County with parts of Maryland and even with Baltimore. Within ten years this proved to be one of the most valuable lines in the county. Through it and connecting lines to the south, Chambersburg and its surrounding area not only had access to the rich Shenandoah region but to southern markets as far away as Savannah and New Orleans.

Utilities

Perhaps the most far reaching development of the post war period, which touched the lives of those who lived through these years and the generations that followed, came with the advent of privately owned or public utilities. Although a private water system provided water through wooden pipes to customers as early as 1818 in Chambersburg, the town's first municipal system came in 1875 when a reservoir was built on the heights of the northwestern portion of the borough. However, by the end of the century, the county seat could boast of a system that furnished water from the mountain streams of the Caledonia region, which is the origin of the town's present day water supply.

Manufactured gas came to Chambersburg as early as 1856 when a generating facility was erected on the west bank of the creek opposite the Baptist Church on West Queen Street. This did not become a publicly owned operation until the middle of the present century, however.

Electricity came to town in 1889 when a steam plant began generating power for lighting the town's streets. In 1892 the first electricity for homes and for business and industry came. On into the new century, electric power continued to be produced by the borough until World War II, when the western portion of the town began using power furnished by the South Penn Company.

Telephone service came to Franklin County in 1883 when a line was erected to connect Hagerstown with Waynesboro. Chambersburg then became interested in phone service, and in 1890 the Franklin Electric Company, with headquarters in the county seat, was organized. Conflict with the Bell Company of Harrisburg, which held prior rights in this part of the state, eventually resulted in the formation of the Cumberland Valley Telephone in 1900. This occurred after the Bell Company's patents had expired.

All of these utilities, whose roots extended into the postwar years, became the basic foundation upon which modern living exists. Perhaps no other development from this era touches all who live today more than pure water, gas fuel, electricity, and the telephone. Only those who lived in the nineties or early years of the present century can fully understand the importance of this part of our heritage.

Fire Protection

Fire protection following the war became more mechanized as steam powered equipment became available. By 1885 the boroughs of the county had organized fire companies trained to use this new kind of equipment. These organizations replaced the earlier fire brigades that fought fires with only two basic tools, buckets and axes along with hand-powered pumping machines.

The coming of steam powered pumping engines and the advent of central water systems, which made possible fire hydrants placed along borough streets, brought better fire protection to all county towns.

Chambersburg, through the post war era, could boast of having the most and best equipped fire companies. When other boroughs could point to one or two companies,

Post war view (after 1869) of Chambersburg where burned ruins once stood. The rebuilt view now displays the steeple of Central Presbyterian Church (center) and to the right the cupola of the Franklin County Courthouse. McGrath's Hotel in the foreground was located at the corner of Second and Queen Streets where the Chamber of Commerce is now located.

the county seat had five such organizations. The Friendship Company had been organized in 1780, and during the post war era it could boast of having 100 members. The Hope Hose Company traced its beginning to 1830, and by 1870 it carried a membership of 50 firemen.

The years following the war witnessed the arrival of more fire fighting organizations. Two of these included the Junior Hose Company founded in 1869 and the Goodwill Hose Company founded in 1877.

By the end of the century, Waynesboro had two fire companies. The earliest, known as the Mechanics Steam Fire Engine and Hose Company, was established in 1879. It succeeded the town's very first fire fighting body, established in 1840, and was known as the Washington Engine Company. A later body of fire fighters, incorporated in 1882, is known today as the Always There Hook and Ladder Company.

Greencastle traces its present company, the Rescue Hose organization, established in 1896, to an earlier group, the American Steam Fire Engine Company, founded in 1884.

The earliest fire fighters in Mercersburg were organized into the Eclipse Fire Company in 1885 when a steam powered pumper was first used.

Such advances in fire fighting brought greater security to townspeople during the post war years. However, rural families continued to have only the devices their ancestors used - buckets, axes, and prayers for divine intervention.

A North Main Street view from the square prior to 1876 when the fountain was built.

Churches

Prior to the war, there were 54 church bodies in the county, and ten of these were in Chambersburg. Those in the county seat included the Falling Spring Presbyterians and those of German origin, the Lutherans and Reformeds. There were also the congregations whose roots lay in the early Mennonite doctrine, and these included the Brethren in Christ, the Church of the Brethren, the German Baptists as well as the United Brethren. In addition to these congregations, there were the followers of John Wesley known as the Methodists. Catholicism had come to the town following the American Revolution. Jewish families appeared on local records as early as 1837; however, there was no synagogue until after World War II. Negro families of Chambersburg worshipped in the Bethel African Methodist Church as early as 1812.

Most of the congregations throughout the rest of the county followed doctrinal or theological origins similar to those of the Chambersburg churches. However, there were several deviations from this pattern. There were the Covenentors, a fundamentalist group of Presbyterians, whose congregations came into being during the post-Revolutionary period. This group, however, had generally disappeared before the Civil War.

Another body of worshippers, numbering approximately 150 men, women, and children, was a group of apostate Mormons led by Sidney Rigdon, who founded a colony west of Greencastle in 1846 and left the area the following year. A small Episcopal congregation in the Mont Alto community erected a sanctuary in 1854. Its membership, however, declined through the post war years, and by the turn of the century, the congregation had disappeared. (The sanctuary still stands as one of the county's historic spots. Tradition holds that John Brown taught Sunday School there prior to the raid in Harpers Ferry.)

After the war there were no evident trends beyond those found in the older church bodies. Twenty-one new congregate bodies did come into the county after the war with nearly half of them in Antrim Township. They, however, appeared as new congregations who separated from their mother churches. Such a trend occurred in Chambersburg when second churches of the same denomination appeared. By the end of the century, the county seat had two congregations of Presbyterians, Methodists, United Brethrens, and African Methodists, along with those who remained as they were prior to the war.

Schools

The Chambersburg Academy

Early schools of Franklin County were privately owned and operated by individual teachers, churches, or corporate bodies. Representative of these was The Chambersburg Academy located on a site at the corner of East Queen and Third Streets. This distinguished institution was chartered by the state in 1797 although its seeds had been planted in the town as early as 1793 when James Ross, a teacher of languages at Dickinson College, established a school that later became the academy.

The building was destroyed during the McCausland Raid and was rebuilt in 1868, making it the leading preparatory school of south central Pennsylvania. This acad-

The King Street School, used as a hospital for the sick and wounded soldiers during the Civil War, was not burned by the Confederates in 1864. The building now gone was a landmark in the community for many generations.

emy served the youth of the area until the high school movement was well established by the end of the century. Because of declining enrollments, it was abandoned in 1908, and the grounds became the site of Chambersburg's first high school building.

Free Schools

The Free School Act of 1834 and subsequent strengthening of the law in 1836, gave cities, boroughs, and townships the right to establish schools supported by local taxation. Although districts were not compelled to create schools, most of Franklin County's municipalities, over the next three decades, voted to provide free elementary schooling for their children.

Public education was further strengthened by the Act of 1854 which established the office of county superintendent. This law made superintendents responsible for certifying teachers, administering a uniform curriculum, operating a school term of four months, and for working toward creating uniform text books. (At that time there was no free text book law.)

Although important strides were made in the county's schools under provisions of the 1854 law, the war interfered with some of its goals particularly in the area of teacher certifica-

Chambersburg's first public high school located on the northwest corner of Queen and Third Streets where the Central Center (formerly Central Junior High School) now stands.

tion and uniform text books. However, when peace came, greater enthusiasm for education came also. Through the remainder of the century, Franklin County's people saw improved school buildings, expanded school terms, improved teacher training, and the growth of secondary education.

Between 1870 and 1900, more one and two room rural school houses and graded multi-room buildings in towns and cities were built than ever before in the history of the Commonwealth. By 1885 the county had 290 classrooms, accommodating 12,716 children taught by 189 men and 107 women through a six month term. This record does not include the schools of Chambersburg. In 1884 its system withdrew from the county program and began operating as a separate district under the leadership of Superintendent W. H. Hockenberry.

By 1885, Chambersburg's schools had 1,200 children in 33 school rooms taught by 29

The Academy, as it was rebuilt after the Burning of Chambersburg. The building to the left was also part of the academy.

women and 4 men in four buildings. In 1857 the King Street School provided instruction to children at elementary, grammar and secondary levels.

The Washington Street Building, erected in 1877, had a similar curriculum. Two other schools also served the borough. One on West German (Liberty) Street, erected in 1874, housed colored children while the other on East German (Liberty) Street, built in 1885, accommodated students from that part of the borough. Beyond these schools, records indicate that a high school program for boys was started in 1851 on the second story of a building on West Catherine Street. It was known as the Carrstown School. The King Street School's secondary program, from 1859 to 1893, was for girls only. Available records show that a high school of a coed nature did not come into existence until a separate building was erected in 1908.

The Academy . . . the Franklin Railroad tracks on Third Street are in the foreground.

High school programs did not come to Waynesboro until 1870, to Greencastle until 1875, and to Mercersburg until 1878. The teaching of secondary subjects in these schools took place in buildings that also housed elementary and grammar school students. Separate high schools in these districts came later in the new century.

Higher Education

Although higher education had come to Franklin County as early as 1836 when Marshall College was established in Mercersburg and when the Reformed Theological Seminary was founded in 1837, both of these institutions played no role in the post war period. Marshall College had been transferred to Lancaster in 1853 when it became part of the institution known today as Franklin and Marshall College. Seventeen years later, the seminary was also transferred to the same city.

In 1865 the buildings of the seminary and college were brought into use again through the creation of Mercersburg College, which, in 1881, was forced to close for economic reasons. Within the year it was reopened, but by 1890 it had closed again, thus ending the history of higher education in Mercersburg.

In 1893, the Mercersburg Academy was established by Dr. William Mann Irvine. This institution continues today as one of the nation's leading preparatory schools.

Wilson College

Today's Wilson College had its origin when two Presbyterian ministers began a dialogue concerning higher education for women. The Reverend Tyson Edwards of Hagerstown and the Reverend James W. Wightman of Greencastle met in the manse of the Greencastle church to consider possibilities for organizing such a school. Tradition holds that Edwards was first

In 1893, the Mercersburg Academy was established by Dr. William Mann Irvine. This institution continues today as one of the nation's leading preparatory schools.

An 1890s view of local townsfolk at the Franklin Hotel, the current site of the Chamber of Commerce on the corner of Queen and Second Streets. Note the large wheel bicycle of the period on the side-walk.

interested in an institution for women patterned after the finishing school concept, popular at the time. Wightman was convinced that a college should be considered to "extend to young ladies the same high advantages for a thorough education as were available to young men." Eventually both agreed that they should seek support for a degree granting college.

In April 1868, plans for founding a college for women were submitted to the Carlisle Presbytery. Within a year the proposal was accepted, and on March 24, 1869, the state granted a charter which led to the formation of the college. Through a generous gift from Miss Sarah Wilson of the St. Thomas community, the farm lands of Alexander K. McClure, which lay along the northern edge of Chambersburg, were purchased. The palatial residence of the McClure family became the first building of Wilson College, named for the lady whose money made it possible.

An early 1900s view, from the fountain in the square, of the South Main Street of Chambersburg.

The opening of the college was immediate. In 1870, its initial term began on October 12 with a handful of students, and in 1873 its first commencement was held. There were five graduates. At that time, the founders served as administrative officers. Doctor Edwards was the president, and the Reverend Wightman was his vice president. Today Wilson College continues as one of the nation's few remaining colleges for women.

Normal School
The movement to improve public school teachers came through annual institutes held in

Two views of members of the Housum Post 309 at GAR Hall on West Queen Street. Reunions such as these continued into the early decades of the 20th century.

the county seat and summer schools held in various school houses. However, there still was a major need for an institution of higher education designed to train young people for teaching. Establishing such an institution in Chambersburg became the goal that County Superintendent Andrew McElwain pursued during his tenure as county superintendent from 1863 to 1866. This leader attempted to get a Normal School for the state's Seventh District placed in Chambersburg. It required local financing to supplement state monies. Unfortunately, the proposal came at a time when Chambersburg's finances were at their lowest point. There was interest but little money, and eventually the school was erected and went into operation in Shippensburg in 1873. Today that school is known as Shippensburg University, and it offers many types of degree programs other than those aimed at teacher certification.

The following letter written to the editor of the Chambersburg *Public Opinion* was perhaps motivated by the spirit of reconciliation between North and South generated by events such as the Gettysburg Reunion.

Editor of Public Opinion:

Let it be mentioned at the start that the writer of this letter belongs to a famliy "burnt out" in the fire of July 30, 1864 at which time some family relics were lost, that is a matter of regret to this day. This, I take it, confers a right to make the following remarks.

Was it fiendish to burn Chambersburg? Perhaps it was; but was it also fiendish for Sheridan to rush through Virginia with fire and sword, laying it to waste, boasting afterwards that "a crow flying that way after him would have to carry his own provisions?" Was it fiendish of Sherman to cut a fifty mile swath of desolation "from Atlanta to the sea," leaving a barren desert where women and children afterwards starved? The whole South was laid to waste, and its people suffered want, weighed with which the damage and suffering that we met with was a trifle -- and the whole great prosperous North to back us up at that.

We all have a poor opinion of the individual who is blind to his own faults and wide awake to the faults of others. In fact, the New Testament lays down the law unmistakably on that point. Why should nations be different? Have not the blind passions and rages of the war time had leisure to cool, that on each recurring anniversary of the fire that old adjective "fiendish" should creep up? Is it not time to perceive and admit that the war is give and take; and that the evil passions, wrong cruelty and destruction that are an integral part of the "fiendish" game are equally distributed on both sides. In our optimism we thought that the Gettysburg Reunion was the virtual acknowledgement of this; that the brothers had joined hands and admitted that they had been mistaken in attributing each other all sorts of hateful traits; that they now know they were able to see that they were all simply Americans, each fighting for the right as he saw it, and therefore entitled to the respect given to honesty and courage, that all the rest are horrors of the time, including the hatred of American for American, were a kind of prolonged nightmare induced by the war-fiend, whom, Heaven grant, the world will worship no longer.

FAIR PLAY

July 31, 1913

G.A.R.

Following the war, attempts to organize veterans resulted in the formation of groups representing particular segments of the service such as the Society of the Army of Tennessee or the Potomac, or the Loyal Legion, etc. An early Grand Army of the Republic Organization was started in 1867. However, its leadership became too rigid and came under scrutiny when its financial management became suspect. By 1875 its membership had fallen from a high of nearly 200,000 to a mere 25,000.

However, new leadership, beginning in the eighties, from two veterans, Paul Van Cervoort of Nebraska and Robert B. Beath of Philadelphia, brought a revival of interest, and by 1890, 400,000 veterans belonged to the G.A.R. This organization became a powerful political force as it brought into focus the need for national and state legislation aimed at aiding veterans.

A joint committee of the Ladies and Soldiers monumental associations spearheaded efforts to erect monuments around the county. The most prominent one was placed in Chambersburg's Memorial Square in 1878.

Eventually there were seven posts of the Grand Army of the Republic in Franklin County. The first was the Captain John E. Walker Post 287 of Waynesboro, established on September 22, 1882. Roxbury's Lieutenant Peter B. Pomeroy Post 295 came on December 26, 1882. Then on February 21, 1883, the Colonel Peter B. Housum Post 309 came to Chambersburg. Fayetteville's Stevens Post 317 was established on April 3, 1883, and a year later on May 12, the Corporal William Rihl Post 438 came to Greencastle. The last to be chartered were the Mercersburg's Captain J.P. McCullough Post 497, established on October 2, 1885, and the Colonel James G. Elder Post 578 of St. Thomas, which came sometime in the early 90's.

Eventually the G.A.R. became interested in conducting Memorial Day ceremonies to honor those who were war casualties or deceased veterans, in promoting educational programs, in supporting plans to preserve battle sites, in sponsoring reunions

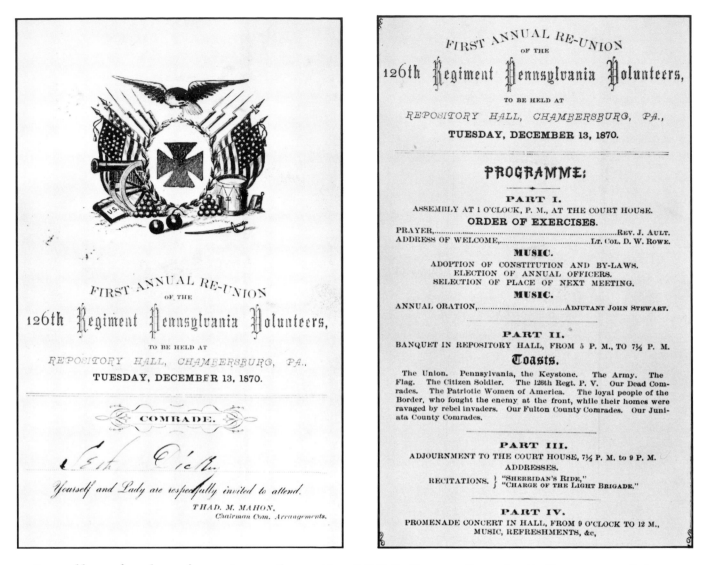

Locally-raised regiments such as the 126th Pennsylvania Infantry and 21st Pennsylvania Cavalry held their reunions in Chambersburg.

at state and federal levels, and, above all, in promoting candidates and legislation to benefit veterans. At the height of its power, the G.A.R. was said to be such a political force that some observers labeled it as the Generally Always Republican Organization.

Of the state legislators from Franklin County between the end of the war and 1900, most were supported by the G.A.R. One outstanding Congressman from the county seat was the Honorable Thaddeus Mahon who served six and a half terms as the area's representative in Congress. His constant re-election came from his advocacy of higher pensions and the promise of collecting war damages for those who had lost property as a result of the war. Although Mahon's success in the "war damage" category was negligible, his help for those with pension problems made him popular. A biography of Mahon

(In the summer of 1896, the Public Opinion ran this article on the GAR encampment in town.)

THE ENCAMPMENT

What the Boys in Blue Have Been Doing in Chambersburg

Speical Correspondence

CHAMBERSBURG, June 3 -- The thirtieth annual encampment of the Department of Pennsylvania, Grand Army of the Republic, began in this city on Monday evening.

The town has since been literally packed with veterans of the late war and many have had trouble in obtaining accommodations.

The first veterans to arrive in town reached here on Sunday afternoon at 1:30 o'clock over the Western Maryland railroad. There were the Lambs of Post 51 of Philadelphia. An immense throng of people met the visitors at the station and cheered them lustily as they marched to Camp Taylor. The Lambs brought with them four cannon and salutes were fired as they entered town and as they marched to camp.

On Monday evening the Department President of Woman's Relief Corps, with her staff, met at Hotel Washington to examine accounts. A meeting of the Department Council was also held at the same time and place.

Yesterday morning the Ladies' Circle G.A.R. opened its annual session in the Central Presbyterian Church. O.C. Bowers, Esq., delivered the address of welcome. The reunion of the Pennsylvania Reserve Association was held at the Montgomery hotel yesterday morning, and a meeting in the interest of the Brookville Home for old people was held in the First Lutheran Church at 10 o'clock a.m. At 1:30 o'clock the thirteenth annual convention of the Woman's Relief Corps of the Department of Pennsylvania was held in the court house. The delegates were welcomed by Hon. W.U. Brewer. The Pennsylvania Memorial Home Association met in the court house yesterday afternoon at 2 o'clock.

The event of importance last evening was the lecture of O.O. Howard, in Rosedale Opera House. The audience that greeted him was large and appreciative.

The program for the remainder of the week will be as follows:

Wednesday -- Parade in which all old soldiers are invited to join. The line will form at 9 o'clock on North Main Street. At 10 o'clock the first business session will be held. The address of welcome will be delivered by Burgess Orr. At 10:30 o'clock the reunion of the 158th P.V. will take place in Housum Post room.

Other reunions will take place to-day as follows: At 3 o'clock the 17th Pa. Cav. will meet in the Columbus lodge room and a reunion of the survivors of the 21st Pa. Vols will be held in the side room of the National Hotel. Joint reunions of the 77th Pa. Vols will be held in the Housum Post room today between the hours of 3:30 and 7 o'clock p.m.

The campfire will be held in Rosedale this evening and Adjutant General Thos. J. Stewart will preside. Addresses will be made by prominent G.A.R. men.

Thursday -- The sessions of the encampment will open at 10 o'clock a.m. At 1 p.m. the reunion of the 49th P.V. regiment will be held in the Housum Post room. In the evening at 8 o'clock Professor Keene will give an entertainment in Rosedale.

On Friday an excursion will be run to Gettysburg over the Western Maryland railroad.

Thus will close one of the largest occasions in the history of Chambersburg.

indicates that during his tenure he was responsible for improving pension claims of 1800 constituents. He was also credited for improving rural mail service and extending railroads in the Cumberland Valley.

Mahon's departure from the political arena came when the political power of the G.A.R. began to wane. This began during the years following World War I, and by 1925 most county posts had disappeared. (The Corporal William Rihl monument along Route 11 north of Greencastle stands today as a constant reminder of the Grand Army of the Republic. It was the Greencastle Post that raised money and, with a grant from the State Assembly, erected this memorial to the first Union soldier killed on Pennsylvania's soil.)

Memorial Fountain

Franklin County's most enduring memorial to those who served the Union cause came after a delay of ten years during which two opposing ideas were eventually reconciled. In 1868 a group of Chambersburg ladies met following a Memorial Day ceremony to discuss the idea of a memorial for the veterans and those who gave their lives to preserve the Union. A permanent organization followed in June with Mrs. Isabel Brotherton as president. This body of women raised money over the years through special programs, festivals, and sales at town functions or county fairs. Eventually this group came to be knows as the Franklin County Monumental Association.

Interest lagged, but by 1877 the Monumental Association could announce that it had $1,300 in its treasury. At a meeting on April 19 of that year, the Association's leader, Mrs. Lyman S. Clarke, proposed that a memorial be placed in the center of the square. Although there was no active G.A.R. post at the time, a soldier's group advocated a monument with no fountain.

This attitude had existed among the veterans from the beginning, but after an editorial by the *Public Opinion* on June 5, 1877, the ex-soldiers agreed to the fountain with a monument. Various designs were considered; then in June, 1878, the fountain, with a soldier, designed by the Motte and Fiske Company of Philadelphia, was chosen by a committee of the women and representatives of the veterans. Both parties agreed that the memorial should be placed in the center of the town square.

A description of the original memorial tells of a cast iron bronzed fountain standing 26 feet high with five metal basins of varied sizes. Four boys were depicted as riders of dolphins attached to a shaft, supporting the basins. The largest basin contained four swans, and the next had four lions All these animals, with water spouting from mouths and nostrils, created the fountain effect. In front of this metallic menagerie stood a lone soldier, at parade rest, looking south. Accompanying the 7-foot tall warrior was a bronze cannon pointing in the same direction.

The entire assemblage was enclosed by a chain fence secured between rails and joined by iron cartridge boxes. A gate, with sabres crossed at its top, had a bronze shield with an appropriate dedicatory inscription on it.

On Saturday, July 20, 1878, the Veterans' Memorial Dedication was preceded at 10 a.m. by a massive two hour, three-mile parade whose procession along the town's "gayly decorated" streets was witnessed by an estimated gathering of 15,000 spectators. Following it, a dedicatory service at the Memorial was held in an afternoon of intense ninety degree heat. The Honorable D. Watson Rowe presided over the ceremonies while the principal oration was delivered by Mayor A. P. Sharpe of Carlisle. His message reminded the audience of the sacrifices of those who had fought for the Union, and he indicated that the work of art standing in the center of the county seat should "warn generations to come of the horrors of fratricidal war."

Fraternal Organizations

The growth of fraternal bodies during the post war period reached a peak that remains unmatched in any other era of the county's history. Although the Independent Order of Odd Fellows was a part of life in many towns before the war, this lodge continued to grow and prosper during the post war period. Mercersburg's Marshall Lodge was founded in 1847, Waynesboro's the same year, and the Conococheague Lodge of Greencastle in 1846. However, Chambersburg was home to three Odd Fellow bodies, those being the Columbus Lodge of 1842, the Olive Branch Body of 1844, and the Chambersburg Chapter in 1846.

> **By the end of the century, one society found in all communities was the Women's Christian Temperance Union.**

Chambersburg's George Washington Lodge No. 143 of the Masonic Fraternal Body was founded in 1816. However, in 1830, the anti-Masonic movement forced it to disband, but in 1845 this pioneer fellowship was reactivated. It continued to prosper through the war, surviving the McCausland fire and serving as the mother lodge of Greencastle's Mt. Pisgah Lodge, No. 443, founded in 1869. Waynesboro's Acacia Lodge, No. 586, was constituted in 1891, and by the end of the century, these three lodges remained as the sole representatives of Masonic brotherhood in the county.

Beyond the Odd Fellows and Masonry, a host of other fraternal organizations came to the county after the war. Greencastle was home for many of these lodges or societies, which included the Knights of Honor, the Legion of Honor, the Knights of Redmen, the Conococheague Council of Royal Arcanum, the Junior Order of United American Mechanics, and the Daughters of Liberty.

Waynesboro had two bodies beyond the Odd Fellows and Masons. They were the Knights of Pythias and the Improved Order of Redmen. In addition to the Odd Fellows, Mercersburg was host to a group known as the Sons of Veterans.

The county seat, also, was home for many other fraternal groups such as the Junior Order of United American Mechanics, the Franklin Guards, the Sons of Veterans, a Cumberland Valley Council of Royal Arcanum, an Order of Improved Heptasophs, and the Y.M.C.A.

By the end of the century, one society found in all communities was the Women's Christian Temperance Union. This body, although composed largely of women, also attracted male members. Its influence, found in practically every state, became a major political force in the effort that eventually brought Prohibition to the nation in 1920.

Entertainment

The years following the war brought new kinds of entertainment to most towns. Although town halls came to Waynesboro and Greencastle, this kind of center had been part of Chambersburg's social and business life prior to the war. Franklin Hall, in the county seat, had been burned in the fire of 1864; however, a new structure replaced the earlier one on the northeast corner of the Square adjacent to the Court House. It was called Repository Hall, which was a three- storied structure with store rooms on the ground floor, an auditorium at the second level, and rooms for lodge meetings or other small group gatherings on the top floor.

By 1875, Greencastle had a three-storied town hall, and Waynesboro could point to a two-storied building, topped by a town clock, which had an auditorium on the second floor. The ground floor housed the town's fire company and a general store.

These halls were used for concerts, dances, community suppers, home talent or minstrel shows, and events such as school graduations, town meetings or political rallies. They also accommodated traveling dramatic troupes, magicians, musical ensembles, lecturers, magic lantern exhibitions, and other types of entertainment. Chambersburg's Repository Hall also served as a meeting place for county teacher institutes. Minutes of the institutes indicate that the hall was ideal for meetings since it had an organ that could be used for musical programs and group singing.

The Rosedale Opera House, located on North Main Street, was built on the site of the Rosedale Seminary, a girls' school that had been destroyed in the McCausland fire. In 1888 the teacher institutes moved to the opera house, where its well lighted auditorium could seat a thousand patrons not only for daytime but evening entertainment. Professional vocal artists and instrumental groups plus prominent orators of the day became part of the billing for not only the teacher institutes, but also, for public performances.

By the end of the century, town halls and the opera house were still a part of community

> **Wolf's Lake was an amusement park that developed around an impound- ment of the Conoco- cheague Creek to form the dam that powered the Wolf Company's various shops.**

life. However, by 1920, the coming of motion pictures ended their importance although some, like the Rosedale building, were converted into movie theaters.

Beyond town halls and theaters, traditional entertainments continued. People still found pleasure in picnicking, church socials, singing schools, dances, quilting parties, and husking bees. Rural schools became community centers that accommodated song fests, spelling bees, holiday programs, lectures, and debates.

Perhaps the most anticipated entertainment during the warm weather seasons came from the traveling tent shows and circuses. Hotel registers of most towns of the post war period provide evidence of the different performers associated with these traveling companies. Such records tell of the nation's greatest circus, the Bailey and Company Circus and Menagerie, playing towns of the county in August of 1865.

In the midst of these entertainments, there came to Chambersburg, perhaps the most prestigious entertainment center in the county's history. It was knows as Wolf's Lake, an amusement park that developed around an impoundment of the Conococheague Creek to form the dam that powered the Wolf Company's various shops.

The lake and its attractions evolved through the years, and by the century's end the park featured a dance floor knows as "Dreamland;" a resort type hotel for visitors that rose to a height of 100 feet above the lake's clear and crystal waters; a swimming area with a "bath house;" a boat house, where canoes and row boats could be rented; a playing field for all seasons; and a railway siding to accommodate excursion parties.

Pictures of this massive entertainment area, found in a booklet printed at the turn of the century, reveal a long view from the rooming center. Of special interest was a scene showing "Round Island," connected to both sides of the lake by a highly ornate bridge. Also, the rail line can be seen as a winding track following turns of the creek along its eastern edge. Another scene shows the "Boat House" with a caption that tells of "nearly fifty boats, including naptha launches, each headed by a 'captain.'" The caption also tells of "many row boats for fishermen."

The coming of trolley lines in the early years of the new century brought more amusement parks. When Red Bridge Park came to the Chambersburg area, Wolf Lake's days were numbered, and it eventually disappeared from the local scene.

Band Music

In the early years of the Civil War, there were 618 bands in the Union forces. Someone has calculated that this amounted to one musician for every 41 soldiers. However, this "music overkill" finally stopped when Congress learned that the War Department had spent $4,000,000 on bands in the first year and a half of the war. The obvious boondoggle ended when band funds were stopped. From then to war's end, the only bands were those attached to regiments, and they were limited to sixteen musicians each. One of the memories veterans brought home from the war was that band music, and in the post war years this resulted in a mania that brought bands throughout the North. By the time Franklin County celebrated its centennial in 1884, there were 21 bands and four drum corps representing towns and villages throughout the county. This can be seen in the fact that all of them took part in the huge parades that were part of this celebration. These bands and drum corps collectively accounted for 317 musicians with Roxbury having the largest with 21 pieces and Greencastle having the smallest with 11 players in its Junior Order of United American Mechanics' Band. All of these bands were primarily brass bands with only a few reed instruments in the entire lot.

Chambersburg was represented by two bands - a junior organization of fourteen pieces and the regular Chambersburg Band which was the only one in the county prior to the Civil War. It was a brass band mentioned in accounts of political parades of both the 1860 and 1864 election campaigns. This organization served communities throughout the county when such music was needed for special occasions.

Interest in bands continued until the last part of the century. By 1910 most of them had disappeared. Only one, the St. Thomas band of today, can trace its origins to that era of music following the war.

> **Chambersburg was represented by two bands - a junior organization of fourteen pieces and the regular Chambersburg Band which was the only one in the county prior to the Civil War.**

Baseball

Returning soldiers brought with them not only a love for band music but an enthusiasm for a new game that they had learned to play in the encampments. It was called baseball, and within a decade after the war, towns and villages began fielding teams. By the 1870's, this new kind of recreation was all the rage.

By modern standards these early teams were laughable. Scores of 80 to 37 or 52 to 46 are on record as results of contests between teams from Greencastle and Waynesboro. Similar scores were likely throughout other parts of the county because the games were quite different from those of today.

Players had no gloves; pitchers tossed the ball underhanded; the catcher stood at a distance back of the batter so as to catch the ball on the first bounce. Base runners could be "put out" by being hit with thrown balls as they ran between bases; batters called for balls at certain heights. If the pitch was not in his zone of preference, the umpire, the sole official, called it a ball.

That the game improved is evident in the recognition the sport later received in the county newspapers. Contests between teams representing the area towns became matters of "life and death." Box scores and accounts of victories or defeats appeared on the front pages of the county's journals and were often accompanied by praise or criticism of managers or players.

Today's interest in this sport, exemplified by the many county teams participating at the Little and Pony league levels, in high school athletic programs, in American Legion competition, and at the adult league level reflects kindly on the unbroken tradition of the game, whose origin rests solely in the decade following the end of the Civil War.

Automobiles

Despite the impact of baseball, nothing from the late post war era can surpass the influence of self propelled vehicles known as horseless carriages. Later known as automobiles, they first came into Franklin County in the nineties. There is a record of one of these, known as a Locomobile, being shown at the Franklin County Fair of September, 1900. (A production record shows that 750 of this make were turned out in 1900. In fact there were only 2,200 cars made by six companies that year.)

The coming of motor cars also meant the end of the toll roads that had been serving Chambersburg and the rest of the county as early as 1820. By 1930 these had disappeared to become state highways. (Incidentally, eighteen manufacturers made 2,663,780 cars that year.)

Let this be the last evidence of developments that came into the life of the county seat and its neighbors following the Civil War. Of all these social changes during the post war years, the automobile has had more influence on living patterns than any other development since the Civil War. With its coming, America's Age of Innocence, typified by the late 19th century, was gone forever.

Signal Corps/Montgomery Diary

The following are excerpts from the diary of James H. Montgomery of St. Thomas who served in the Signal Corps detachment which was organized and trained in Chambersburg in early 1864. The diary begins in February, 1864 and continues through late June, about one month prior to the Burning of Chambersburg.

Wednesday, Feb. 10, 1864 - Mr. . . . Reames kindly gave us seats in his conveyance to Chambersburg . . . called to see Captain H. Clay Snyder, Chief Signal Officer of Dept. of Susquehanna. After examination (to his satisfaction) is orthography, reading, writing, geography, grammar and arithmetic we signed enlistment papers for service in Signal Corps . . . took the cars to Harrisburg to be mustered into the service of the U.S. . . . arriving at Harrisburg at 4:30 p.m.

Thursday, February 11 - Arose at 6 o'clock a.m. and breakfasted at 9 . . . Sackmen, Reamer, and myself visited "Camp Washington" when the 20th Pa. Cavalry are now lying. Met our boys from St. Thomas viz - Lt. Jacob Deatrick . . . Nelson Polsgrove, John Elliott, James Sellers, Wesly Kridler, Samuel Harley and Philip Rautraff and others . . .

Friday, February 12 - . . . visited the capitol buildings today and the river banks. The scenery very fine. Visited Mr. C.M. Burkholder ticket agent Central R.R. and formerly a citizen of our place.

Saturday, February 13 - Received of Capt. H. Clay Snyder a certificate of enlistment upon which I am to draw my bounty. Left Harrisburg for camp at Hagerstown but by leave I went home where I arrived at "early candle lighting." Rec'd of Mr. John Croft one hundred dollars local bounty - St. Thomas Township.

Sunday, February 14 - Weather very stormy. No preaching today. Attended Sabbath school. John A. Sellers and myself visited some of my friends . . .

Monday, February 15 - Weather continues cool and stormy. After bidding farewell to my dear little family wife and mother and friends I proceeded to my school when I managed my business and bid my pupils farewell. Arrived at Chambersburg 10:30 o'clock at 11:30 o'clock I took cars for Hagerstown at which place I arrived at 12:30 o'clock. Dinner at "Washington House." 50ct. Supper and bed at . . . Byers private boarding house - 50 ct.

Tuesday, February 16 - Weather very stormy and cold. Snows all day. Went out to see the camp of Signal Corps, an awful place to be called a camp. Everything in confusion, nobody in charge. Horses scattered over three square miles. Capt. Snyder gone to Harrisburg for more men, for rations for the men and feed for the horses.

All the enlisted men are boarding in town. Supper and night at Byers - 50 ct.

(Editor's Note: For the next several days Montgomery wrote about the poor conditions at what the soldiers called "Camp Desolution." Temperatures dropped to twelve below zero and the men were still in their civilian clothes as uniforms had not yet been issued. On February 20 Montgomery's tailor-made uniform arrived from White's clothing store in Chambersburg. It cost him $27. On February 25, orders were issued to move the camp to Chambersburg.)

Friday, February 26 - Reveille 4 o'clock. Struck tents and took up the line of March for Chambersburg, Pa. noon at Greencastle. Arrived at Chambersburg at 4:30 o'clock and was ordered to go into camp at Allens Grove near the residence of Josiah Allen Jr. . . .

(Editor's Note: The grove was located west of Chambersburg on the road to St. Thomas.)

Saturday, February 27 - Having rained all the roads were very muddy . . . worked all day on tents. 20th Cavalry arrived and went into camp 3/4 mile west of us on Groves farm. . .

Sunday, February 28 - the 20th and 21st PA Cavalry both regiments are camped on Grove's farm . . .

(Editor's Note: Those regiments were raised as six-month outfits during Lee's invasion but reorganized for three-year service in February, 1864 in Chambersburg. Some men from the county served in the 20th, while all or part of companies A, B, D, E, F, G, K, L, and M of the 21st were from Franklin County.)

Monday, February 29 - . . . spent the day building camp . . . all well except myself, having an attack of dysentary. Feel very sick.

Sgt. James Montgomery

Tuesday, March 1st - Snowing very fast all day. Went to St. Thomas tailors to get jacket and overcoat altered. Bought tin cup, plate, knife, fork and spoon. Sister Allen presented us with a very good apple pie. Cooking was hard and food not very palatable. In that such presents are always very acceptable . . .

Wednesday, March 2 - Weathers very cold. Clothing arrived and was issued to men. Social singing at school house. Neely presented us with fine chicken . . .

Thursday, March 3 - Arose early. Weather clear . . . . Traded horses with Joseph Foreman . . . Chicken pot pie for dinner prepared by Sister Allen . . .

Friday, March 4 - Arose early. Weather very cold . . . Wife went with Allen and wife to brother-in-law . . . near Marion. Children spent part of the day at the Center School house.

Saturday, March 5 - Weather very disagreeable, rains

all day . . . Spent evening and night with wife and children at Allen's.

Sunday, March 6 - Weather very fine . . . All well . . . Left camp at 9:00 o'clock attended church. Preaching by Rev. Thomas. Text Mark 10 chapter, 21st verse . . . Dinner at house with family . . . Evening at preaching. Rev. _____ United Brethern officiated . . .

Monday, March 7 - Left house at 5:00 o'clock, arrived at camp at 6:00 o'clock . . . all well . . . Capt. on camp making out rolls . . . Flagging commenced today.

Tuesday, March 8 - Day spent changing the arrangement of our camp. Rolls prepared and signed for government bounty. W.W. Allison returned from home bringing a load of "good things" . . .

Wednesday, March 9 - Order no. 6 read today. Roll call hereafter at 6:00 a.m. and 7:00 p.m. Flag drill 7:30 to 9:00 a.m. and 5:00 - 6:30 p.m. No liquor to be used. Profanity will be tolerated on no account.

Thursday, March 10 - Weather very bad - rain, rain, rain.

Saturday, March 12 - Maj. Gen. Couch visited camp today "in-cog" but was recognized by several of the boys. Capt. Snyder only call on us once per day - his time appears to be entirely taken up by the ladies of Chambersburg.
(Editor's Note: Couch was commander of the Department of the Susquehanna. Montgomery apparently means he came incognito.)

Sunday, March 13 - Attended Sabbath School and afterwards preaching. Sermon by Rev. A.K. Nelson . . . Returned to camp at 3:30 . . . Bible class organized . . . at Centre School house near our camp. Also preaching at the same place by the Rev. Meade - a member of the Corps . . . The best of order was maintained and the strictest attention paid by the audience to the minister . . . 11:30 PM Messenger arrived from Fayetteville announcing the death of my brother-in-law Leonard Sellers. Poor sister and children. There (sic) best friend is gone. God help them.

March 14 - Weather cold. Arose early and conveyed the sad news of brothers death to my family and friends and obtained "leave of absence" to attend funeral . . . Flag drill as usual everyday. Maj. Schultz (sic) A.A.G. visits camp today.
(Editors note: Major John S. Schultze was Gen. Couch's adjutant.)

Tuesday, March 15 - Arose early and went to Fayetteville. Service at the house of Rev. Nichols. Funeral very large. Buried at Presbyterian graveyard in Chambersburg.

Wednesday, March 16 - Weather very disagreeable on which account we have no drill . . . Mrs. George W. Betz presents me through Mary (my wife) with a very useful article to the soldier (a "housewife"). Many thanks for such favors.
(Editor's Note: A "housewife" was a nickname given to a small sewing kit carried by soldiers).

Thursday, March 17 - St. Patrick's Day. Went to Brake's saw mill today for boards for Capt. Snyder's tent 288 ft. boards and 68 feet scantling = $4.60. Boxing gloves introduced on camp . . . Drill used by Serg't Neely and Franklin.

Friday, March 18 - Men are leaving enlisted now for the army outside of the Corps. This is to be a "Corps of Instruction" for recruits. Capt. ordered to camp . . . Spring election held in St. Thomas for Township Officers.

Saturday, March 19 - Today the entire camp was policed thoroughly. Long sick and removed to town "Ladies Aid Society."
(Editor's Note: This was Adolphus R. Long, a Franklin County man who had joined the Signal Corps. All across the north local communties had their "Ladies Aid Societies." These volunteer groups were a combination U.S.O. and Red Cross, caring for the sick soldiers, sending them "care packages" at Christmas time and other holidays, and holding "fairs" to raise money for patriotic causes.

The Union signal station (seen above) near Sharpsburg, Maryland in 1862. Stations similar to this were established across the southern part of Franklin County in the summer of 1864. See other stations, left.

Sunday, March 20 - Attended preaching . . . Returned to camp to oyster supper furnished by Allison.

Monday, March 21 - John Walsh arraigned for drunkeness. Pleads not guilty - sentence guilty. Ebright in jail for "drunk" by Provost Marshall. All well.

Tuesday, March 22 - Rations received.

Wednesday, March 23 - Weather very cold today. 21st Reg't PA Cav. received their horses today.

Thursday, March 24 - Weather cool. Snowed the greater part of the day. Raised a sleeping tent in the rear of our other one which we floored. Life very comfortable now.

Friday, March 25 - Continues to snow, which melts as fast as it falls, making the roads very muddy. "Sister Anna" furnished us with another "pot pie."

Saturday, March 26 - Weather very cool. Snow being six in. deep . . . each member of the mess taking a turn as cook.

Sunday, March 27 - Birthday anniversary - family returned home from sisters. Mother along, Mr. Mead preached in St. Thomas today.

Tuesday, March 29 - Singing in St. Thomas tonight

Wednesday, March 30 - A musical club organized tonight.

Thursday, March 31 - A beautiful banner presented to the 21st Cav., Gov. Curtin, Gen. Couch and staff and other dignitaries present. A lot of papers stolen from clerks office. Roll call instituted every two hours during today. Ordered by Captain to take charge of horses.

Friday, April 1 - Weather rainy and disagreeable - a very bad day for persons to change their residence. 20th Ca. broke camp today and left for parts unknown.

Sunday, April 3 - Attended Sabbath School and church.

Monday, April 4 - Rains and snows. Another batch of recruits arrived on camp.

Tuesday, April 5 - Rained and snowed all day.

Wednesday, April 6 - Detail to be made daily to attend to the horses of the corps. I am placed in charge of the detail.

Thursday, April 7 - Inspection here of quarters by Maj. Gen. Couch's staff. A Meerschaum pipe $8.00 presented to Capt. Snyder.

Friday, April 8 - Moved camp from Allen's Grove to Mr. Samuel Coble's field on the site of Gen. Stahl's Headquarters. Lesher and I left without a tent - slept in the commissary tent.
(Editor' Note: This refers to Major General Julius Stahel.)

Saturday, April 9 - Weather very disagreeable today. Still without a tent, promised one tomorrow.

Sunday, April 10 - On camp attending to diseased horses. Still sleep in commissary tent.

Tuesday, April 12 - Spent the forenoon of today putting up poles for horses. At noon Sgt. Neely, myself, Allison, Stewart, Palm, Murray Speer, Neilson and Egolf were detailed to go to Mt. Parnell and open communication with camp (by signal) for practice. Reached there at 5:30 p.m. Pitched tents, had supper and went to bed. Rained all night. Very foggy. Cannot get a glimpse of camp or even one hundred yards from us.

Wednesday, April 13 - Still rainy this morning. Unfit for signaling but cleared off at noon and a more magnificent scene was never unfolded to the eyes of man than was spread out before us. Communications was opened with camp. Stewart was detailed and sent to St. Thomas for bread, cheese. Torches from 8:00 - 10:00 p.m.

Thursday, April 14 - Showers of rain prevented any practice in the forenoon but afternoon was clear and practice kept up pretty constantly till a late hour to night. We enjoy our change it being a relief from the routine of camp duty which become as very tiresome.

Friday, April 15 - Very cold here and few of us slept much last night. Received dispatch to "come in" -Left mountain at 9:30 o'clock a.m. Dined at St. Thomas. Sergeant Strong and Messimer take our places on Parnell and Franklin, McManus, and Long go to Casey's Knob. All well.

Sunday, April 17 - Weather continues. bad. Preaching today by Rev. Thomas. Subject "vices of the day" including gambling, dancing, interpetence.

Monday, April 18 - Returned to camp.

Tuesday, April 19 - Franklin and men return from "Casey" . . . Strong and party also returns. Another batch of recruits arrive on camp. Bought a stove, Lesher and I = $2.00.

Thursday, April 21 - Great trouble with horses. Six cases of diseased foot "rotten hoof". Drew a gum poncho.
(Editors Note: A gum poncho was usually made of Indian rubber.)

Friday, April 22 - Wife and children very sick. Obtained permission and went up to see them returning at midnight.

Saturday, April 23 - Camp in great excitement this morning. Captain Snyder received an order for sixty-three men to be forwarded to Cumberland, MD.

Sunday, April 24 - Went home this afternoon returning at 11:30 a.m. tonight. Wife no better.

Monday, April 25 - Heavy rain this morning. Our comrades (sixty-three in all) left camp for the depot at Chambersburg for Cumberland, MD. Lt. Kennedy of 21st Cav. reported to Capt. Snyder for duty in the Signal Corps. Our Capt. H.C. Snyder ordered under arrest by Major John Bert of Gen. Couch's staff. Charged with being engaged with others in "bounty business".

Wednesday, April 27 - Morning and evening cool but noon the weather was warm and pleasant. Home this evening. Wife better.

Friday, April 29 - Camp guard doubled. Every day bring rule more strict. Rumor says the enemy are advancing down the Shenandoah Valley.

Saturday, April 30 - 21st Cavalry mustered for pay. Our camp is as usual very quiet only the usual daily flagging.

Sunday, May 1 - Communion today at St. Thomas.

Monday, May 2 - . . . continued rumor of the enemy approaching.
(Editors Note: On Tuesday, May 3 Montgomery received pay for his services as a captain - the emergency militia called out for Lee's 1863 invasion.)

Wednesday, May 4 - Major Bert called to see Captain Snyder who was absent on a visit with some ladies at Mr. Wilson's.
(Editor's Note: At this point not all the words are legible but it appears that he wrote, "Major very angry. Ordered me to inform Cpt. Snyder that I await his return to his quarters. Court martial appointed for Saturday.)

Thursday, May 5 - Much sympathy is manifested by our men for our Capt. though some think him guilty. Music on camp this evening by Capt. Snyder on guitar, W. _____ on banjo, Craig and _____ on violins.
(Editors Note: On May 7 Captain Snyder's court martial began and Montgomery notes that their new commander Lt. Amos Thayer reported for duty. Snyder would be found guilty of failure to keep adequate records and submit required reports. He was dismissed from the service.) On Sunday, May 8, Montgomery recorded that Lt. Thayer issued new orders concerning duties in

camp. Life for the detachment would take on a more military bearing.

Monday, on May 9, the following schedule was read at guard mount in the morning and dress parade: Roll call 6:00 a.m., Stable call 6:45 a.m., Breakfast 7:30 a.m., Water call 8:00 a.m., Drill (flag) 8:30 a.m., Inspection (daily) 10:00 a.m., Feed and dinner 12:00 p.m., Roll call 2:00 p.m., Drill 3:00 p.m., Water 5:00 p.m., Dress parade 6:00 p.m., Stable call 9:00 p.m., Taps 10:00 p.m.

Montgomery was sent home on sick leave with a severe bout of neuralgia on Thursday, May 12. This was no doubt aggrevated by heavy rains occurring almost daily. Montgomery returned to camp on Thursday, May 19.)

Thursday, May 19 ... A busy day on camp. A tents are all ordered in and "Shelter tents" issued in their steade. To remedy the usual "dog tent" we are erecting all huts 10 x 8 ft. and 5 ft. high covering with the shelters thereby making a very comfortable "sh-abang." Cutler, Lashell, Neely and myself - acting Sergts. are testing together. Drew new halters, bridles and sabers and pistols - "Colt Navy revolvers."

Friday, May 20 - Erected an arrangement for our horses. A frame covered with fine brush. Tent finished.

Saturday, May 21 - General policing today.

Sunday, May 22 - Was visited by William Finney and County Superintendent McElwain.
(Editors Note: William Finney was a local carpenter who later became prominent in a lumber and coal business in Chambersburg. Andrew J. McElwain was county school superintendent from 1863 - 1866. His house was burned by McCausland's raiders because he had taught blacks.)

Monday, May 23 - Took horses to town for shoeing.

Tuesday, May 24 - Sword exercise by Hershberger.

Wednesday, May 25 - Sabre drill by Lashell.

Friday, May 27 - Staff buttons ordered off uniforms of enlisted men.

Saturday, May 28 - No drill today.

Sunday, May 29 - Arose early. Inspection of men and quarters, horses, stables and equipment at 8:00 o'clock a.m. Attended divine service at St. Thomas by Rev. Thomas, text Prov. 22, 6 verse. Samuel Irwin Allen, son of Josiah and Annier M. Allen parted this life today aged 8 mo. & 18 days.

Monday, May 30 - Attended the burial of Allen's child at cemetery Chambersburg having leave of absence for the day. I returned to the house of mourning for supper. Arrived at camp at 4:00 o'clock p.m. Paymaster on camp - paid us off my wages amounting to $84.23 Paid off all my little debts and gave Mary $30 having $25 with which to purchase boots.

Tuesday, May 31 - Weather very warm. McCarty in the guard house erected for his accommodations.

Saturday, June 4 - Attending singing at St. Thomas.

Sunday, June 5 - Attended dedication ceremonies of the new United Brethern Church, St. Thomas, in company with Mary.

Wednesday, June 8 - Went to town in charge of horses for shoeing.

Friday, June 10 - Weather beautiful a detail made to prepare the Town Hall, Chambersburg for the sanitary fare (sic) to be held next week.

Saturday, June 11 - Reamer says we are to leave here for the front soon.

Monday, June 13 - Detail still made daily for cutting spruce pine for Hall.

Tuesday, June 16 - Fair of Sanitary and Christian Commission opened today.

Pvt. James A. Lashell, Gettysburg

Pvt. Mac Montgomery

Pvt. William A. Fulmer

Capt. H. Clay Snyder, Franklin Co.

R. M. Messimer, Perry County

Pvt. Wentz C. Miller, Perry Co.

Pvt. Charles C. Hackett, Perry Co.

George W. Tressler, Perry Co.

L.E. Palm, Newville

Pvt. David M. Jones, New Bloomfield

Sgt. William Cutler, Cumberland County

Pvt. J.M. Benedict, Chambersburg

Pvt. Robert Allison, Cumberland County

Pvt. W.W. Allison, Carlisle

Pvt. H.H. McClintock, Perry County

George W. Wolfong, Dauphin Co.

Pvt. Samuel L. Maxwell, Chambersburg

Pvt. Samuel H. Eby, Greencastle

Pvt. W. A. Lindsay, Cumberland Co.

David Raffensberger, St. Thomas

History is alive in Franklin County

Chambersburg's historic Memorial Square.

Mary Ritner's house on King Street where John Brown stayed in 1859.

This star on Memorial Square marks the site where Lee made the decision to go to Gettysburg.

Picture credits

Alexander Collection, Ted: 16, 19, 161, 162
Baer, Elizabeth: 183, 185
Battles and Leaders of the Civil War: 78, 82
Beard, Mr. and Mrs. Edward: 40
Brand, Mrs. Louise: 9
First National Bank, Greencastle, Pa.: 76
Gargaro, I.A.: 140
Gottschalk, Robert: (maps) 13, 24, 51, 54,
71, 74, 121, 126, 172, 184
Hoke, Jacob, The Great Invasion: 77
Kauffman Collection, Murray E.: 2, 4, 5, 8,
11, 12, 14, 17, 18, 19 (bottom), 20 80, 94, 96,
97, 100-104, 105 (top), 106-117, 119, 122,
145, 146, 148-158
National Park Service: 64, 66, 172
Pananes Collection, Will and Robert Hol-
land: 27-29, 55, 58, 60, 72, 93
United States Army Military History Insti-
tute: 21, 23, 25, 26, 28 (bottom), 30, 31, 35,
38, 39, 40, 42, 47, 50, 56, 69, 70, 75, 76
(bottom), 79, 81, 83, 84, 91, 95, 98, 99, 133,
159, 170, 176-182
Valley News Echo: 1, 3, 5, 7, 59, 73
West Virginia State Archives: 105

The editors would like to thank J.B. Leib for
providing copies of photographs for the U.S.
Army Military History Institute.

Index

Index

Bibliography

Alexander, Ted ed. The 126th Pennsylvania Shippensburg. Beidel Printing House, Inc. 1984

Atlas of Franklin County, Pennsylvania. Philadelphia. Pomeroy and Beers, 1868

Bates, Samuel P. and Richard J. Fraise. History of Franklin County, Pennsylvania. Chicago. Warner, Beers and Co., 1887

Bates, Samuel P. History of Pennsylvania Volunteers. 1861-65. 5 Vols. Harrisburg, Pa. B. Singerly. 1871

Battles and Leaders of the Civil War. 4 Vols. New York. The Century Company. 1887.

Beach, William H. The First New York (Lincoln) Cavalry: From April 19, 1861 to July 7, 1865. New York. The Lincoln Cavalry Association, 1902

Beyond the Years: The Fountain in the Square. Franklin County Heritage. Chambersburg, Pa. 1978

Biographical Annals of Franklin County, Pennsylvania. Chicago. The Genealogical Publishing Co. 1905.

Blackford, William W. War Years with Jeb Stuart. New York. Charles Scribner's Sons, 1946

Booth, George Wilson. Personal Reminiscences of a Maryland Soldier in the War Between the States 1861-1865. Baltimore. By the Author, 1898

Brown, J. Willard. The Signal Corps, U.S.A. in the War of the Rebellion. Boston. U.S. Veteran Signal Corps Association. 1896

Bushong, Millard K. Old Jube: A Biography of General Jubal A. Early. By the Author, 1955

Conrad, W.P. Franklin County School Superintendents. 1977.

Conrad, W.P., and Alexander, Ted. When War Passed This Way. Greencastle, Pa. Lilian S. Besore Memorial Library, 1982.

Cooper, John M. Recollections of Chambersburg. Chambersburg, Pa: A. Nevin Pomeroy, Publisher, 1900

Douglass, Frederick. Life and Times of Frederick Douglass. New York: The MacMillan Company, 1962, as reprinted from the revised edition of 1892.

Egle, William H. ed. Andrew Gregg Curtin: His Life and Services. Philadelphia. Civil Printing Co. 1895

Gilmor, Harry. Four Years in the Saddle. New York. Harper and Brothers, 1866

Henninger, Louie B. Recollections of the Old Chambersburg of 60 Years Ago. 1920.

History of Bedford, Somerset and Fulton County, PA. Chicago, Waterman, Watkin Co., 1884

History of the Cumberland Valley. Harrisburg. The Susquehanna History Association. 1930.

History of Franklin County, Pennsylvania. Chicago. Warner, Beers and Co. 1887.

Hoke, Jacob. The Great Invasion of 1863; or, General Lee in Pennsylvania. Dayton. W.J. Shuey, 1887.

Hoke, Jacob. Historical Reminiscences of the War or Incidents Which Transpired in and About Chambersburg During the War of the Rebellion. Chambersburg, M.A. Foltz, Printer and Publisher, 1884

Hutton, A.J. White. History of Chambersburg. 1930

Lord, Walter. The Fremantle Diary. Boston. Little, Brown and Company. 1954

McCauley, I.H. Historical Sketch of Franklin County, Pennsylvania. Chambersburg, Pa. John M. Pomeroy. 1877.

Mohr, James C. Ed., The Cormany Diaries: A Northern Family in the Civil War. Pittsburgh. University of Pittsburgh Press, 1982.

Montgomery, William E. Ed. One Hundred and Fifty Years of Free Masonry in Chambersburg, Pennsylvania, 1800-1950. Chambersburg. 1959.

Morrison, Robert D. Zion Reform Church Through Two Hundred Years, 1778-1985. Chambersburg, Consistory of Zion Reform Church. 1986.

Murfin, James V. The Gleam of Bayonets: The Battle of Antietam and the Maryland Campaign of 1862. New York. Thomas Yoseloff. 1965.

National Bank of Chambersburg: The History of its Progress Through its First Century. Chambersburg, Pennsylvania. Press of Henderson and Mong. 1909.

Newcomer, C. Armour. Coles Cavalry, or Three Years in the Saddle in the Shenandoah Valley. Baltimore. Cushing and Co. 1895.